WEBSTER'S NEW WORLD

MISPELLER'S
DICTIONERY

D0034299

15,000 common
misspellings <u>and</u> their
correct spellings

*

WEBSTER'S NEW WORLD

MISPELLER'S DICTIONARY

Prepared by the editors of
Webster's New World Dictionary

PRENTICE HALL PRESS

Library of Congress Catalog Card Number: 83-60107
ISBN: 0-671-46864-2

FOREWORD

Before the eighteenth century, people spelled English words just about as they wanted to. That made for considerable confusion, and as literacy became more widespread, dictionary makers, such as Samuel Johnson, attempted to standardize English spelling, mainly on the basis of word origins. Those efforts resulted in a relatively stabilized English orthography. But as pronunciations continued to change and spellings remained fixed, confusion arose again, and today even writers of intellectual standing often hesitate about whether to use an *s* or a *z* in *exercise* or find themselves writing "miniscule." And dictionary editors often hear the plaint, "How do I find it in a dictionary if I can't spell it?"

This book has been prepared to help you do just that. If you have sought a word in a dictionary and have been unable to find it, or if you are just uncertain about a word, look for it in this list under the spelling you think it may have. Chances are good that you will find it here, for the left-hand columns consist of an alphabetical list of common misspellings, phonetic respellings, and homonyms (words that sound alike but are spelled differently and that are sometimes confused). The right-hand columns contain the correct spellings, in boldface type and, as an added feature, tiny centered dots that show where the words are conventionally broken at the ends of lines. In the case of homonyms or of words that look somewhat alike (such as *marital* and *martial*), you will find an identifying word or phrase, set in italic type within parentheses.

In selecting misspelled forms to show in this word list, often more than one for a word, the editors have concentrated on those errors that are commonly made, especially in the following general categories:

1) uncertainty about whether a consonant is doubled, as *mispelling, Massachusets, gallactic,* etc.
2) uncertainty about the order of vowels, as *siezure, seige,* etc.
3) errors resulting from mispronunciation, as *momento, dias, mushmelon,* etc.
4) homonyms, or words that have the same pronunciation but different meanings, as *bore* and *boar, maze* and *maize,* etc.
5) unrelated words that have similar spellings that cause confusion, as *dairy* and *diary*
6) the dropping or slurring over of a vowel or syllable in pronunciation, as *menstrate, mathmatics,* etc.
7) the adding of a vowel, as *mayorality, athelete,* etc.
8) the confusion of one word with some other well-known word, as *hairbrained, cold slaw,* etc.
9) complete confusion, which covers all the other possibilities that require a phonetic respelling

In addition we have also indicated pairings of words that often cause confusion:

1) singulars and plurals, as *crisis* and *crises, basis* and *bases,* etc.
2) masculine and feminine forms, as *fiance´* and *fiancée, alumni* and *alumnae,* etc.
3) nouns and verbs, as *breath* and *breathe*

Such pairs or groups of words also have identifying notes in italics and within parentheses following the correct spelling. In addition to brief definitions, other information may be given to assist in identifying the correct spelling. The following abbreviations are used:

adj.	adjective	*poss.*	possessive
adv.	adverb	*pp.*	past participle
aux.v.	auxiliary verb	*prep.*	preposition
conj.	conjunction	*pron.*	pronoun
f.	feminine	*prp.*	present participle
interj.	interjection	*pt.*	past tense
m.	masculine	*sing.*	singular
n.	noun	*v.*	verb
pl.	plural		

For words having more than one acceptable spelling, only the first spelling given in *Webster's New World Dictionary,* Second College Edition, is shown here.

If the spelling cannot be found in the misspelled words column, the following Word Finder Table may help in determining the correct spelling. Pronounce the word as correctly as possible, think of it in terms of its pronounced syllables, and consult the table for the most common spellings for the sounds of those syllables.

If the sound is like the . . .	try also the spelling . . .	as in the words . . .
a in fat	ai, au	pl*ai*d, dr*au*ght
a in lane	ai, ao, au, ay, ea, ei, eigh, et, ey	r*ai*n, g*ao*l, g*au*ge, r*ay*, br*ea*k, r*ei*n, w*ei*gh, sach*et*, th*ey*
a in care	ai, ay, e, ea, ei	*ai*r, pr*ay*er, th*e*re, w*ea*r, th*ei*r
a in father	au, e, ea	g*au*nt, s*e*rgeant, h*ea*rth
a in ago	e, i, o, u, *and combinations, as* ou	*a*g*e*nt, san*i*ty, c*o*mply, foc*u*s, vici*ou*s

If the sound is like the . . .	try also the spelling . . .	as in the words . . .
b in big	bb	ru*bb*er
ch in chin	tch, ti, tu	ca*tch*, ques*ti*on, na*tu*re
d in do	dd, ed	pu*dd*le, call*ed*
e in get	a, ae, ai, ay, ea, ei, eo, ie, u	*a*ny, *ae*sthete, s*ai*d, s*ay*s, br*ea*d, h*ei*fer, l*eo*pard, fr*ie*nd, b*u*ry
e in equal	ae, ay, ea, ee, ei, eo, ey, i, ie, oe	alumn*ae*, qu*ay*, l*ea*n, fr*ee*, dec*ei*t, p*eo*ple, k*ey*, mach*i*ne, ch*ie*f, ph*oe*be
e in here	ea, ee, ei, ie	*ea*r, ch*ee*r, w*ei*rd, b*ie*r
er in over	ar, ir, or, our, re, ur, ure, yr	li*ar*, elix*ir*, auth*or*, glam*our*, ac*re*, aug*ur*, meas*ure*, zeph*yr*
f in fine	ff, gh, lf, ph	cli*ff*, lau*gh*, ca*lf*, *ph*rase
g in go	gg, gh, gu, gue	e*gg*, *gh*oul, *gu*ard, prolo*gue*
h in hat	wh	*wh*o
i in it	a, e, ee, ia, ie, o, u, ui, y	us*a*ge, *E*nglish, b*ee*n, carr*ia*ge, s*ie*ve, w*o*men, b*u*sy, b*ui*lt, h*y*mn
i in kite	ai, ay, ei, ey, ie, igh, uy, y, ye	*ai*sle, *ay*e, sl*ei*ght, *ey*e, t*ie*, n*igh*, b*uy*, fl*y*, r*ye*
j in jam	d, dg, di, dj, g, gg	gra*d*uate, ju*dg*e, sol*di*er, a*dj*ective, ma*g*ic, exa*gg*erate
k in keep	c, cc, ch, ck, cqu, cu, lk, q, qu, que	*c*an, a*cc*ount, *ch*orus, ta*ck*, la*cqu*er, bis*cu*it, wa*lk*, *q*uick, li*qu*or, baro*que*
l in let	ll, sl	ca*ll*, i*sl*e
m in me	chm, gm, lm, mb, mm, mn	dra*chm*, paradi*gm*, ca*lm*, li*mb*, dru*mm*er, hy*mn*
n in no	gn, kn, mn, nn, pn	*gn*u, *kn*eel, *mn*emonic, di*nn*er, *pn*eumatic
ng in ring	n, ngue	pi*n*k, to*ngue*

vi

If the sound is like the...	try also the spelling...	as in the words...
o in go	au, eau, eo, ew, oa, oe, oh, oo, ou, ough, ow	m*au*ve, b*eau*, y*eo*man, s*ew*, b*oa*t, t*oe*, *oh*, br*oo*ch, s*ou*l, d*ough*, r*ow*
o in long	a, ah, au, aw, oa, ou	*a*ll, Ut*ah*, fr*au*d, th*aw*, br*oa*d, *ou*ght
oo in tool	eu, ew, o, oe, ou, ough, u, ue, ui	man*eu*ver, dr*ew*, m*o*ve, sh*oe*, gr*ou*p, thr*ough*, r*u*le, bl*ue*, fr*ui*t
oo in look	o, ou, u	w*o*lf, w*ou*ld, p*u*ll
oi in oil	oy	t*oy*
ou in out	ough, ow	b*ough*, cr*ow*d
p in put	pp	cli*pp*er
r in read	rh, rr, wr	*rh*yme, be*rr*y, *wr*ong
s in sew	c, ce, ps, sc, sch, ss	*c*ent, ri*ce*, *ps*ychology, *sc*ene, *sch*ism, mi*ss*
sh in ship	ce, ch, ci, s, sch, sci, se, si, ss, ssi, ti	o*ce*an, ma*ch*ine, fa*ci*al, *s*ure, *sch*wa, con*sci*ence, nau*se*ous, ten*si*on, i*ss*ue, fi*ssi*on, na*ti*on
t in top	ed, ght, pt, th, tt	walk*ed*, bou*ght*, *pt*omaine, *th*yme, be*tt*er
u in cuff	o, oe, oo, ou	s*o*n, d*oe*s, fl*oo*d, d*ou*ble
u in use	eau, eu, eue, ew, ieu, iew, ue, ui, you, yu	b*eau*ty, f*eu*d, qu*eue*, f*ew*, ad*ieu*, v*iew*, c*ue*, s*ui*t, *you*th, *yu*le
ur in fur	ear, er, eur, ir, or, our, yr	l*ear*n, g*er*m, haut*eur*, b*ir*d, w*or*d, sc*our*ge, m*yr*tle
v in vat	f, lv, ph	o*f*, sa*lv*e, Ste*ph*en
w in will	o, u, wh	ch*o*ir, q*u*aint, *wh*eat
y in you	i, j	on*i*on, halle*lu*jah
z in zero	s, sc, ss, x, zz	bu*s*y, di*sc*ern, sci*ss*ors, *x*ylophone, bu*zz*er

If the sound is like the...	try also the spelling...	as in the words...
z in azure	ge, s, si, zi	ga*r*a*ge*, lei*s*ure, fu*si*on, gla*zi*er

Sometimes, certain letter combinations (rather than single sounds) cause problems when you are trying to find a word. Here are some common ones:

If you've tried...	then try...	If you've tried...	then try...	If you've tried...	then try...
pre	per, pro, pri, pra, pru	cks, gz	x	fiz	phys
		us	ous	ture	teur
per	pre, pir, pur, par, por	tion	sion, cion, cean, cian	tious	seous
is	us, ace, ice	le	tle, el, al	air	are
ere	eir, ear, ier	kw	qu	ance	ence
wi	whi	cer	cre	ant	ent
we	whe	ei	ie	able	ible
zi	xy	si	psy, ci	sin	syn, cin, cyn

As a final note, when you find the word you are seeking, allow your eye to set the correct spelling, in boldface type, syllable by syllable in your mind. In that way you may discover that just one or two referrals to the word will fix it for you permanently.

This listing has been prepared by the following editors on the staff of *Webster's New World Dictionary:* Jonathan Goldman, Jennifer Robinson, and Donald Stewart.

A

WRONG	RIGHT	WRONG	RIGHT
abalish	**abol·ish**	abhorent	**ab·hor·rent**
abaminable	**abom·i·na·ble**	abillity	**abil·i·ty**
abarigine	**ab·o·rig·i·ne**	abiss	**abyss**
abayance	**abey·ance**	abjeck	**ab·ject**
abbacus	**ab·a·cus**	abjective	**ob·jec·tive**
abbandon	**aban·don**	abligation	**ob·li·ga·tion**
abbatement	**abate·ment**	abligatory	**ob·lig·a·to·ry**
abberation	**ab·er·ra·tion**	abliterate	**ob·lit·er·ate**
abbolition	**ab·o·li·tion**	ablong	**ob·long**
abbortion	**abor·tion**	abnormallity	**ab·nor·mal·i·ty**
abbundant	**abun·dant**	abnormel	**ab·nor·mal**
abcence	**ab·sence**	abnoxious	**ob·nox·ious**
abcess	**ab·scess**	abominible	**abom·i·na·ble**
abdacate	**ab·di·cate**	abored	**aboard**
abdaminal	**ab·dom·i·nal**	aborrigine	**ab·o·rig·i·ne**
abducktion	**ab·duc·tion**	abowt	**about**
abedience	**obe·di·ence**	abrasieve	**ab·ra·sive**
abel	**able**	abrazion	**ab·ra·sion**
abelisk	**ob·e·lisk**	abrest	**abreast**

1

WRONG	*RIGHT*
abreviate	**ab·bre·vi·ate**
abriged	**abridged**
abrup	**abrupt**
absalutely	**ab·so·lute·ly**
absalve	**ab·solve**
abscand	**ab·scond**
abscene	**ob·scene**
abscent	**ab·sent**
abscure	**ob·scure**
absense	**ab·sence**
absequious	**ob·se·qui·ous**
abserd	**ab·surd**
absess	**ab·scess**
absession	**ob·ses·sion**
absidian	**ob·sid·i·an**
abskond	**ab·scond**
absolete	**ob·so·lete**
absolutly	**ab·so·lute·ly**
absorbant	**ab·sorb·ent**
absorbtion	**ab·sorp·tion**
abstacle	**ob·sta·cle**
abstane	**ab·stain**
abstanent	**ab·sti·nent**
abstetrics	**ob·stet·rics**
abstinant	**ab·sti·nent**
abstinense	**ab·sti·nence**
abstrack	**ab·stract**
abtrusive	**ob·tru·sive**
abundent	**abun·dant**
abusave	**abu·sive**
abuze	**abuse**
abzolve	**ab·solve**

WRONG	*RIGHT*
abzorb	**ab·sorb** *(take in)*
abzurd	**ab·surd**
academicly	**aca·dem·i·cal·ly**
a capella	**a cap·pel·la**
accademy	**acad·e·my**
Accapulco	**Aca·pul·co**
accede	**ex·ceed** *(surpass)*
accellerator	**ac·cel·er·a·tor**
accept	**ex·cept** *(omit)*
accepted	**ex·cept·ed** *(left out)*
acceptible	**ac·cept·a·ble**
access	**ex·cess** *(surplus)*
accessable	**ac·ces·si·ble**
accessary	**ac·ces·so·ry**
accidently	**ac·ci·den·tal·ly**
acclusion	**oc·clu·sion**
accollade	**ac·co·lade**
accomodation	**ac·com·mo·da·tion**
accompanyment	**ac·com·pa·ni·ment**
accoustic	**acous·tic**
accrew	**ac·crue**
accross	**across**
accult	**oc·cult**
accummulate	**ac·cu·mu·late**
accupational	**oc·cu·pa·tion·al**
accupuncture	**acu·punc·ture**
accurasy	**ac·cu·ra·cy**
accurrate	**ac·cu·rate**
accute	**acute**
accuzation	**ac·cu·sa·tion**

WRONG	RIGHT	WRONG	RIGHT
acede	**ac·cede** (agree)	Acquarius	**Aquar·i·us**
acedemically		acquiesence	**ac·qui·es·cence**
	aca·dem·i·cal·ly	acrabat	**ac·ro·bat**
acelerator	**ac·cel·er·a·tor**	acrage	**acre·age**
acent	**ac·cent** (emphasis)	acramonious	**acri·mo·ni·ous**
acept	**ac·cept** (receive)	acrilic	**acryl·ic**
aceptable	**ac·cept·a·ble**	acrue	**ac·crue**
acepted	**ac·cept·ed** (approved)	acsend	**as·cend**
acerage	**acre·age**	acsent	**ac·cent** (emphasis)
acess	**ac·cess** (approach)	acsent	**as·cent** (a rising)
acetiline	**acet·y·lene**	acsept	**ac·cept** (receive)
acheivement	**achieve·ment**	acsertain	**as·cer·tain**
achord	**ac·cord**	acsetic	**as·cet·ic** (austere)
acidentally	**ac·ci·den·tal·ly**	actavate	**ac·ti·vate**
aclaim	**ac·claim**	acter	**ac·tor**
aclectic	**ec·lec·tic**	activety	**ac·tiv·i·ty**
aclimate	**ac·cli·mate**	actoress	**ac·tress**
a'clock	**o'clock**	actualy	**ac·tu·al·ly**
acme	**ac·ne** (pimples)	acuemen	**acu·men**
acne	**ac·me** (peak)	acumulate	**ac·cu·mu·late**
acolade	**ac·co·lade**	acurate	**ac·cu·rate**
acommodation		acurracy	**ac·cu·ra·cy**
	ac·com·mo·da·tion	acursed	**ac·curs·ed**
acompaniment		acusation	**ac·cu·sa·tion**
	ac·com·pa·ni·ment	acuse	**ac·cuse**
acomplice	**ac·com·plice**	acustic	**acous·tic**
acomplish	**ac·com·plish**	acustom	**ac·cus·tom**
acord	**ac·cord**	ad	**add** (combine)
acordion	**ac·cor·di·on**	adament	**ad·a·mant**
acost	**ac·cost**	adanoids	**ad·e·noids**
acount	**ac·count**	adapt	**ad·ept** (expert)
acquaintence	**ac·quaint·ance**	adapt	**adopt** (choose)

WRONG	RIGHT
adaptible	**adapt·a·ble**
adaquate	**ad·e·quate**
add	**ad** *(advertisement)*
addage	**ad·age**
addative	**ad·di·tive**
addept	**ad·ept** *(expert)*
addick	**ad·dict**
addition	**edi·tion** *(book issue)*
additionaly	**ad·di·tion·al·ly**
adeiu	**adieu** *(goodbye)*
adelweiss	**edel·weiss**
adendum	**ad·den·dum**
adep	**ad·ept** *(expert)*
ader	**ad·der** *(snake)*
adhear	**ad·here**
adhezive	**ad·he·sive**
adict	**ad·dict**
adige	**ad·age**
adition	**ad·di·tion** *(adding)*
aditive	**ad·di·tive**
adjunck	**ad·junct**
adjurn	**ad·journ**
adjutent	**ad·ju·tant**
admanish	**ad·mon·ish**
admeral	**ad·mi·ral**
admeration	**ad·mi·ra·tion**
adminester	**ad·min·is·ter**
adminestration	**ad·min·is·tra·tion**
administrater	**ad·min·is·tra·tor**
admirible	**ad·mi·ra·ble**

WRONG	RIGHT
admision	**ad·mis·sion**
admissable	**ad·mis·si·ble**
admitance	**ad·mit·tance**
ad nauzeam	**ad nau·se·am**
adnoids	**ad·e·noids**
ado	**adieu** *(goodbye)*
adolescant	**ad·o·les·cent**
adom	**at·om**
adoo	**ado** *(fuss)*
adopt	**adapt** *(adjust)*
adorible	**ador·a·ble**
adrennalin	**ad·ren·al·in**
adress	**ad·dress**
adue	**ado** *(fuss)*
adultarate	**adul·ter·ate**
adultry	**adul·tery**
advacate	**ad·vo·cate**
advancment	**ad·vance·ment**
advantagious	**ad·van·ta·geous**
adventureous	**ad·ven·tur·ous**
adverse	**averse** *(unwilling)*
adversery	**ad·ver·sary**
advertisment	**ad·ver·tise·ment**
advice	**ad·vise** *(v.)*
advisary	**ad·vi·so·ry**
advise	**ad·vice** *(n.)*
adzorb	**ad·sorb** *(collect on surface)*
Aegian	**Ae·ge·an**
aeresol	**aer·o·sol**

WRONG	RIGHT	WRONG	RIGHT
aeronatical	**aer·o·nau·ti·cal**	aforism	**aph·o·rism**
afable	**af·fa·ble**	aformentioned	....
afair	**af·fair**		**afore·men·tioned**
afasia	**apha·sia**	afrayed	**afraid**
afect	**af·fect** (to influence)	Afreca	**Af·ri·ca**
afectionate	**af·fec·tion·ate**	afrodisiac	**aph·ro·dis·i·ac**
afective	**af·fec·tive** (emotional)	afront	**af·front**
affadavit	**af·fi·da·vit**	afterward	**af·ter·word**
affare	**af·fair**		(epilogue)
affect	**ef·fect** (result)	afterword	**af·ter·ward** (later)
affective	**ef·fec·tive**	aganize	**ag·o·nize**
	(having effect)	agast	**aghast**
affend	**of·fend**	agensy	**agen·cy**
affible	**af·fa·ble**	agetate	**ag·i·tate**
afficionado	**afi·cio·nado**	aggresion	**ag·gres·sion**
affilliate	**af·fil·i·ate**	aggrivate	**ag·gra·vate**
affirmitive	**af·firm·a·tive**	agitater	**ag·i·ta·tor**
affluent	**ef·flu·ent** (flowing)	agled	**ogled**
affraid	**afraid**	agnastic	**ag·nos·tic**
affusive	**ef·fu·sive**	agraculture	**agri·cul·ture**
Afganistan	**Afghan·i·stan**	agravate	**ag·gra·vate**
aficcionado	**afi·cio·nado**	agreegious	**egre·gious**
afid	**aphid**	agreeible	**agree·a·ble**
afidavit	**af·fi·da·vit**	agregate	**ag·gre·gate**
afiliate	**af·fil·i·ate**	agrerian	**agrar·i·an**
afinity	**af·fin·i·ty**	agression	**ag·gres·sion**
afirm	**af·firm**	ahed	**ahead**
afirmative	**af·firm·a·tive**	aid	**aide** (assistant)
afix	**af·fix**	aide	**aid** (help)
afliction	**af·flic·tion**	ail	**ale** (a drink)
afluent	**af·flu·ent** (rich)	ailmint	**ail·ment**
aford	**af·ford**	air	**err** (be wrong)

WRONG	RIGHT	WRONG	RIGHT
air	**heir** (inheritor)	albetross	**al·ba·tross**
airate	**aer·ate**	albinoes	**al·bi·nos**
airess	**heir·ess**	albumen	**al·bu·min**
airial	**aer·i·al**		(class of proteins)
airid	**ar·id**	albumin	**al·bu·men**
airie	**aer·ie** (nest)		(egg white)
airobic	**aer·o·bic**	alchoholic	**al·co·hol·ic**
airodynamics		ale	**ail** (be ill)
	aer·o·dy·nam·ics	aleet	**elite** (best)
aironautical	**aer·o·nau·ti·cal**	alege	**al·lege**
airosol	**aer·o·sol**	alegiance	**al·le·giance**
airospace	**aer·o·space**	alegory	**al·le·go·ry**
airplain	**air·plane**	alegro	**al·le·gro**
aisle	**isle** (island)	alergy	**al·ler·gy**
ajacent	**ad·ja·cent**	aleviate	**al·le·vi·ate**
ajective	**ad·jec·tive**	alfactory	**ol·fac·to·ry**
ajenda	**agen·da**	algabra	**al·ge·bra**
ajoining	**ad·join·ing**	algie	**al·gae**
ajourn	**ad·journ**	Algiria	**Al·ge·ria**
ajulation	**ad·u·la·tion**	alian	**al·ien**
ajunct	**ad·junct**	aliance	**al·li·ance**
ajust	**ad·just**	alied	**al·lied**
ajutant	**ad·ju·tant**	aligator	**al·li·ga·tor**
ake	**ache**	alimentary	**ele·men·ta·ry**
aknowledge	**ac·knowl·edge**		(basic)
akorn	**acorn**	alinement	**align·ment**
akrid	**ac·rid**	alius	**ali·as**
a la cart	**a la carte**	alkaholic	**al·co·hol·ic**
alamony	**al·i·mo·ny**	alkeline	**al·ka·line**
alay	**al·lay** (relieve)	all	**awl** (tool)
Albaquerque	**Albu·quer·que**	Allabama	**Al·a·bama**
albem	**al·bum**	allabaster	**al·a·bas·ter**

WRONG	RIGHT
allacation	**al·lo·ca·tion**
allbatross	**al·ba·tross**
allderman	**al·der·man**
alledge	**al·lege**
allegience	**al·le·giance**
allert	**alert**
alley	**al·ly** *(join; partner)*
allibi	**al·i·bi**
allience	**al·li·ance**
allies	**al·leys**
	(pl.; narrow lanes)
alligater	**al·li·ga·tor**
allignment	**align·ment**
allimentary	**ali·men·ta·ry**
	(nourishing)
allimony	**al·i·mo·ny**
allive	**ol·ive**
allmanac	**al·ma·nac**
allmighty	**al·mighty**
allmost	**al·most**
alloting	**al·lot·ting**
alloud	**aloud** *(loudly)*
allowence	**al·low·ance**
allready	**al·ready**
allthough	**al·though**
alltogether	**al·to·geth·er**
allude	**elude** *(escape)*
alluminum	**alu·mi·num**
allusion	**elu·sion** *(an escape)*
allusion	**il·lu·sion** *(false idea)*
allusive	**elu·sive**
	(hard to grasp)
allusive	**il·lu·sive** *(deceptive)*
allways	**al·ways**
ally	**al·ley** *(sing.; narrow lane)*
almend	**al·mond**
alocation	**al·lo·ca·tion**
alotting	**al·lot·ting**
aloud	**al·lowed** *(permitted)*
alowance	**al·low·ance**
alowed	**al·lowed** *(permitted)*
aloy	**al·loy**
alphebet	**al·pha·bet**
altar	**al·ter** *(to change)*
altatude	**al·ti·tude**
alter	**al·tar** *(table for worship)*
alterior	**ul·te·ri·or**
alterration	**alter·a·tion**
alturnate	**al·ter·nate**
alude	**al·lude** *(refer to)*
alumnae	**alum·ni** *(m., pl.)*
alumni	**alum·nae** *(f., pl.)*
alure	**al·lure**
alusion	**al·lu·sion** *(reference)*
alusive	**al·lu·sive** *(referring to)*
amature	**am·a·teur**
amazment	**amaze·ment**
ambaguity	**am·bi·gu·i·ty**
ambasador	**ambas·sa·dor**
ambeance	**am·bi·ance**
ambedextrous	
	am·bi·dex·trous
ambiant	**am·bi·ent**
ambitous	**am·bi·tious**

WRONG	RIGHT	WRONG	RIGHT
ambivalance	**am·biv·a·lence**	amuk	**amok**
ambudsman	**om·buds·man**	amunition	**ammu·ni·tion**
ambulence	**am·bu·lance**	anackronism	**anach·ro·nism**
ameanable	**ame·na·ble**	analisis	**anal·y·sis** *(sing.)*
amego	**ami·go**	analitic	**an·a·lyt·ic**
ameible	**ami·a·ble**	analize	**an·a·lyze**
amelet	**om·e·let**	anallogy	**anal·o·gy**
amelliorate	**amel·io·rate**	anals	**an·nals** *(records)*
amend	**emend** *(correct)*	analysis	**anal·y·ses** *(pl.)*
amenible	**ame·na·ble**	analyst	**an·nal·ist**
ameno	**ami·no**		*(writer of annals)*
amfetamine	**amphet·a·mine**	anamation	**an·i·ma·tion**
amfibian	**am·phib·i·an**	anamosity	**an·i·mos·i·ty**
amicible	**am·i·ca·ble**	anasthetic	**an·es·thet·ic**
ammendment	**amend·ment**	anatamy	**anat·o·my**
ammends	**amends**	anceint	**an·cient**
ammoral	**amor·al**	ancester	**an·ces·tor**
ammorous	**am·o·rous**	ancilary	**an·cil·lary**
ammorphous	**amor·phous**	ancor	**an·chor**
ammortize	**am·or·tize**	anecdote	**an·ti·dote** *(remedy)*
ammount	**amount**	aneckdote	**an·ec·dote** *(story)*
ammulet	**am·u·let**	anemal	**an·i·mal**
amnezia	**am·ne·sia**	anex	**an·nex**
amnibus	**om·ni·bus**	angel	**an·gle** *(corner; aspect)*
amnisty	**am·nes·ty**	angenue	**in·gé·nue**
amond	**al·mond**	angery	**an·gry**
amonia	**am·mo·nia**	angle	**an·gel** *(spirit)*
amore	**amour**	angwish	**an·guish**
ampear	**am·pere**	anice	**an·ise** *(plant)*
ampitheater	**am·phi·the·a·ter**	anigma	**enig·ma**
amplefy	**am·pli·fy**	anihilate	**an·ni·hi·late**
ampletude	**am·pli·tude**	animasity	**an·i·mos·i·ty**

WRONG	RIGHT
aniss	**anus** *(fundament)*
aniversary	**anni·ver·sa·ry**
anjina	**an·gi·na**
ankel	**an·kle**
anker	**an·chor**
annal	**anal** *(of the anus)*
annalgesic	**an·al·ge·sic**
annalist	**an·a·lyst**
	(one who analyzes)
annalog	**an·a·log**
annalogy	**anal·o·gy**
annalysis	**anal·y·sis** *(sing.)*
annarchist	**an·ar·chist**
annatation	**an·no·ta·tion**
annewity	**an·nu·i·ty**
annialate	**an·ni·hi·late**
anniversory	**anni·ver·sa·ry**
annix	**an·nex**
annoint	**anoint**
annomaly	**anom·a·ly**
annonymous	**anon·y·mous**
annorexia	**an·o·rex·ia**
announcment	
	an·nounce·ment
annualy	**an·nu·al·ly**
annule	**an·nu·al**
annull	**an·nul**
annunciate	**enun·ci·ate**
	(pronounce)
anomally	**anom·a·ly**
anonemous	**anon·y·mous**
anorrexia	**an·o·rex·ia**

WRONG	RIGHT
anotation	**an·no·ta·tion**
anouncement	
	an·nounce·ment
anoy	**an·noy**
anser	**an·swer**
ansestor	**an·ces·tor**
ansillary	**an·cil·lary**
ant	**aunt** *(relative)*
antadote	**an·ti·dote** *(remedy)*
antaginistic	**an·tag·o·nis·tic**
antalope	**an·te·lope**
antanym	**an·to·nym**
antartic	**ant·arc·tic**
antasid	**ant·ac·id**
antchovy	**an·cho·vy**
ante	**an·ti** *(opposed)*
anteak	**an·tique**
antebiotic	**an·ti·bi·ot·ic**
antecedant	**an·te·ced·ent**
anteclimax	**an·ti·cli·max**
antedepressant	
	an·ti·de·pres·sant
antefreeze	**an·ti·freeze**
antehistamine	
	an·ti·his·ta·mine
antena	**an·ten·na**
antepasto	**an·ti·pas·to**
anteperspirant	
	an·ti·per·spir·ant
antequated	**an·ti·quat·ed**
anteseedent	**an·te·ced·ent**
anteseptic	**an·ti·sep·tic**

9

WRONG	RIGHT	WRONG	RIGHT
anthalogy	**an·thol·o·gy**	anziety	**anx·i·e·ty**
anthrapology	**an·thro·pol·o·gy**	apacalypse	**apoc·a·lypse**
anti	**an·te** *(stake; share)*	apacryphal	**apoc·ry·phal**
antibiatic	**an·ti·bi·ot·ic**	Apalachia	**Appa·la·chia**
anticapate	**an·tic·i·pate**	apall	**ap·pall**
anticedent	**an·te·ced·ent**	aparatus	**ap·pa·ra·tus**
antidate	**an·te·date**	aparel	**ap·par·el**
antidepressent	**an·ti·de·pres·sant**	aparently	**ap·par·ent·ly**
antidote	**an·ec·dote** *(story)*	aparition	**ap·pa·ri·tion**
antihistamean	**an·ti·his·ta·mine**	apartmint	**apart·ment**
antiperspirent	**an·ti·per·spir·ant**	apastle	**apos·tle**
antisipate	**an·tic·i·pate**	apature	**ap·er·ture**
antithasis	**an·tith·e·sis** *(sing.)*	apeal	**ap·peal**
antithesis	**an·tith·e·ses** *(pl.)*	apearance	**ap·pear·ance**
antlur	**ant·ler**	apeasement	**ap·pease·ment**
antonim	**an·to·nym**	apecks	**apex**
antrepreneur	**en·tre·pre·neur**	apellate	**ap·pel·late**
anual	**an·nu·al**	apendage	**ap·pend·age**
anuity	**an·nu·i·ty**	apendicitis	**ap·pen·di·ci·tis**
anull	**an·nul**	apendix	**ap·pen·dix**
anullment	**an·nul·ment**	apethetic	**ap·a·thet·ic**
anunciate	**an·nun·ci·ate** *(announce)*	apetite	**ap·pe·tite** *(hunger)*
anvel	**an·vil**	apharism	**aph·o·rism**
anxeity	**anx·i·e·ty**	aphradisiac	**aph·ro·dis·i·ac**
anxous	**anx·ious**	aplaud	**ap·plaud**
anywere	**an·y·where**	aplause	**ap·plause**
anyx	**on·yx**	aple	**ap·ple**
		apliance	**ap·pli·ance**
		aplication	**ap·pli·ca·tion**
		aplom	**aplomb**
		aply	**ap·ply**
		apocalipse	**apoc·a·lypse**

WRONG	RIGHT	WRONG	RIGHT
apocrephal	**apoc·ry·phal**	apploud	**ap·plaud**
apointment	**ap·point·ment**	appocalypse	**apoc·a·lypse**
apolegy	**apol·o·gy**	appocryphal	**apoc·ry·phal**
apollogetic	**apol·o·get·ic**	Appolo	**Apol·lo**
Apolo	**Apol·lo**	appologetic	**apol·o·get·ic**
aportionment		appology	**apol·o·gy**
	ap·por·tion·ment	appostle	**apos·tle**
apossum	**opos·sum**	appostrophe	**apos·tro·phe**
apostrophies	**apos·tro·phes**		*(sing.)*
	(pl.)	apprahend	**ap·pre·hend**
apostrophy	**apos·tro·phe**	appraise	**ap·prise** *(inform)*
	(sing.)	appraximate	**ap·prox·i·mate**
Appalachia	**Appa·la·chia**	appricot	**apri·cot**
appathetic	**ap·a·thet·ic**	apprise	**ap·praise** *(estimate)*
appatite	**ap·pe·tite** *(hunger)*	approachible	**ap·proach·a·ble**
appeerence	**ap·pear·ance**	appropos	**ap·ro·pos**
appeasment	**ap·pease·ment**	appropreate	**ap·pro·pri·ate**
appeel	**ap·peal**	approvel	**ap·prov·al**
appel	**ap·ple**	apracot	**apri·cot**
appelate	**ap·pel·late**	apraisal	**ap·prais·al**
appendacitis	**ap·pen·di·ci·tis**	apraise	**ap·praise** *(estimate)*
appendege	**ap·pend·age**	apreciate	**ap·pre·ci·ate**
appendicks	**ap·pen·dix**	aprehend	**ap·pre·hend**
apperatus	**ap·pa·ra·tus**	aprentice	**ap·pren·tice**
apperel	**ap·par·el**	aprise	**ap·prise** *(inform)*
apperently	**ap·par·ent·ly**	aproachable	**ap·proach·a·ble**
apperture	**ap·er·ture**	apropoe	**ap·ro·pos**
applacation	**ap·pli·ca·tion**	apropriate	**ap·pro·pri·ate**
applaws	**ap·plause**	aproval	**ap·prov·al**
applie	**ap·ply**	aprove	**ap·prove**
applience	**ap·pli·ance**	aproximate	**ap·prox·i·mate**
applomb	**aplomb**	aptatude	**ap·ti·tude**

WRONG	RIGHT	WRONG	RIGHT
aptic	**op·tic**	arithmatic	**arith·me·tic**
aquaduct	**aq·ue·duct**	arival	**ar·riv·al**
aquaintance	**ac·quaint·ance**	arizing	**aris·ing**
aquamurine	**aq·ua·ma·rine**	ark	**arc** (curve)
aquareum	**aquar·i·um**	arkade	**ar·cade**
Aquerius	**Aquar·i·us**	arkaic	**ar·cha·ic**
aquiduct	**aq·ue·duct**	arkangel	**arch·an·gel**
aquiescence	**ac·qui·es·cence**	Arkensaw	**Ar·kan·sas**
aquire	**ac·quire**	arkeology	**ar·chae·ol·o·gy**
aquitted	**ac·quit·ted**	arkives	**ar·chives**
araign	**ar·raign**	armachure	**ar·ma·ture**
arange	**or·ange**	armadilo	**ar·ma·dil·lo**
arangement	**ar·range·ment**	armastice	**ar·mi·stice**
arangutan	**orang·u·tan**	armement	**ar·ma·ment**
aray	**ar·ray**	armer	**ar·mor**
arbatrate	**ar·bi·trate**	armery	**ar·mory**
arbitrery	**ar·bi·trary**	arogance	**ar·ro·gance**
arc	**ark** (enclosure)	arouze	**arouse**
archangle	**arch·an·gel**	arow	**ar·row**
archary	**arch·ery**	arrain	**ar·raign**
archipellago	**ar·chi·pel·ago**	arrangment	**ar·range·ment**
architechure	**ar·chi·tec·ture**	arrogence	**ar·ro·gance**
arduos	**ar·du·ous**	arromatic	**ar·o·mat·ic**
ardvark	**aard·vark**	arrouse	**arouse**
area	**aria** (melody)	arsenel	**ar·se·nal**
arears	**ar·rears**	arsinic	**ar·se·nic**
Arees	**Ar·i·es**	arsinist	**ar·son·ist**
aregano	**oreg·a·no**	artachoke	**ar·ti·choke**
arest	**ar·rest**	artacle	**ar·ti·cle**
arguement	**ar·gu·ment**	artafact	**ar·ti·fact**
aria	**ar·ea** (region)	artaficial	**arti·fi·cial**
aristacratic	**aris·to·crat·ic**	artary	**ar·tery**

WRONG	RIGHT	WRONG	RIGHT
artfull	**art·ful**	asimilation	**as·sim·i·la·tion**
artheritis	**ar·thri·tis**	asistance	**as·sist·ance**
artic	**arc·tic**	asociation	**as·so·ci·a·tion**
artickle	**ar·ti·cle**	asorted	**as·sort·ed**
artifack	**ar·ti·fact**	aspeck	**as·pect**
artilery	**ar·til·lery**	asperagus	**as·par·a·gus**
artirial	**ar·te·ri·al**	asperin	**as·pi·rin**
artisticly	**artis·ti·cal·ly**	aspholt	**as·phalt**
arye	**awry**	aspin	**as·pen**
asailant	**as·sail·ant**	asprin	**as·pi·rin**
asassin	**as·sas·sin**	aspyre	**as·pire**
asassinate	**assas·si·nate**	assailent	**as·sail·ant**
asault	**as·sault**	assalt	**as·sault**
asay	**as·say** *(analyze)*	assasanate	**assas·si·nate**
ascent	**as·sent** *(consent)*	assasin	**as·sas·sin**
ascent	**ac·cent** *(emphasis)*	assay	**es·say** *(try; composition)*
ascertane	**as·cer·tain**	assembley	**as·sem·bly**
ase	**ace**	assent	**as·cent** *(a rising)*
asembly	**as·sem·bly**	assimulation	**as·sim·i·la·tion**
asent	**as·sent** *(consent)*	assinement	**as·sign·ment**
aserbic	**acer·bic**	assinine	**as·i·nine**
asert	**as·sert**	assistence	**as·sist·ance**
asess	**as·sess**	assparagus	**as·par·a·gus**
asetate	**ac·e·tate**	assurence	**as·sur·ance**
asetic	**as·cet·ic** *(austere)*	assurt	**as·sert**
asett	**as·set**	asswage	**as·suage**
asetylene	**acet·y·lene**	astanish	**as·ton·ish**
asfault	**as·phalt**	astarisk	**as·ter·isk**
asfixiate	**as·phyx·i·ate**	astaroid	**as·ter·oid**
asidic	**acid·ic**	astensible	**os·ten·si·ble**
asignment	**as·sign·ment**	astigmatism	**stig·ma·tism**
asilum	**asy·lum**		*(condition of normal lens)*

WRONG	RIGHT	WRONG	RIGHT
astoot	**as·tute**	atorney	**at·tor·ney**
astralogy	**as·trol·o·gy**	atract	**at·tract**
astranaut	**as·tro·naut**	atraphy	**at·ro·phy**
astrangement		atrasity	**atroc·i·ty**
	es·trange·ment	atribution	**at·tri·bu·tion**
astranomy	**as·tron·o·my**	atrition	**at·tri·tion**
astringint	**as·trin·gent**	atrocous	**atro·cious**
astronot	**as·tro·naut**	atrofy	**at·ro·phy**
asuage	**as·suage**	atrotious	**atro·cious**
asume	**as·sume**	attanement	**at·tain·ment**
asumption	**as·sump·tion**	attashay	**at·ta·ché**
asurance	**as·sur·ance**	attemp	**at·tempt**
ataché	**at·ta·ché**	attendence	**at·tend·ance**
atachment	**at·tach·ment**	attension	**at·ten·tion**
atack	**at·tack**	attentave	**at·ten·tive**
atainment	**at·tain·ment**	atter	**ot·ter**
atamic	**atom·ic**	attonement	**atone·ment**
atempt	**at·tempt**	attorny	**at·tor·ney**
atendance	**at·tend·ance**	atum	**at·om**
atention	**at·ten·tion**	atune	**at·tune**
atest	**at·test**	audable	**au·di·ble**
athaletics	**ath·let·ics**	audasity	**au·dac·i·ty**
athelete	**ath·lete**	audatorium	**au·di·to·ri·um**
athiestic	**athe·is·tic**	audeo	**au·dio**
athoritarian	**author·i·tar·i·an**	audiance	**au·di·ence**
athority	**au·thor·i·ty**	Augist	**Au·gust**
atic	**at·tic**	aukward	**awk·ward**
atire	**at·tire**	aul	**awl** *(tool)*
atitude	**at·ti·tude**	auning	**awn·ing**
atlus	**at·las**	aunt	**ant** *(insect)*
atmaspheric	**atmos·pher·ic**	aural	**oral** *(of the mouth)*
atonment	**atone·ment**	aurel	**au·ral** *(of the ear)*

auspaces	**aus·pi·ces**	avrage	**av·er·age**
auspitious	**aus·pi·cious**	avud	**av·id**
austairity	**aus·ter·i·ty**	avursion	**aver·sion**
austeer	**aus·tere**	awate	**await**
autagraph	**au·to·graph**	awburn	**au·burn**
autamatic	**au·to·mat·ic**	awdacity	**au·dac·i·ty**
autamobile	**au·to·mo·bile**	awdible	**au·di·ble**
autanamous	**au·ton·o·mous**	awdience	**au·di·ence**
autapsy	**au·top·sy**	awdio	**au·dio**
auther	**au·thor**	awdition	**au·di·tion**
autherize	**au·thor·ize**	awditorium	**au·di·to·ri·um**
authoratarian		awear	**aware**
	author·i·tar·i·an	awefully	**aw·ful·ly**
autockracy	**au·toc·ra·cy**	awesum	**awe·some**
autoes	**au·tos**	awfuly	**aw·ful·ly**
automabile	**au·to·mo·bile**	awile	**awhile**
autonomos	**au·ton·o·mous**	awktion	**auc·tion**
autum	**au·tumn**	awkword	**awk·ward**
auxilary	**aux·il·ia·ry**	aword	**award**
avacado	**av·o·ca·do**	awsome	**awe·some**
availible	**avail·a·ble**	awthentic	**au·then·tic**
avalanch	**av·a·lanche**	awthor	**au·thor**
avanue	**av·e·nue**	awthorize	**au·thor·ize**
avarage	**av·er·age**	awtistic	**au·tis·tic**
avaricous	**ava·ri·cious**	awtocracy	**au·toc·ra·cy**
avaunt–guarde	**avant–garde**	awtopsy	**au·top·sy**
aveation	**avi·a·tion**	awtumn	**au·tumn**
avelanche	**av·a·lanche**	axel	**ax·le**
avericious	**ava·ri·cious**	axes	**ax·is** *(sing.)*
averse	**ad·verse** *(opposed)*	axis	**ax·es** *(pl.)*
avinue	**av·e·nue**	azbestos	**as·bes·tos**
avoidible	**avoid·a·ble**	azthma	**asth·ma**

B

WRONG	RIGHT
babboon	**ba·boon**
Babelonian	**Bab·y·lo·ni·an**
babled	**bab·bled**
babling	**bab·bling**
babooshka	**ba·bush·ka**
babtism	**bap·tism**
babtist	**bap·tist**
babtize	**bap·tize**
babyed	**ba·bied**
Babyllonian	**Bab·y·lo·ni·an**
bacallaureate	**bac·ca·lau·re·ate**
baccanal	**bac·cha·nal**
bacchanallean	**bac·cha·na·li·an**
baccilus	**ba·cil·lus**
Baccus	**Bac·chus**
bach	**batch** (quantity)
bachalor	**bach·e·lor**
bachannal	**bac·cha·nal**
Bachus	**Bac·chus**
backake	**back·ache**
backalaureate	**bac·ca·lau·re·ate**
backammon	**back·gam·mon**
backanal	**bac·cha·nal**
backanalian	**bac·cha·na·li·an**
backbord	**back·board**
backbraking	**back·break·ing**
backgamen	**back·gam·mon**

WRONG	RIGHT
backloged	**back·logged**
backpak	**back·pack**
backround	**back·ground**
backword	**back·ward**
bactiria	**bac·te·ria**
badder	**bat·ter**
baddering	**bat·ter·ing**
baddery	**bat·tery**
bade	**bayed** (howled)
badjer	**badg·er**
badminten	**bad·min·ton**
badmitten	**bad·min·ton**
baffeling	**baf·fling**
bafling	**baf·fling**
bafoon	**buf·foon**
bagage	**bag·gage**
bagammon	**back·gam·mon**
bager	**badg·er**
bagle	**ba·gel**
baid	**bade**
baige	**beige**
bail	**bale** (bundle)
bailful	**bale·ful**
bait	**bate** (lessen)
bakrey	**bak·ery**
bakteria	**bac·te·ria**
balad	**bal·lad**
balancable	**bal·ance·a·ble**
balancible	**bal·ance·a·ble**
balast	**bal·last**
balcany	**bal·co·ny**
bale	**bail** (money)

WRONG	RIGHT	WRONG	RIGHT
bale bond	**bail bond**	Baltamore	**Bal·ti·more**
balefull	**bale·ful**	bambu	**bam·boo**
balence	**bal·ance**	banall	**ba·nal**
balerina	**bal·le·ri·na**	bananza	**bo·nan·za**
balero	**bo·le·ro**	banaster	**ban·is·ter**
balet	**bal·let** (dance)	banbon	**bon·bon**
baliff	**bai·liff**	banbox	**band·box**
balister	**bal·us·ter**	band	**banned** (forbidden)
balistic	**bal·lis·tic**	bandade	**Band–Aid**
Balivia	**Bo·liv·ia**	bandet	**ban·dit**
Balken	**Bal·kan**	bandie	**ban·dy**
balkony	**bal·co·ny**	bandige	**band·age**
ball	**bawl** (cry)	bandjo	**ban·jo**
ballance	**bal·ance**	bands	**banns**
ballarina	**bal·le·ri·na**		(marriage announcement)
ballay	**bal·let** (dance)	bandwagen	**band·wag·on**
ballcony	**bal·co·ny**	banel	**ba·nal**
ballderdash	**bal·der·dash**	baner	**ban·ner**
ballet	**bal·lot** (voting slip)	banign	**be·nign**
ballid	**bal·lad**	banjoe	**ban·jo**
balligerance	**bel·lig·er·ence**	bankett	**ban·quette** (bench)
ballister	**bal·us·ter**	bankrupcy	**bank·rupt·cy**
ballistik	**bal·lis·tic**	bankwet	**ban·quet** (feast)
ballsa	**bal·sa**	bannana	**ba·nana**
ballsam	**bal·sam**	bannish	**ban·ish**
ballust	**bal·last**	bannister	**ban·is·ter**
balogna	**bo·lo·gna**	banns	**bans** (forbids)
balona	**bo·lo·gna**	banquit	**ban·quet** (feast)
baloon	**bal·loon**	bans	**banns**
balot	**bal·lot** (voting slip)		(marriage announcement)
balroom	**ball·room**	bansai	**bon·sai** (tree shaping)
balsom	**bal·sam**	banstand	**band·stand**

17

WRONG	RIGHT
bantom	**ban·tam**
banwagon	**band·wag·on**
baptest	**bap·tist**
baptizm	**bap·tism**
baracks	**bar·racks**
baracuda	**bar·ra·cu·da**
barage	**bar·rage**
barbacue	**bar·be·cue**
barbarrian	**bar·bar·i·an**
barbel	**bar·bell** (weights)
barbell	**bar·bel**
	(hairlike growth)
barberian	**bar·bar·i·an**
barberous	**bar·ba·rous**
barbery	**bar·ber·ry**
barbichurate	**bar·bi·tu·rate**
barble ..	**bar·bel** (hairlike growth)
Barcilona	**Bar·ce·lo·na**
bare	**bear** (animal; carry)
bared	**barred** (excluded)
ba–relief	**bas–re·lief**
baren	**bar·ren** (sterile)
baren	**bar·on** (noble)
baret	**bar·rette** (hair clasp)
barfoot	**bare·foot**
bargan	**bar·gain**
baricade	**bar·ri·cade**
barier	**bar·ri·er**
bariness	**bar·on·ess**
baring	**bar·ring** (preventing)
barister	**bar·ris·ter**
barly	**bar·ley**

WRONG	RIGHT
barnicle	**bar·na·cle**
baroke	**ba·roque**
baron	**bar·ren** (sterile)
baronness	**bar·on·ess**
baroom	**bar·room**
barracade	**bar·ri·cade**
barred	**bard** (poet)
barren	**bar·on** (noble)
barret	**bar·rette** (hair clasp)
barricks	**bar·racks**
barricuda	**bar·ra·cu·da**
barristor	**bar·ris·ter**
barritone	**bar·i·tone**
barrol	**bar·rel**
barrometer	**ba·rom·e·ter**
barron	**bar·ren** (sterile)
barroque	**ba·roque**
barrow	**bor·row**
	(take temporarily)
Barsilona	**Bar·ce·lo·na**
bartendor	**bar·tend·er**
basanet	**bas·i·net** (helmet)
basanet	**bas·si·net** (baby bed)
baschion	**bas·tion**
base	**bass** (voice)
based	**baste** (sew; moisten)
basel	**bas·il** (herb)
basel	**bas·al** (basic)
basemint	**base·ment**
basen	**ba·sin**
base–relief	**bas–re·lief**
baserk	**ber·serk**

WRONG	RIGHT	WRONG	RIGHT
bases	**ba·sis** (sing.)	battallion	**bat·tal·ion**
bashfull	**bash·ful**	batton	**bat·ten** (fasten)
basicly	**bas·i·cal·ly**	batton	**ba·ton** (stick)
basil	**bas·al** (basic)	baud	**bawd** (prostitute)
basillica	**ba·sil·i·ca**	baudy	**bawdy**
basillus	**ba·cil·lus**	baught	**bought** (purchased)
basinet	**bas·si·net** (baby bed)	bauk	**balk**
basis	**ba·ses** (pl. of basis)	baul	**bawl** (cry)
baskit	**bas·ket**	Baveria	**Ba·var·ia**
baskitball	**bas·ket·ball**	bawble	**bau·ble**
basment	**base·ment**	bawd	**baud** (measurement)
basoon	**bas·soon**	bawk	**balk**
basque	**bask** (warm)	bawl	**ball** (sphere)
basquet	**bas·ket**	bawxite	**baux·ite**
bass	**base** (foundation)	bayanet	**bay·o·net**
bassanet	**bas·si·net** (baby bed)	bayliff	**bai·liff**
bassilica	**ba·sil·i·ca**	baynal	**ba·nal**
bassit	**bas·set**	bayonnet	**bay·o·net**
bass–relief	**bas–re·lief**	bayoo	**bay·ou**
basterd	**bas·tard**	bazaar	**bi·zarre** (odd)
bata	**be·ta**	bazare	**ba·zaar** (market)
batallion	**bat·tal·ion**	bazil	**bas·il** (herb)
batchelor	**bach·e·lor**	be	**bee** (insect)
bate	**bait** (lure)	beach	**beech** (tree)
bateak	**ba·tik**	beachead	**beach·head**
bated	**bat·ted** (hit)	beachnut	**beech·nut**
batery	**bat·tery**	beakon	**bea·con**
bath	**bathe** (v.)	beanary	**bean·ery**
bathas	**ba·thos**	bear	**beer** (drink)
bathe	**bath** (n.)	bear	**bare** (naked)
bathouse	**bath·house**	bearfoot	**bare·foot**
bating	**bat·ting** (hitting)	bearly	**bare·ly**

19

beastial	**bes·tial**	begining	**be·gin·ning**
beastiary	**bes·ti·ary**	behaf	**be·half**
beat	**beet** (vegetable)	behavor	**be·hav·ior**
beateous	**beau·te·ous**	behemuth	**be·he·moth**
beatle	**bee·tle**	belaber	**be·la·bor**
beattitude	**be·at·i·tude**	beleif	**be·lief** (n.)
beautey	**beau·ty**	beleive	**be·lieve** (v.)
beautious	**beau·te·ous**	Belgiam	**Bel·gium**
beautitian	**beau·ti·cian**	belicose	**bel·li·cose**
becken	**beck·on**	belief	**be·lieve** (v.)
becom	**be·calm**	believe	**be·lief** (n.)
bedazle	**be·daz·zle**	believeable	**be·liev·a·ble**
bedclose	**bed·clothes**	beliggerance	**bel·lig·er·ence**
bedlum	**bed·lam**	bell	**belle** (woman)
bedsted	**bed·stead**	bellacose	**bel·li·cose**
beech	**beach** (shore)	belles–letters	**belles-let·tres**
beecon	**bea·con**	bellfry	**bel·fry**
beed	**bead**	Bellgium	**Bel·gium**
beefstake	**beef·steak**	bell–lettres	**belles-let·tres**
beegle	**bea·gle**	bellow	**be·low** (down)
beeker	**beak·er**	below	**bel·low** (roar)
beem	**beam**	ben	**been** (pp. of be)
been	**bean** (legume)	benadiction	**ben·e·dic·tion**
beenery	**bean·ery**	benaficial	**ben·e·fi·cial**
beer	**bier** (coffin platform)	beneeth	**be·neath**
beet	**beat** (strike)	benefacter	**ben·e·fac·tor**
beever	**bea·ver**	benefficial	**ben·e·fi·cial**
befudle	**be·fud·dle**	beneficiery	**ben·e·fi·ci·ary**
begger	**beg·gar**	benefitted	**ben·e·fit·ed**
beggin	**be·gin**	benevolance	**be·nev·o·lence**
beggining	**be·gin·ning**	benevolant	**be·nev·o·lent**
begile	**be·guile**	Bengel	**Ben·gal**

benidiction	**ben·e·dic·tion**	bersitis	**bur·si·tis**
benifactor	**ben·e·fac·tor**	bersurk	**ber·serk**
benificiary	**ben·e·fi·ci·ary**	berth	**birth** *(origin)*
benifited	**ben·e·fit·ed**	bery	**ber·ry** *(fruit)*
benine	**be·nign**	beschial	**bes·tial**
bennevolent	**be·nev·o·lent**	beseige	**be·siege**
benzene	**ben·zine**	beserk	**ber·serk**
	(cleaning fluid)	bestiery	**bes·ti·ary**
benzine ...	**ben·zene** *(chemistry)*	bestro	**bis·tro**
bequeathe	**be·queath**	Bethleham	**Beth·le·hem**
berch	**birch**	betrothe	**be·troth**
bereev	**be·reave**	betwene	**be·tween**
berg	**burg** *(town)*	beuty	**beau·ty**
berger	**burgh·er** *(citizen)*	beval	**bev·el**
berger	**bur·ger** *(hamburger)*	beverege	**bev·er·age**
berglar	**bur·glar**	bevvel	**bev·el**
Bergundy	**Bur·gun·dy**	bewillder	**be·wil·der**
berial	**bur·i·al**	bewt	**butte** *(hill)*
beritone	**bar·i·tone**	bewteous	**beau·te·ous**
berl	**burl**	bewtician	**beau·ti·cian**
berlap	**bur·lap**	bewty	**beau·ty**
berlesque	**bur·lesque**	biagraphy	**bi·og·ra·phy**
berly	**bur·ley** *(tobacco)*	bialogical	**bi·o·log·i·cal**
berly	**bur·ly** *(rough)*	biasses	**bi·as·es**
berometer	**ba·rom·e·ter**	bibleography ..	**bib·li·og·ra·phy**
beroque	**ba·roque**	bibliofile	**bib·li·o·phile**
berp	**burp**	bicalm	**be·calm**
berray	**be·ret** *(cap)*	bicarbanate	**bi·car·bon·ate**
berrel	**bar·rel**	bicentenial	**bi·cen·ten·ni·al**
berrier	**bar·ri·er**	bich	**bitch**
berrow	**bar·row**	bicicle	**bi·cy·cle**
berry	**bury** *(cover)*	bicusped	**bi·cus·pid**

WRONG	RIGHT	WRONG	RIGHT
bidazzle	**be·daz·zle**	biochemestry	....
bideck	**be·deck**		**bi·o·chem·is·try**
biding	**bid·ding** (offering)	biodegradible	....
biege	**beige**		**bi·o·de·grad·a·ble**
bigatry	**big·ot·ry**	bioengeneering	....
biggamy	**big·a·my**		**bi·o·en·gi·neer·ing**
biggot	**big·ot**	biogerphy	**bi·og·ra·phy**
biggotry	**big·ot·ry**	biolegy	**bi·ol·o·gy**
bight	**byte** (string of bits)	biorythm	**bi·o·rhythm**
bigomy	**big·a·my**	biotecnology	....
bigonia	**be·gon·ia**		**bi·o·tech·nol·o·gy**
biguile	**be·guile**	bipartesan	**bi·par·ti·san**
bihemoth	**be·he·moth**	bipass	**by·pass**
biker	**bick·er** (squabble)	bipassed	**by·passed**
bilabor	**be·la·bor**	biproduct	**by·prod·uct**
bilatteral	**bi·lat·er·al**	bireave	**be·reave**
bilboard	**bill·board**	biret	**be·ret** (cap)
bild	**build**	birth	**berth** (space)
bilding	**build·ing**	bisalt	**ba·salt**
biliards	**bil·liards**	biscut	**bis·cuit**
bilion	**bil·lion**	biseech	**be·seech**
bilje	**bilge**	bisen	**bi·son**
billay	**be·lay**	bisentennial	**bi·cen·ten·ni·al**
billingual	**bi·lin·gual**	biseps	**bi·ceps**
billionnnaire	**bil·lion·aire**	bisexule	**bi·sex·u·al**
billious	**bil·ious**	bisiege	**be·siege**
billon	**bil·lion**	bisk	**bisque**
bindary	**bind·ery**	biskit	**bis·cuit**
bineath	**be·neath**	bisness	**busi·ness**
binery	**bi·na·ry**	bissexual	**bi·sex·u·al**
binevolent	**be·nev·o·lent**	bissoon	**bas·soon**
binnocular	**bin·oc·u·lar**	bistander	**by·stand·er**

WRONG	RIGHT
bit	**bitt** (post)
bit	**bite** (chomp)
bit	**byte** (string of bits)
bite	**bight** (curve)
bite	**byte** (string of bits)
bitern	**bit·tern**
bitoominous	**bi·tu·mi·nous**
bitray	**be·tray**
bitt	**bit** (binary digit)
bitumenous	**bi·tu·mi·nous**
biuld	**build**
biulding	**build·ing**
bivouaced	**biv·ou·acked**
bivuac	**biv·ou·ac**
biway	**by·way**
biwilder	**be·wil·der**
biyou	**bay·ou**
bizaar	**bi·zarre** (odd)
Bizantine	**By·zan·tine**
bizarre	**ba·zaar** (market)
bizness	**busi·ness**
bizooka	**ba·zoo·ka**
blackmale	**black·mail**
blair	**blare**
blamless	**blame·less**
blanche	**blanch**
blandeshment	**blan·dish·ment**
blankit	**blan·ket**
blarny	**blar·ney**
blasfeme	**blas·pheme**
blasphamy	**blas·phe·my**

WRONG	RIGHT
blatency	**bla·tan·cy**
blatent	**bla·tant**
blatter	**blad·der**
blazen	**bla·zon**
blead	**bleed**
bleap	**bleep**
bleechers	**bleach·ers**
bleek	**bleak**
bleery	**bleary**
blemesh	**blem·ish**
blend	**blende** (ore)
blende	**blend** (mix)
blesed	**bless·ed**
blew	**blue** (color)
blisful	**bliss·ful**
blisster	**blis·ter**
blite	**blight**
blith	**blithe**
blithly	**blithe·ly**
blits	**blitz**
blizard	**bliz·zard**
bloc	**block** (mass)
blochy	**blotchy**
block	**bloc** (group)
blockadge	**block·age**
blockaid	**block·ade**
blodily	**blood·i·ly**
blody	**bloody**
blokade	**block·ade**
bloodally	**blood·i·ly**
bloodey	**bloody**
bloored	**blurred**

WRONG	RIGHT	WRONG	RIGHT
blosome	**blos·som**	bodess	**bod·ice**
blossum	**blos·som**	boggey	**bog·gy** *(marshy)*
blotchey	**blotchy**	bogy	**bo·gey** *(golf term)*
blote	**bloat**	bohemean	**bo·he·mi·an**
blowse	**blouse**	boicott	**boy·cott**
blubbry	**blub·bery**	boistrous	**bois·ter·ous**
bluberry	**blue·ber·ry**	bokay	**bou·quet**
blubonnet	**blue·bon·net**	bolder	**boul·der** *(rock)*
blud	**blood**	bole	**boll** *(pod)*
bluddy	**bloody**	bole	**bowl** *(round container)*
blue	**blew** *(gusted)*	boll	**bole** *(tree trunk)*
bluebonet	**blue·bon·net**	bolla	**bo·la**
blugeon	**bludg·eon**	bollder	**bold·er** *(more daring)*
blume	**bloom**	bollder	**boul·der** *(rock)*
blured	**blurred**	bollero	**bo·le·ro**
blurr	**blur**	Bollivia	**Bo·liv·ia**
bo	**beau** *(boyfriend)*	bollster	**bol·ster**
boar	**boor** *(rude person)*	bolony	**bo·lo·gna**
boar	**bore** *(dull person)*	bom	**bomb** *(explosive)*
boarish	**boor·ish**	bom	**balm** *(ointment)*
bobalink	**bob·o·link**	bomb	**balm** *(ointment)*
bobben	**bob·bin**	bombadier	**bom·bar·dier**
bobbie pin	**bob·by pin**	bommy	**balmy** *(mild)*
bobed	**bobbed**	bomshell	**bomb·shell**
bobin	**bob·bin**	bonana	**ba·nana**
bobushka	**ba·bush·ka**	bondege	**bond·age**
bobwite	**bob·white**	bondfire	**bon·fire**
boch	**botch**	boney	**bony**
bochulism	**bot·u·lism**	bonnbonn	**bon·bon**
boddice	**bod·ice**	bonnfire	**bon·fire**
boddy	**bawdy**	bonsai	**ban·zai** *(cry)*
boddy	**body**	bonusses	**bo·nus·es**

WRONG	RIGHT	WRONG	RIGHT
bonyness	**bon·i·ness**	borsh	**borsch**
bonzai	**ban·zai** *(cry)*	bosum	**bos·om**
bonzai	**bon·sai** *(tree shaping)*	botannical	**bo·tan·i·cal**
Boodist	**Bud·dhist**	botanny	**bot·a·ny**
boodoir	**bou·doir**	botchulism	**bot·u·lism**
boofant	**bouf·fant**	botten	**but·ton**
bookeeper	**book·keep·er**	bottum	**bot·tom**
boolevard	**boul·e·vard**	boudwar	**bou·doir**
boollabaisse	**bouil·la·baisse**	boufont	**bouf·fant**
boollion	**bul·lion** *(metal)*	bough	**bow** *(bend)*
boomarang	**boom·er·ang**	bought	**bout** *(fight)*
booquet	**bou·quet**	bouillebais	**bouil·la·baisse**
boor	**bore** *(dull person)*	bouillon	**bul·lion** *(metal)*
boor	**boar** *(hog)*	boulavard	**boul·e·vard**
boorgeois	**bour·geois**	boullibase	**bouil·la·baisse**
bootcher	**butch·er**	boullion	**bouil·lon** *(broth)*
bootee	**boo·ty** *(loot)*	boullion	**bul·lion** *(metal)*
bootique	**bou·tique**	boundry	**bound·a·ry**
booty	**boot·ee** *(shoe)*	bounse	**bounce**
borch	**borsch**	bounteful	**boun·ti·ful**
bord	**bored** *(weary)*	bountey	**boun·ty**
bord	**board** *(wood)*	bountious	**boun·te·ous**
bore	**boor** *(rude person)*	bourben	**bour·bon**
bore	**boar** *(hog)*	bourden	**bur·den** *(load)*
bored	**board** *(wood)*	bourgen	**bur·geon**
borish	**boor·ish**	bourgeosie	**bour·geoi·sie**
born	**borne** *(carried)*	bourgois	**bour·geois**
borow	**bor·row**	boursar	**bur·sar**
	(take temporarily)	bout	**bought** *(purchased)*
borron	**bo·ron**	bouteak	**bou·tique**
borrough	**bor·ough** *(town)*	bouttoniere	**bou·ton·niere**
borrow	**bor·ough** *(town)*	bouy	**buoy** *(floater)*

WRONG	RIGHT	WRONG	RIGHT
bouyancy	**buoy·an·cy**	braselet	**brace·let**
boveen	**bo·vine**	brasen	**bra·zen**
bow	**beau** (boyfriend)	brasier	**bra·zier** (grill)
bow	**bough** (branch)	brasiere	**bras·siere** (bra)
bowel	**bowl** (round container)	brasure	**bra·zier** (grill)
bowl	**boll** (pod)	brauth	**broth**
bowl	**bow·el** (intestine)	Braylle	**Braille**
bowl	**bole** (tree trunk)	braze	**braise** (cook)
bowla	**bo·la**	brazeness	**bra·zen·ness**
bowlder	**boul·der** (rock)	brazier	**bras·siere** (bra)
bowlderize	**bowd·ler·ize**	brazure	**bra·zier** (grill)
bowllegged	**bow·leg·ged**	breach	**breech** (bottom)
bowndary	**bound·a·ry**	bread	**breed** (produce)
bownteous	**boun·te·ous**	bread	**bred** (produced)
bowntiful	**boun·ti·ful**	break	**brake** (stop)
bownty	**boun·ty**	breakible	**break·a·ble**
bowt	**bout** (fight)	breath	**breadth** (width)
bowvine	**bo·vine**	breath	**breathe** (v.)
boxite	**baux·ite**	breathe	**breath** (n.)
boy	**buoy** (floater)	breaze	**breeze**
boycot	**boy·cott**	bred	**bread** (loaf)
boysterous	**bois·ter·ous**	bredfruit	**bread·fruit**
bozum	**bos·om**	bredth	**breadth** (width)
brackin	**brack·en**	breech	**breach** (break)
braggard	**brag·gart**	breezally	**breez·i·ly**
Braile	**Braille**	breezey	**breezy**
braise	**braze** (solder)	breif	**brief**
braize	**braise** (cook)	breth	**breath** (n.)
braize	**braze** (solder)	brethern	**breth·ren**
braizen	**bra·zen**	Breton	**Brit·on** (Celt)
brake	**break** (burst)	brevery	**bre·vi·ary**
braker	**break·er** (wave)	brevety	**brev·i·ty**

breviery	**bre·vi·ary**	brokerege	**bro·ker·age**
brewnet	**bru·nette**	brokoli	**broc·co·li**
brewry	**brew·ery**	brokrage	**bro·ker·age**
bribary	**brib·ery**	broncheal	**bron·chi·al** *(adj.)*
brickette	**bri·quette**	bronchial	**bron·chi·ole** *(n.)*
bridal	**bri·dle** *(of a horse)*	bronchitus	**bron·chi·tis**
bridle	**brid·al** *(of a bride)*	bronkial	**bron·chi·al** *(adj.)*
brieviary	**bre·vi·ary**	bronkiole	**bron·chi·ole** *(n.)*
brigadeer	**brig·a·dier**	bronkitis	**bron·chi·tis**
brige	**bridge**	Bronks	**Bronx**
brik–a–brak	**bric-a-brac**	broo	**brew**
brillience	**bril·liance**	brooch	**broach** *(introduce)*
brillient	**bril·liant**	Brooklin	**Brook·lyn**
briney	**briny**	broom	**brougham** *(carriage)*
briquett	**bri·quette**	broom	**brume** *(mist)*
brisle	**bris·tle**	broonet	**bru·nette**
Britain	**Brit·on** *(Celt)*	broose	**bruise**
Britainy	**Brit·ta·ny**	broot	**brut** *(champagne)*
Britania	**Bri·tan·nia**	broot	**brute** *(beast)*
Brittain	**Brit·ain** *(Great Britain)*	broshure	**bro·chure**
Brittainy	**Brit·ta·ny**	broughm	**brougham** *(carriage)*
Brittania	**Bri·tan·nia**	brouse	**browse**
Brittanica	**Bri·tan·nica**	browny	**brown·ie**
Brittony	**Brit·ta·ny**	browth	**broth**
broach	**brooch** *(jewelry)*	browze	**browse**
broague	**brogue**	bruit	**brut** *(champagne)*
brocaid	**bro·cade**	bruit	**brute** *(beast)*
broche	**brooch** *(jewelry)*	bruitish	**brut·ish**
broche	**broach** *(introduce)*	bruize	**bruise**
brocolli	**broc·co·li**	brume	**brougham** *(carriage)*
broge	**brogue**	brume	**broom** *(sweeper)*
brokade	**bro·cade**	bruse	**bruise**

WRONG	RIGHT	WRONG	RIGHT
Brussle sprouts	**Brus·sels sprouts**	buldog	**bull·dog**
brut	**bruit** *(rumor)*	buldozer	**bull·doz·er**
brutallity	**bru·tal·i·ty**	bulet	**bul·let**
brutallize	**bru·tal·ize**	buletin	**bul·le·tin**
brute	**bruit** *(rumor)*	bulevard	**boul·e·vard**
brute	**brut** *(champagne)*	bullbous	**bul·bous**
bubbley	**bub·bly**	bullegged	**bow·leg·ged**
bucanneer	**buc·ca·neer**	bullie	**bul·ly**
buccolic	**bu·col·ic**	bullion	**bouil·lon** *(broth)*
bucher	**butch·er**	bullit	**bul·let**
buckaneer	**buc·ca·neer**	bulliten	**bul·le·tin**
bucksome	**bux·om**	bullrush	**bul·rush**
bucollic	**bu·col·ic**	bullwark	**bul·wark**
bucskin	**buck·skin**	bullwip	**bull·whip**
Budda	**Bud·dha**	bulwork	**bul·wark**
budder	**but·ter**	bumlebee	**bum·ble·bee**
budderfly	**but·ter·fly**	bungelow	**bun·ga·low**
buddie	**bud·dy**	bunyon	**bun·ion**
Buddist	**Bud·dhist**	buoyency	**buoy·an·cy**
budgit	**budg·et**	burbon	**bour·bon**
budgitery	**budg·et·ary**	burch	**birch**
budoir	**bou·doir**	burdgeon	**bur·geon**
bufay	**buf·fet**	bureaukrat	**bureau·crat**
buffelo	**buf·fa·lo**	bureucracy	**bureau·cra·cy**
bufoon	**buf·foon**	burg	**berg** *(iceberg)*
buget	**budg·et**	Burgandy	**Bur·gun·dy**
bugetary	**budg·et·ary**	burgeler	**bur·glar**
buggey	**bug·gy**	burgeoisie	**bour·geoi·sie**
buiscut	**bis·cuit**	burger	**burgh·er** *(citizen)*
bukolic	**bu·col·ic**	burgh	**burg** *(town)*
bukskin	**buck·skin**	burgher	**bur·ger** *(hamburger)*
		burgler	**bur·glar**

WRONG	RIGHT	WRONG	RIGHT
burlesk	**bur·lesque**	butt	**butte** *(hill)*
burley	**bur·ly** *(rough)*	buttary	**but·tery**
Burlin	**Ber·lin**	butte	**butt** *(end)*
burly	**bur·ley** *(tobacco)*	butten	**but·ton**
burm	**berm**	buttoneer	**bou·ton·niere**
Burmuda	**Ber·mu·da**	buttox	**but·tocks**
burocracy	**bureau·cra·cy**	buttrass	**but·tress**
burow	**bur·row** *(dig)*	buttuck	**but·tock**
burrage	**bar·rage**	buxem	**bux·om**
burrial	**bur·i·al**	buy	**bye** *(secondary)*
burro	**bur·row** *(dig)*	buzom	**bos·om**
burrow	**bor·ough** *(town)*	buzzar	**ba·zaar** *(market)*
burrow	**bor·row**	buzzar	**bi·zarre** *(odd)*
	(take temporarily)	buzzerd	**buz·zard**
burrow	**bur·ro** *(donkey)*	by	**buy** *(purchase)*
burrsitis	**bur·si·tis**	by	**bye** *(secondary)*
burry	**bury** *(cover)*	byases	**bi·as·es**
burser	**bur·sar**	bycicle	**bi·cy·cle**
burserk	**ber·serk**	bye	**buy** *(purchase)*
bus	**buss** *(kiss)*	byfocals	**bi·fo·cals**
busness	**busi·ness**	byle	**bile**
busom	**bos·om**	bynary	**bi·na·ry**
buss	**bus** *(coach)*	byological	**bi·o·log·i·cal**
bussle	**bus·tle**	byology	**bi·ol·o·gy**
but	**butt** *(end)*	byprodduct	**by·prod·uct**
butain	**bu·tane**	bystanderd	**by·stand·er**
butchary	**butch·ery**	byte	**bit** *(binary digit)*
bute	**butte** *(hill)*	byte	**bight** *(curve)*
buter	**but·ter**	bywey	**by·way**
buterfly	**but·ter·fly**	Byzentine	**By·zan·tine**
butlar	**but·ler**		
butress	**but·tress**		

C

WRONG	RIGHT
cabage	**cab·bage**
cabaray	**cab·a·ret**
cabboose	**ca·boose**
cabel	**ca·ble** (thick rope)
cabenet	**cab·i·net**
caberet	**cab·a·ret**
cable	**ca·bal** (secret group)
cacao	**co·coa** (chocolate)
cacaphony	**ca·coph·o·ny**
Cacasian	**Cau·ca·sian**
caccus	**cau·cus**
cacky	**kha·ki**
cacoon	**co·coon**
cactis	**cac·tus**
caddaver	**ca·dav·er**
caddie	**cad·dy** (tea tray)
cadette	**ca·det**
cadie	**cad·die** (golfer)
cadry	**ca·dre**
cady	**cad·dy** (tea tray)
Caeser	**Cae·sar**
Caezarean	**Cae·sar·e·an**
cafateria	**caf·e·te·ria**
cafeine	**caf·feine**
caffe	**ca·fé**
caffee	**cof·fee**
caffeteria	**caf·e·te·ria**
caffiene	**caf·feine**
caften	**caf·tan**
Cajin	**Ca·jun**

WRONG	RIGHT
cajoll	**ca·jole**
caktus	**cac·tus**
calaber	**cal·i·ber**
Calafornia	**Cal·i·for·nia**
calammity	**ca·lam·i·ty**
calandar	**cal·en·dar** (table of dates)
calarie	**cal·o·rie**
calasthenics	**cal·is·then·ics**
calcalate	**cal·cu·late**
calculater	**cal·cu·la·tor**
cale	**kale**
caleidoscope	**ka·lei·do·scope**
calender	**col·an·der** (strainer)
caligraphy	**cal·lig·ra·phy**
calipso	**ca·lyp·so**
calistenics	**cal·is·then·ics**
callamine	**cal·a·mine**
callamity	**ca·lam·i·ty**
calldron	**cal·dron**
callendar	**cal·en·dar** (table of dates)
calliber	**cal·i·ber**
callico	**cal·i·co**
calliflower	**cau·li·flower**
callorie	**cal·o·rie**
callous	**cal·lus** (hardened skin)
callus	**cal·lous** (insensitive)
calsium	**cal·ci·um**
calvary	**cav·al·ry** (troops)
Calvery	**Cal·va·ry** (Biblical place)

camaflage	**cam·ou·flage**	cannapé	**ca·na·pé** *(appetizer)*
camasole	**cam·i·sole**	cannary	**ca·nary**
cameleon	**cha·me·le·on**	cannasta	**ca·nas·ta**
camfor	**cam·phor**	cannen	**can·non** *(large gun)*
camio	**cam·eo**	cannidate	**can·di·date**
cammel	**cam·el**	cannine	**ca·nine**
cammera	**cam·era**	canning	**can·ing** *(flogging)*
cammomile	**cham·o·mile**	cannister	**can·is·ter**
cammouflage	**cam·ou·flage**	cannon	**can·on** *(church law)*
campane	**cam·paign**	canon	**can·non** *(large gun)*
campas	**cam·pus**	canopy	**ca·na·pé** *(appetizer)*
campound	**com·pound**	cansel	**can·cel**
camra	**cam·era**	canser	**can·cer**
Canadien	**Ca·na·di·an**	cant	**can't** *(cannot)*
canapé	**can·o·py** *(awning)*	cantalever	**can·ti·le·ver**
canapée	**ca·na·pé** *(appetizer)*	cantalope	**can·ta·loupe**
canaster	**can·is·ter**	cantene	**can·teen**
cancelation	**can·cel·la·tion**	canter	**can·tor** *(singer)*
cancker	**can·ker**	cantor	**can·ter** *(gallop)*
candadate	**can·di·date**	canue	**ca·noe**
canded	**can·did**	canvas	**can·vass** *(poll)*
candedacy	**can·di·da·cy**	canvass	**can·vas** *(cloth)*
candel	**can·dle**	canyun	**can·yon**
candellabrum		capabel	**ca·pa·ble**
	can·de·la·brum	capasity	**ca·pac·i·ty**
cander	**can·dor**	capatal	**cap·i·tal** *(city; chief)*
candyed	**can·died**	capchure	**cap·ture**
canen	**can·on** *(church law)*	capeble	**ca·pa·ble**
canery	**ca·nary**	capichulate	**capit·u·late**
canibal	**can·ni·bal**	capilary	**cap·il·lary**
caning	**can·ning** *(preserving)*	capital	**cap·i·tol** *(building)*
cannal	**ca·nal**	capitol	**cap·i·tal** *(city; chief)*

WRONG	RIGHT
capitolism	**cap·i·tal·ism**
capitualate	**capit·u·late**
cappaccino	**cap·puc·cino**
cappillary	**cap·il·lary**
cappitulate	**capit·u·late**
Capracorn	**Cap·ri·corn**
caprise	**ca·price**
capsle	**cap·sule**
captan	**cap·tain**
captavate	**cap·ti·vate**
captave	**cap·tive**
capter	**cap·tor**
capter	**cap·ture**
captian	**cap·tion**
capuccino	**cap·puc·cino**
Carabbean	**Car·ib·be·an**
carachteristic	**char·ac·ter·is·tic**
caracter	**char·ac·ter** *(personality)*
Caralina	**Car·o·li·na**
carat	**car·et** *(proofreader's mark)*
carat	**car·rot** *(vegetable)*
carban	**car·bon**
carbanated	**car·bon·at·ed**
carbarater	**car·bu·ret·or**
carbene	**car·bine**
carberetor	**car·bu·ret·or**
carbind	**car·bine**
carbond	**car·bon**
carburator	**car·bu·ret·or**

WRONG	RIGHT
carcanoma	**car·ci·no·ma**
carcus	**car·cass**
cardagan	**car·di·gan**
cardbord	**card·board**
cardeac	**car·di·ac**
cardeology	**car·di·ol·o·gy**
cardeovascular	**car·di·o·vas·cu·lar**
cardiak	**car·di·ac**
cardialogy	**car·di·ol·o·gy**
cardinel	**car·di·nal**
cardiovasclar	**car·di·o·vas·cu·lar**
cardnal	**car·di·nal**
carear	**ca·reer**
carefull	**care·ful**
carefuly	**care·ful·ly**
carel	**car·rel** *(study desk)*
caremel	**car·a·mel**
caret	**car·at** *(gem weight)*
caret	**car·rot** *(vegetable)*
caret	**kar·at** *(1/24)*
carfully	**care·ful·ly**
cariage	**car·riage**
caricature	**char·ac·ter** *(personality)*
caricture	**car·i·ca·ture** *(picture)*
carier	**car·ri·er**
caries	**car·ries** *(form of carry)*
carion	**car·ri·on**
carisma	**cha·ris·ma**

WRONG	RIGHT	WRONG	RIGHT
carivan	**car·a·van**	carrot	**car·et**
carma	**kar·ma**		*(proofreader's mark)*
carmel	**car·a·mel**	carrotene	**car·o·tene**
carnaval	**car·ni·val**	carrouse	**ca·rouse**
carnavore	**car·ni·vore**	carsinogen	**car·cin·o·gen**
carnege	**car·nage**	carsinoma	**car·ci·no·ma**
carnel	**car·nal**	cartalage	**car·ti·lage**
carniverous	**car·niv·o·rous**	cart blanche	**carte blanche**
carol	**car·rel** *(study desk)*	cart blanche	**carte blanche**
carosene	**ker·o·sene**	cartell	**car·tel**
carot	**car·rot** *(vegetable)*	carten	**car·ton**
carotted	**ca·rot·id**	cartillage	**car·ti·lage**
carouze	**ca·rouse**	cartrige	**car·tridge**
carpetting	**car·pet·ing**	cartune	**car·toon**
carpinter	**car·pen·ter**	casally	**cas·u·al·ly**
carpit	**car·pet**	caseing	**cas·ing**
carrafe	**ca·rafe**	caseno	**ca·si·no**
carrage	**car·riage**		*(gambling room)*
carrasel	**car·rou·sel**	caserole	**cas·se·role**
carravan	**car·a·van**	casette	**cas·sette**
carrel	**car·ol** *(song)*	cashe	**cache** *(hiding place)*
carress	**ca·ress**	casheer	**cash·ier**
Carribbean	**Car·ib·be·an**	cashmeer	**cash·mere**
carricature	**car·i·ca·ture**	cashou	**cash·ew**
	(picture)	cashually	**cas·u·al·ly**
carridge	**car·riage**	cashualty	**cas·u·al·ty**
carrien	**car·ri·on**	casino	**cas·si·no** *(card game)*
carries	**car·ies** *(decay)*	caskade	**cas·cade**
carring	**car·ry·ing**	caskit	**cas·ket**
carrob	**car·ob**	casment	**case·ment**
carrol	**car·ol** *(song)*	casock	**cas·sock**
carrot	**car·at** *(gem weight)*	cassarole	**cas·se·role**

WRONG	RIGHT	WRONG	RIGHT
casscade	**cas·cade**	cattegory	**cat·e·go·ry**
cassel	**cas·tle**	cattel	**cat·tle**
casseno	**cas·si·no** *(card game)*	catterpillar	**cat·er·pil·lar**
casset	**cas·sette**	caulaflower	**cau·li·flower**
cassino	**ca·si·no**	cautius	**cau·tious**
	(gambling room)	cavaleir	**cav·a·lier**
casstanets	**cas·ta·nets**	Cavalry	**Cal·va·ry**
cast	**caste** *(social rank)*		*(Biblical place)*
castagate	**cas·ti·gate**	cavaty	**cav·i·ty**
caster	**cas·tor** *(oil)*	cavear	**cav·i·ar**
castor	**cast·er** *(wheel)*	cavelcade	**cav·al·cade**
castrait	**cas·trate**	cavelier	**cav·a·lier**
casulty	**cas·u·al·ty**	cavelry	**cav·al·ry** *(troops)*
catachism	**cat·e·chism**	cavurn	**cav·ern**
cataclism	**cat·a·clysm**	cawk	**caulk**
catacome	**cat·a·comb**	cayak	**kay·ak**
catagory	**cat·e·go·ry**	cayote	**coy·o·te**
catalist	**cat·a·lyst**	Ceasarean	**Cae·sar·e·an**
catalitic	**cat·a·lyt·ic**	cecada	**ci·ca·da**
catapalt	**cat·a·pult**	ceder	**ce·dar**
catapillar	**cat·er·pil·lar**	ceese	**cease**
catarack	**cat·a·ract**	ceiling	**seal·ing** *(fastening)*
catastrophies	**ca·tas·tro·phes**	celabrate	**cel·e·brate**
catastrophy	**ca·tas·tro·phe**	celebrety	**ce·leb·ri·ty**
catchew	**cash·ew**	celery	**sal·a·ry** *(pay)*
cateclism	**cat·a·clysm**	celesstial	**ce·les·tial**
catelog	**cat·a·log**	cell	**sell** *(trade for money)*
Cathalic	**Cath·o·lic**	cellar	**sell·er** *(vendor)*
cathater	**cath·e·ter**	cellebrate	**cel·e·brate**
cathedrel	**ca·the·dral**	cellebrity	**ce·leb·ri·ty**
Cathlic	**Cath·o·lic**	celler	**cel·lar** *(basement)*
cattalog	**cat·a·log**	cellery	**cel·e·ry** *(vegetable)*

WRONG	RIGHT
cellestial	**ce·les·tial**
cellibacy	**cel·i·ba·cy**
cellofane	**cel·lo·phane**
celophane	**cel·lo·phane**
celp	**kelp**
Celsus	**Cel·si·us**
celulite	**cel·lu·lite**
celuloid	**cel·lu·loid**
cematery	**cem·e·tery**
cemical	**chem·i·cal**
cemint	**ce·ment**
cemotherapy	**chem·o·ther·a·py**
censer	**cen·sor** (prohibiter)
censor	**cen·sure** (blame)
censor	**cen·ser** (incense box)
censor	**sen·sor** (detection device)
censure	**cen·sor** (prohibiter)
cent	**sent** (pt. of send)
cent	**scent** (smell)
centagrade	**cen·ti·grade**
centameter	**cen·ti·me·ter**
centapede	**cen·ti·pede**
centenial	**cen·ten·ni·al**
centerpeice	**cen·ter·piece**
centery	**cen·tu·ry**
centrel	**cen·tral**
centrifagle	**cen·trif·u·gal**
centrifical	**cen·trif·u·gal**
cepter	**scep·ter**
ceptic	**sep·tic**

WRONG	RIGHT
cerafe	**ca·rafe**
ceramik	**ce·ram·ic**
ceramony	**cer·e·mo·ny**
cercumstance	**cir·cum·stance**
cerdential	**cre·den·tial**
cereal	**se·ri·al** (in a series)
cerebrel	**cer·e·bral**
ceriel	**ce·re·al** (grain)
cerramic	**ce·ram·ic**
cerrebral	**cer·e·bral**
cerremony	**cer·e·mo·ny**
certan	**cer·tain**
certifacate	**cer·tif·i·cate**
certifyable	**cer·ti·fi·a·ble**
cervex	**cer·vix**
Cesar	**Cae·sar**
cession	**ses·sion** (meeting)
Chabley	**Cha·blis**
chairiot	**char·i·ot**
chairwoman	**char·wom·an** (cleaning person)
chalay	**cha·let**
chalenge	**chal·lenge**
challet	**cha·let**
challice	**chal·ice**
chammeleon	**cha·me·le·on**
chammy	**cham·ois**
champaign	**cham·pagne** (wine)
champeon	**cham·pi·on**
chancelor	**chan·cel·lor**

WRONG	RIGHT	WRONG	RIGHT
chandalier	**chan·de·lier**	chateu	**châ·teau**
chane	**chain**	chaufer	**chauf·feur** *(driver)*
chanel	**chan·nel**	chauvanism	**chau·vin·ism**
changable	**change·a·ble**	cheap	**cheep** *(chirp)*
changeing	**chang·ing**	chearful	**cheer·ful**
chansellor	**chan·cel·lor**	cheatah	**chee·tah**
chaparone	**chap·er·on**	checanery	**chi·can·ery**
chaplin	**chap·lain**	Checkoslovakia	
chappel	**chap·el**		**Czech·o·slo·va·kia**
chaptor	**chap·ter**	Chedar	**Ched·dar**
character	**car·i·ca·ture**	cheek	**chic** *(fashionable)*
	(picture)	cheep	**cheap** *(inexpensive)*
charactoristic		cheeze	**cheese**
	char·ac·ter·is·tic	cheif	**chief** *(leader)*
charaty	**char·i·ty**	cheif	**chef** *(cook)*
charcole	**char·coal**	chello	**cel·lo**
chariat	**char·i·ot**	chematherapy	
charish	**cher·ish**		**chem·o·ther·a·py**
charizma	**cha·ris·ma**	chemestry	**chem·is·try**
charrade	**cha·rade**	chemize	**che·mise**
chartreuze	**char·treuse**	chennille	**che·nille**
charwoman	**chair·wom·an**	cherade	**cha·rade**
	(person in charge)	cherisma	**cha·ris·ma**
chase longue	**chaise longue**	cherity	**char·i·ty**
chasen	**chas·ten**	chern	**churn**
chasim	**chasm**	cherrish	**cher·ish**
chassy	**chas·sis**	cherrubic	**che·ru·bic**
chastaty	**chas·ti·ty**	chessnut	**chest·nut**
chastize	**chas·tise**	chic	**sheik** *(Arab chief)*
Chatanooga	**Chat·ta·nooga**	chicery	**chic·o·ry**
chatel	**chat·tel**	chickory	**chic·o·ry**
chater	**chat·ter**	chieftan	**chief·tain**

WRONG	RIGHT
chiken	**chick·en**
chilli	**chili** (pepper)
chily	**chilly** (cold)
chiminey	**chim·ney**
chinchila	**chin·chilla**
chintsy	**chintzy**
chior	**choir**
chipmonk	**chip·munk**
chiractor	**chi·ro·prac·tor**
chire	**choir**
chisle	**chis·el**
chivallry	**chiv·al·ry**
Chiwawa	**Chi·hua·hua**
chloranate	**chlo·ri·nate**
chloraphyl	**chlo·ro·phyll**
chlorene	**chlo·rine**
chocalate	**choc·o·late**
chock	**chalk** (white powder)
choise	**choice**
cholestrol	**cho·les·ter·ol**
chollera	**chol·era**
choosen	**cho·sen**
choral	**cor·al** (shell)
chord	**cord** (string)
chorreography	**chor·e·og·ra·phy**
chouder	**chow·der**
chow main	**chow mein**
chozen	**cho·sen**
chranic	**chron·ic**
chranological	**chron·o·log·i·cal**

WRONG	RIGHT
chrisanthemum	**chrys·an·the·mum**
chrissen	**chris·ten**
Christanity	**Chris·ti·an·i·ty**
chromasome	**chro·mo·some**
chronacle	**chron·i·cle**
chuckel	**chuck·le**
cianide	**cy·a·nide**
Cianti	**Chi·an·ti**
cicle	**cy·cle**
ciclone	**cy·clone**
cieling	**ceil·ing** (overhead covering)
cigerette	**cig·a·rette**
cilinder	**cyl·in·der**
cillia	**cil·ia**
cinama	**cin·e·ma**
cinammon	**cin·na·mon**
Cinncinnati	**Cin·cin·nati**
circalate	**cir·cu·late**
circas	**cir·cus**
circeler	**cir·cu·lar**
circiut	**cir·cuit**
circomscribe	**cir·cum·scribe**
circomstantial	**cir·cum·stan·tial**
circuler	**cir·cu·lar**
circumfrence	**cir·cum·fer·ence**
circumsize	**cir·cum·cise**
circumspeck	**cir·cum·spect**
circumstanse	**cir·cum·stance**

WRONG	RIGHT	WRONG	RIGHT
circumstansial		cleerance .... **clear·ance**	
	.... **cir·cum·stan·tial**	cleet .... **cleat**	
cirhosis .... **cir·rho·sis**		cleevage .... **cleav·age**	
ciropractor ...... **chi·ro·prac·tor**		clemmency .... **clem·en·cy**	
cirrosis .... **cir·rho·sis**		clenser .... **cleans·er**	
cist .... **cyst** *(sac)*		cleptomaniac	
cisturn .... **cis·tern**		.... **klep·to·ma·ni·ac**	
citazen .... **cit·i·zen**		clever ...... **cleav·er** *(large knife)*	
cite .... **site** *(location)*		cliantele .... **cli·en·tele**	
cite .... **sight** *(vision)*		click .... **clique** *(group of people)*	
cittadel .... **cit·a·del**		clientell .... **cli·en·tele**	
civilazation .... **civ·i·li·za·tion**		climactic .... **cli·mat·ic**	
civillian .... **ci·vil·ian**		*(of a climate)*	
clairavoyance .. **clair·voy·ance**		climatic .... **cli·mac·tic**	
clame .... **claim**		*(of a climax)*	
clammor .... **clam·or**		climet .... **cli·mate**	
claranet .... **clar·i·net**		clinicly .... **clin·i·cal·ly**	
claraty .... **clar·i·ty**		clishay .... **cli·ché**	
clarefy .... **clar·i·fy**		cloke .... **cloak**	
clarical .... **cler·i·cal**		clorinate .... **chlo·ri·nate**	
clarinnet .... **clar·i·net**		clorophyl .... **chlo·ro·phyll**	
clarvoyance ..... **clair·voy·ance**		close .... **clothes** *(apparel)*	
classafication		clostrophobia	
.... **clas·si·fi·ca·tion**		.... **claus·tro·pho·bia**	
clastrophobia		cloth .... **clothe** *(v.)*	
.... **claus·tro·pho·bia**		clothe .... **cloth** *(n.)*	
claws .... **clause** *(grammar)*		clotheing .... **cloth·ing**	
clearence .... **clear·ance**		clothes .... **close** *(shut)*	
cleavedge .... **cleav·age**		cloyster .... **clois·ter**	
cleaver .... **clev·er** *(sly)*		cluch .... **clutch**	
cleche .... **cli·ché**		clumsey .... **clum·sy**	
cleek .... **clique** *(group of people)*		clurgy .... **cler·gy**	

WRONG	RIGHT	WRONG	RIGHT
coagalate	**co·ag·u·late**	colar	**col·lar** *(neck band)*
coaless	**co·a·lesce**	colateral	**col·lat·er·al**
coallition	**co·a·li·tion**	cold slaw	**cole·slaw**
coarse	**course** *(way; class)*	cole	**coal** *(mineral)*
cobolt	**co·balt**	coleague	**col·league**
cocane	**co·caine**	colector	**col·lec·tor**
cocanut	**co·co·nut**	colege	**col·lege** *(school)*
cocao	**ca·cao** *(tree)*	colegiate	**col·le·giate**
coccoon	**co·coon**	colen	**co·lon**
coch	**coach**	coler	**col·or**
cockaroach	**cock·roach**	colera	**chol·era**
cocoa	**ca·cao** *(tree)*	colesce	**co·a·lesce**
cocoe	**co·coa** *(chocolate)*	colesterol	**cho·les·ter·ol**
codefy	**cod·i·fy**	colide	**col·lide**
codiene	**co·deine**	colision	**col·li·sion**
codle	**cod·dle**	colition	**co·a·li·tion**
coersion	**co·er·cion**	collage	**col·lege** *(school)*
cofee	**cof·fee**	collander	**col·an·der** *(strainer)*
coffen	**cof·fin**	collapseable	**col·laps·i·ble**
cogatate	**cog·i·tate**	collecter	**col·lec·tor**
cogenital	**con·gen·i·tal**	college	**col·lage** *(art form)*
cognizent	**cog·ni·zant**	collegue	**col·league**
coherense	**co·her·ence**	coller	**col·lar** *(neck band)*
cohesave	**co·he·sive**	collerd	**col·lard** *(kale)*
coifure	**coif·fure** *(hair style)*	collic	**col·ic**
coincidance	**co·in·ci·dence**	colliseum	**col·i·se·um**
coinside	**co·in·cide**	collitis	**co·li·tis**
colaborate	**col·lab·o·rate**	collogne	**co·logne**
colage	**col·lage** *(art form)*	collonial	**co·lo·ni·al**
colander	**cal·en·dar** *(table of dates)*	collonnade	**col·on·nade**
		Collorado	**Col·o·rado**
colapse	**col·lapse**	collossal	**co·los·sal**

39

WRONG	RIGHT	WRONG	RIGHT
collum	**col·umn**	comitment	**com·mit·ment**
collumnist	**col·um·nist**	comitted	**com·mit·ted**
colonade	**col·on·nade**	comittee	**com·mit·tee**
colone	**co·logne**	comm	**comb**
coloquial	**col·lo·qui·al**	comma	**co·ma** *(stupor)*
colosal	**co·los·sal**	commadore	**com·mo·dore**
columist	**col·um·nist**	comman	**com·mon**
columm	**col·umn**	commatose	**co·ma·tose**
coma	**com·ma**	commemrative	
	(punctuation mark)		**com·mem·o·ra·tive**
comand	**com·mand**	commensement	
combatave	**com·bat·ive**		**com·mence·ment**
combustable	**com·bus·ti·ble**	commentater	**com·men·ta·tor**
comedianne	**co·me·di·enne**	commerse	**com·merce**
	(f.)	commisary	**com·mis·sary**
comedien	**co·me·di·an** *(m.)*	commision	**com·mis·sion**
comedien	**co·me·di·enne** *(f.)*	commited	**com·mit·ted**
comeing	**com·ing**	commitee	**com·mit·tee**
comemorative		committment	**com·mit·ment**
	com·mem·o·ra·tive	commizerate	**com·mis·er·ate**
comencement		commodaty	**com·mod·i·ty**
	com·mence·ment	commonist	**com·mu·nist**
comend	**com·mend**	communacible	
comentary	**com·men·tary**		**com·mu·ni·ca·ble**
comerce	**com·merce**	comode	**com·mode**
comfert	**com·fort**	comodity	**com·mod·i·ty**
comfiscate	**con·fis·cate**	comon	**com·mon**
comfortible	**com·fort·a·ble**	comotion	**com·mo·tion**
comidy	**com·e·dy**	compack	**com·pact**
comiserate	**com·mis·er·ate**	compackor	**com·pac·tor**
comissary	**com·mis·sary**	compacter	**com·pac·tor**
comission	**com·mis·sion**	compannion	**com·pan·ion**

WRONG	RIGHT
compareable	**com·pa·ra·ble**
comparitively	
	com·par·a·tive·ly
compas	**com·pass**
compasionate	
	com·pas·sion·ate
composition	**com·po·si·tion**
compatable	**com·pat·i·ble**
compatence	**com·pe·tence**
compatition	**com·pe·ti·tion**
compell	**com·pel**
compeny	**com·pa·ny**
competance	**com·pe·tence**
competative	**com·pet·i·tive**
competeing	**com·pet·ing**
compettiter	**com·pet·i·tor**
compinsation	
	com·pen·sa·tion
complacation	**com·pli·ca·tion**
complacent	**com·plai·sant**
	(obliging)
complaisant	**com·pla·cent**
	(smug)
complane	**com·plain**
complecated	**com·pli·cat·ed**
complection	**com·plex·ion**
complement	**com·pli·ment**
	(praise)
complementry	
	com·ple·men·ta·ry
completly	**com·plete·ly**
complient	**com·pli·ant**

WRONG	RIGHT
compliment	**com·ple·ment**
	(part of a whole)
complimentry	
	com·pli·men·ta·ry
complisity	**com·plic·i·ty**
componant	**com·po·nent**
composet	**com·pos·ite**
composor	**com·pos·er**
comprable	**com·pa·ra·ble**
compramise	**com·pro·mise**
comprehensable	
	com·pre·hen·si·ble
comprize	**com·prise**
compulsery	**com·pul·so·ry**
comrad	**com·rade**
comunal	**com·mu·nal**
comunicable	
	com·mu·ni·ca·ble
comunication	
	com·mu·ni·ca·tion
comunion	**com·mun·ion**
comunist	**com·mu·nist**
comunity	**com·mu·ni·ty**
comuter	**com·mut·er**
conbine	**com·bine**
conceed	**con·cede**
conceivible	**con·ceiv·a·ble**
concensus	**con·sen·sus**
concherto	**con·cer·to**
concideration	
	con·sid·er·a·tion
conciet	**con·ceit**

concievable	**con·ceiv·a·ble**	confeti	**con·fet·ti**
concommitant	**con·com·i·tant**	confidance	**con·fi·dence**
concordence	**con·cord·ance**	confidensial	**con·fi·den·tial**
concorse	**con·course**	confinment	**con·fine·ment**
concreet	**con·crete**	confirmation	**con·for·ma·tion**
concurent	**con·cur·rent**		*(shape)*
concusion	**con·cus·sion**	conflick	**con·flict**
condament	**con·di·ment**	conformation	**con·fir·ma·tion**
condaminium			*(ceremony; verification)*
	con·do·min·i·um	confrence	**con·fer·ence**
condansation		conglommerate	
	con·den·sa·tion		**con·glom·er·ate**
condascend	**con·de·scend**	congradulate	**con·grat·u·late**
condem	**con·demn** *(censure)*	congragation	**con·gre·ga·tion**
condence	**con·dense**	congruance	**con·gru·ence**
condesend	**con·de·scend**	conivance	**con·niv·ance**
condimint	**con·di·ment**	conjagate	**con·ju·gate**
condit	**con·duit**	conjenial	**con·gen·ial**
condolance	**con·do·lence**	conjenital	**con·gen·i·tal**
condominimum		conjer	**con·jure**
	con·do·min·i·um	conjestion	**con·ges·tion**
conducter	**con·duc·tor**	conklave	**con·clave**
condusive	**con·du·cive**	Conneticut	**Con·nect·i·cut**
Conecticut	**Con·nect·i·cut**	connivence	**con·niv·ance**
conection	**con·nec·tion**	connoiseur	**con·nois·seur**
confascate	**con·fis·cate**	conotation	**con·no·ta·tion**
confecktion	**con·fec·tion**	conquerer	**con·quer·or**
confedence	**con·fi·dence**	consaquence	**con·se·quence**
confedercy	**con·fed·er·a·cy**	consceince	**con·science**
confered	**con·ferred**		*(morals)*
conferrence	**con·fer·ence**	consceintious	
confesion	**con·fes·sion**		**con·sci·en·tious**

WRONG	RIGHT	WRONG	RIGHT
conscience	**con·scious** *(aware)*	consumate	**con·sum·mate**
conscious	**con·science** *(morals)*	consummé	**con·som·mé**
conseal	**con·ceal**	contack	**con·tact**
consede	**con·cede**	contageous	**con·ta·gious**
conseit	**con·ceit**	contamanate	**con·tam·i·nate**
consentrate	**con·cen·trate**	contane	**con·tain**
consentric	**con·cen·tric**	contemparary	**con·tem·po·rary**
conseptual	**con·cep·tu·al**	contemptable	**con·tempt·i·ble**
conserned	**con·cerned**	contenental	**con·ti·nen·tal**
consert	**con·cert**	conterdiction	**con·tra·dic·tion**
conservitave	**con·ser·va·tive**	contestent	**con·test·ant**
consession	**con·ces·sion**	continnuation	**con·tin·u·a·tion**
consicrate	**con·se·crate**	continous	**con·tin·u·ous**
consiliatory	**con·cil·i·a·to·ry**	continuence	**con·tin·u·ance**
consious	**con·scious** *(aware)*	contoor	**con·tour**
consise	**con·cise**	contrabution	**con·tri·bu·tion**
consistancy	**con·sis·ten·cy**	contrack	**con·tract**
consoladation	**con·sol·i·da·tion**	contraseption	**con·tra·cep·tion**
consome	**con·som·mé**	contraversial	**con·tro·ver·sial**
consonent	**con·so·nant**	contrery	**con·trary**
conspirecy	**con·spir·a·cy**	contrivence	**con·triv·ance**
constapation	**con·sti·pa·tion**	controling	**con·trol·ling**
constatution	**con·sti·tu·tion**	conubial	**con·nu·bi·al**
constelation	**con·stel·la·tion**	convalesence	**con·va·les·cence**
constent	**con·stant**	conveneince	**con·ven·ience**
construcktion	**con·struc·tion**	conversent	**con·ver·sant**
consul	**coun·sel** *(advice)*	convertable	**con·vert·i·ble**
consul	**coun·cil** *(legislature)*	convienence	**con·ven·ience**
consultent	**con·sult·ant**		

conyac	**cogn·ac**	corpse	**corps** (group of people)
coo	**coup** (revolt)	corpusle	**cor·pus·cle**
coolent	**cool·ant**	correspondance	
coopon	**cou·pon**		**cor·re·spond·ence**
coordenation	**co·or·di·na·tion**	correspondent	**co·re·spond·ent**
coparison	**com·par·i·son**		(legal term)
coper	**cop·per**	corrollary	**cor·ol·lary**
copyer	**cop·i·er**	corruptable	**cor·rupt·i·ble**
corageous	**cou·ra·geous**	cortizone	**cor·ti·sone**
coral	**cho·ral** (music)	corugated	**cor·ru·gat·ed**
coral	**cor·ral** (pen)	coruptible	**cor·rupt·i·ble**
cord	**chord** (music)	corus	**cho·rus**
cordaroy	**cor·du·roy**	cosign	**co·sine**
cordgial	**cor·dial**		(mathematics term)
cordination	**co·or·di·na·tion**	cosine	**co·sign** (sign jointly)
coreck	**cor·rect**	cosmapolitan	
corection	**cor·rec·tion**		**cos·mo·pol·i·tan**
corelation	**cor·re·la·tion**	costic	**caus·tic**
corenary	**cor·o·nary**	cotage	**cot·tage**
coreography		cotemtible	**con·tempt·i·ble**
	chor·e·og·ra·phy	coterize	**cau·ter·ize**
corespondence		coton	**cot·ton**
	cor·re·spond·ence	council	**coun·sel** (advice)
corespondent	**cor·re·spond·ent**	counsel	**con·sul**
	(writer)		(government representative)
coridor	**cor·ri·dor**	counsel	**coun·cil** (legislature)
coroborate	**cor·rob·o·rate**	countenence	**coun·te·nance**
coronery	**cor·o·nary**	counterfit	**coun·ter·feit**
corosion	**cor·ro·sion**	countrey	**coun·try**
corparation	**cor·po·ra·tion**	coup	**coupe** (car)
corperal	**cor·po·ral**	coupe	**coup** (revolt)
corps	**corpse** (dead body)	coupel	**cou·ple**

WRONG	RIGHT	WRONG	RIGHT
couragious	**cou·ra·geous**	crickit	**crick·et**
courrage	**cour·age**	criminel	**crim·i·nal**
courrier	**cou·ri·er**	criple	**crip·ple**
course	**coarse** *(rough)*	criptic	**cryp·tic**
courtecy	**cour·te·sy**	crises	**cri·sis** *(sing.)*
courtious	**cour·te·ous**	crisis	**cri·ses** *(pl.)*
court–marshall		cristal	**crys·tal**
	court–mar·tial	Cristianity	**Chris·ti·an·i·ty**
covanant	**cov·e·nant**	criticizm	**crit·i·cism**
cowardace	**cow·ard·ice**	critisize	**crit·i·cize**
cowerdly	**cow·ard·ly**	crocadile	**croc·o·dile**
coxe	**coax**	croche	**cro·chet**
cozmetic	**cos·met·ic**	crochety	**crotch·ety**
cozmic	**cos·mic**	croisant	**crois·sant** *(roll)*
craby	**crab·by**	crokay	**cro·quet** *(game)*
crayen	**cray·on**	crokette	**cro·quette** *(food)*
creachure	**crea·ture** *(animal)*	crome	**chrome**
creak	**creek** *(stream)*	cromosome	**chro·mo·some**
creap	**creep**	cronic	**chron·ic**
creater	**cre·a·tor**	cronicle	**chron·i·cle**
	(one who creates)	cronological	**chron·o·log·i·cal**
creater	**crea·ture** *(animal)*	crooton	**crou·ton**
credance	**cre·dence**	croquet	**cro·quette** *(food)*
creditible	**cred·it·a·ble**	croquette	**cro·quet** *(game)*
creek	**creak** *(squeak)*	croshet	**cro·chet**
cressant	**crois·sant** *(roll)*	crucefy	**cru·ci·fy**
cressent	**cres·cent**	cruel	**crew·el** *(needlework)*
crevasse	**crev·ice**	crulty	**cru·el·ty**
	(narrow cleft)	crum	**crumb**
crevice	**cre·vasse**	crusial	**cru·cial**
	(deep fissure)	crusible	**cru·ci·ble**
crewel	**cru·el** *(mean)*	crusifix	**cru·ci·fix**

WRONG	RIGHT	WRONG	RIGHT
crusify	**cru·ci·fy**	curiousity	**cu·ri·os·i·ty**
crysanthemum		curius	**cu·ri·ous**
	chrys·an·the·mum	curlycue	**curl·i·cue**
crystalize	**crys·tal·lize**	curmugeon	**cur·mudg·eon**
cubberd	**cup·board**	curnel	**ker·nel** *(grain)*
cubical	**cu·bi·cle** *(small room)*	currant	**cur·rent** *(stream)*
cubicle	**cu·bi·cal**	current	**cur·rant** *(raisin)*
	(cube–shaped)	curricullum	**cur·ric·u·lum**
cuboard	**cup·board**	cursury	**cur·so·ry**
cudly	**cud·dly**	curtale	**cur·tail**
cudos	**ku·dos**	curteous	**cour·te·ous**
cue	**queue** *(line)*	curtesy	**cour·te·sy**
cuepon	**cou·pon**	curtin	**cur·tain**
cugel	**cudg·el**	cushon	**cush·ion**
cuizine	**cui·sine**	cusine	**cui·sine**
cullinary	**cu·li·nary**	custady	**cus·to·dy**
culmanate	**cul·mi·nate**	customer	**cus·tom·er** *(patron)*
culpible	**cul·pa·ble**	custem	**cus·tom**
culpret	**cul·prit**	custerd	**cus·tard**
cultavate	**cul·ti·vate**	customery	**cus·tom·ary**
cultureal	**cul·tur·al**	cutacle	**cut·i·cle**
cummulative	**cumu·la·tive**	cuting	**cut·ting**
cumpass	**com·pass**	cymbal	**sym·bol** *(mark)*
cumquot	**kum·quat**	cynecal	**cyn·i·cal**
cuning	**cun·ning**	cypras	**cy·press**
cupbord	**cup·board**	Czechaslovakia	
curage	**cour·age**		**Czech·o·slo·va·kia**
curant	**cur·rant** *(raisin)*		
curater	**cu·ra·tor**		**D**
curcuit	**cir·cuit**		
curent	**cur·rent** *(stream)*	dabris	**de·bris**
curiculum	**cur·ric·u·lum**	dacore	**dé·cor**

| --- | --- | --- | --- |
dacorum	**de·cor·um**	dashbord	**dash·board**
dacquiri	**dai·qui·ri**	dashhound	**dachs·hund**
daes	**da·is**	dasturdly	**das·tard·ly**
dafodil	**daf·fo·dil**	dasy	**dai·sy**
dager	**dag·ger**	data	**da·tum** *(sing.)*
dairey	**dairy** *(milk farm)*	dateing	**dat·ing**
daja vu	**dé·jà vu**	datente	**dé·tente**
dalfin	**dol·phin**	datum	**da·ta** *(pl.)*
dalia	**dahl·ia**	daudle	**daw·dle**
dalight	**day·light**	dauter	**daugh·ter**
dalying	**dal·ly·ing**	davinity	**di·vin·i·ty**
dam	**damn** *(condemn)*	davinport	**dav·en·port**
damedge	**dam·age**	dawb	**daub**
damestic	**do·mes·tic**	dawntless	**daunt·less**
dammable	**dam·na·ble**	daylite	**day·light**
dammage	**dam·age**	dayly	**dai·ly**
damn	**dam** *(animal; barrier)*	days	**daze** *(stun)*
dandrif	**dan·druff**	daze	**days** *(pl. of day)*
dandylion	**dan·de·li·on**	dazle	**daz·zle**
dane	**deign** *(condescend)*	dazy	**dai·sy**
dangel	**dan·gle**	deactavate	**de·ac·ti·vate**
dangrous	**dan·ger·ous**	deadlyer	**dead·li·er**
dannilion	**dan·de·li·on**	deadning	**dead·en·ing**
danse	**dance**	deaffen	**deaf·en**
danty	**dain·ty**	dealling	**deal·ing**
daper	**dap·per**	dealor	**deal·er**
dappeled	**dap·pled**	dear	**deer** *(animal)*
dappreciate	**de·pre·ci·ate**	debackle	**de·ba·cle**
daquiri	**dai·qui·ri**	debanair	**deb·o·nair**
dareing	**dar·ing**	debass	**de·base**
darey	**dairy** *(milk farm)*	debatible	**de·bat·a·ble**
darlling	**dar·ling**	debbit	**deb·it**

WRONG	RIGHT	WRONG	RIGHT
debillitate	**de·bil·i·tate**	deen	**dean**
debochery	**de·bauch·ery**	deer	**dear** *(beloved)*
deboner	**deb·o·nair**	defacate	**def·e·cate**
debreif	**de·brief**	defacit	**def·i·cit**
debrie	**de·bris**	defalt	**de·fault**
debter	**debt·or**	defammation	**def·a·ma·tion**
debue	**de·but**	defanitely	**def·i·nite·ly**
decadance	**dec·a·dence**	defase	**de·face**
decadant	**dec·a·dent**	defecit	**def·i·cit**
decapatate	**de·cap·i·tate**	defeck	**de·fect**
decarate	**dec·o·rate**	defectave	**de·fec·tive**
decathalon	**de·cath·lon**	defeet	**de·feat**
decendant	**de·scend·ant**	defendent	**de·fend·ant**
decent	**de·scent** *(going down)*	deference	**dif·fer·ence**
decent	**dis·sent** *(disagreement)*		*(being different)*
decible	**dec·i·bel**	deferrment	**de·fer·ment**
decieitful	**de·ceit·ful**	deffend	**de·fend**
decieve	**de·ceive**	deffensive	**de·fen·sive**
decimel	**dec·i·mal**	deffinition	**def·i·ni·tion**
deckade	**dec·ade**	deffrost	**de·frost**
deckadence	**dec·a·dence**	deficeincy	**de·fi·cien·cy**
decleration	**dec·la·ra·tion**	defience	**de·fi·ance**
decmal	**dec·i·mal**	defind	**de·fined**
decon	**dea·con**	definitly	**def·i·nite·ly**
deconjestant	**de·con·gest·ant**	deformaty	**de·form·i·ty**
decrepet	**de·crep·it**	defrawd	**de·fraud**
decriminilize		degridation	**deg·ra·da·tion**
	de·crim·i·nal·ize	dehidrated	**de·hy·drat·ed**
ded	**dead**	dehumidafy	**de·hu·mid·i·fy**
dedacate	**ded·i·cate**	dein	**deign** *(condescend)*
deductable	**de·duct·i·ble**	deisel	**die·sel**
deel	**deal**	dejeckted	**de·ject·ed**

WRONG	RIGHT
dejenerate	**de·gen·er·ate**
dekay	**de·cay**
delacatessen	**del·i·ca·tes·sen**
delagate	**del·e·gate**
delectible	**de·lec·ta·ble**
deleet	**de·lete**
delektable	**de·lec·ta·ble**
delerious	**de·lir·i·ous**
delicous	**de·li·cious**
delinquancy	**de·lin·quen·cy**
delite	**de·light**
deliverence	**de·liv·er·ance**
delivry	**de·liv·ery**
Dellaware	**Del·a·ware**
dellicacy	**del·i·ca·cy**
dellicatessen	**del·i·ca·tes·sen**
dellta	**del·ta**
dellude	**de·lude**
delluge	**del·uge**
delt	**dealt**
delux	**de·luxe**
demacracy	**de·moc·ra·cy**
demacratic	**dem·o·crat·ic**
demagraphic	**demo·graph·ic**
demalition	**dem·o·li·tion**
deman	**de·mon**
demanstrable	**de·mon·stra·ble**
demeaner	**de·mean·or**
demension	**di·men·sion**
demigog	**dem·a·gogue**
deminish	**di·min·ish**

WRONG	RIGHT
demize	**de·mise**
demmitasse	**dem·i·tasse**
democricy	**de·moc·ra·cy**
demollish	**de·mol·ish**
demollition	**dem·o·li·tion**
demonstrater	**dem·on·stra·tor**
demur	**de·mure** *(coy)*
demure	**de·mur** *(object)*
denamination	**de·nom·i·na·tion**
dence	**dense**
denchers	**den·tures**
denem	**den·im**
deniel	**de·ni·al**
denomonater	**de·nom·i·na·tor**
denounciation	**de·nun·ci·a·tion**
denounse	**de·nounce**
densaty	**den·si·ty**
dentel	**den·tal**
dentest	**den·tist**
denyed	**de·nied**
deodorant	**de·o·dor·ant**
departmentallize	**de·part·men·tal·ize**
dependance	**de·pend·ence**
dependible	**de·pend·a·ble**
depick	**de·pict**
depillatory	**de·pil·a·to·ry**
depleet	**de·plete**
deplorible	**de·plor·a·ble**

depositatory	**de·pos·i·to·ry**	Desember	**De·cem·ber**
deposet	**de·pos·it**	desency	**de·cen·cy**
deppo	**de·pot**	desent	**de·cent** (proper)
depravation	**dep·ri·va·tion**	desent	**de·scent** (going down)
	(loss)	desent	**dis·sent** (disagreement)
depravaty	**de·prav·i·ty**	deseption	**de·cep·tion**
depreshiate	**de·pre·ci·ate**	desert	**des·sert** (food)
depresion	**de·pres·sion**	deserveing	**de·serv·ing**
depressent	**de·pres·sant**	desibel	**dec·i·bel**
deprivation	**dep·ra·va·tion**	deside	**de·cide**
	(a corrupting)	desiduous	**de·cid·u·ous**
depriveing	**de·priv·ing**	desimal	**dec·i·mal**
deputey	**dep·u·ty**	desine	**de·sign**
deragatory	**de·rog·a·to·ry**	desipher	**de·ci·pher**
deravation	**der·i·va·tion**	desireable	**de·sir·a·ble**
deregalate	**de·reg·u·late**	desizion	**de·ci·sion**
derelick	**der·e·lict**	despach	**dis·patch**
derick	**der·rick**	despare	**de·spair**
derigible	**dir·i·gi·ble**	despensable	**dis·pen·sa·ble**
derregulate	**de·reg·u·late**	desperate	**dis·pa·rate**
derrelict	**der·e·lict**		(not alike)
desacrate	**des·e·crate**	despicible	**des·pi·ca·ble**
desalate	**des·o·late**	despize	**de·spise**
desastrous	**dis·as·trous**	despondant	**de·spond·ent**
descendent	**de·scend·ant**	desprate	**des·per·ate**
descent	**de·cent** (proper)		(hopeless)
descent	**dis·sent**	dessegergation	
	(disagreement)		**de·seg·re·ga·tion**
desciple	**dis·ci·ple**	dessert	**des·ert** (dry area)
deseased	**de·ceased** (dead)	dessert	**de·sert** (abandon)
deseased	**dis·eased** (ill)	desserts	**de·serts** (rewards)
desegragate	**de·seg·re·gate**	desserving	**de·serv·ing**

WRONG	RIGHT
dessignated	**des·ig·nat·ed**
destany	**des·tiny**
destatute	**des·ti·tute**
destenation	**des·ti·na·tion**
destructave	**de·struc·tive**
detale	**de·tail**
detane	**de·tain**
detant	**dé·tente**
detatched	**de·tached**
detektive	**de·tec·tive**
deterent	**de·ter·rent**
detergant	**de·ter·gent**
deterierate	**de·te·ri·o·rate**
detestible	**de·test·a·ble**
deth	**death**
detnate	**det·o·nate**
detoor	**de·tour**
detrack	**de·tract**
detramental	**det·ri·men·tal**
dettonate	**det·o·nate**
dettor	**debt·or**
deuse	**deuce**
devalluation	**de·val·u·a·tion**
deveant	**de·vi·ant**
develope	**de·vel·op**
developement	
	de·vel·op·ment
device	**de·vise** (invent)
devide	**di·vide**
devient	**de·vi·ant**
devillish	**dev·il·ish**
devine	**di·vine**

WRONG	RIGHT
devisable	**di·vis·i·ble**
	(dividable)
devise	**de·vice** (mechanism)
devision	**di·vi·sion**
devistation	**dev·as·ta·tion**
devius	**de·vi·ous**
devulge	**di·vulge**
dew	**due** (owed)
dexteraty	**dex·ter·i·ty**
dextrus	**dex·ter·ous**
diabeetis	**di·a·be·tes**
diabollic	**di·a·bol·ic**
diacese	**di·o·cese**
diafram	**di·a·phragm**
diaganal	**di·ag·o·nal**
diagnoses	**di·ag·no·sis** (sing.)
diagnosis	**di·ag·no·ses** (pl.)
dialeck	**di·a·lect**
dialisis	**di·al·y·sis**
diamater	**di·am·e·ter**
diaphram	**di·a·phragm**
diarey	**di·a·ry** (journal)
diarrea	**di·ar·rhea**
dias	**da·is**
diatetic	**di·e·tet·ic**
diatitian	**di·e·ti·tian**
dibacle	**de·ba·cle**
dibark	**de·bark**
dibase	**de·base**
dibatable	**de·bat·a·ble**
dibilitate	**de·bil·i·tate**
dicanter	**de·cant·er**

WRONG	RIGHT
dicapitate	**de·cap·i·tate**
dicathlon	**de·cath·lon**
diceased	**de·ceased** (dead)
diceitful	**de·ceit·ful**
diceive	**de·ceive**
Dicember	**De·cem·ber**
diception	**de·cep·tion**
dich	**ditch**
dicide	**de·cide**
dicipher	**de·ci·pher**
dicision	**de·ci·sion**
diclension	**de·clen·sion**
dicline	**de·cline**
dicorum	**de·co·rum**
dicrease	**de·crease**
dicrepit	**de·crep·it**
dicriminalize	**de·crim·i·nal·ize**
dictater	**dic·ta·tor**
dictionery	**dic·tion·ary**
die	**dye** (tint)
diefy	**de·i·fy**
diel	**di·al**
dielect	**di·a·lect**
dierhea	**di·ar·rhea**
diery	**di·a·ry** (journal)
diesle	**die·sel**
dietician	**di·e·ti·tian**
diety	**de·i·ty**
difault	**de·fault**
difective	**de·fec·tive**
diferent	**dif·fer·ent**

WRONG	RIGHT
diferment	**de·fer·ment**
differance	**dif·fer·ence** (being different)
difference	**def·er·ence** (yielding)
diffrent	**dif·fer·ent**
diffuzion	**dif·fu·sion**
difiance	**de·fi·ance**
dificiency	**de·fi·cien·cy**
dificulty	**dif·fi·cul·ty**
difile	**de·file**
diflect	**de·flect**
diformity	**de·form·i·ty**
difraud	**de·fraud**
difrost	**de·frost**
diftheria	**diph·the·ria**
difuse	**dif·fuse**
difusion	**dif·fu·sion**
digatal	**dig·it·al**
digestable	**di·gest·i·ble**
digetal	**dig·it·al**
digings	**dig·gings**
dignafied	**dig·ni·fied**
dignatary	**dig·ni·tary**
dignaty	**dig·ni·ty**
dignifyed	**dig·ni·fied**
digree	**de·gree**
diktator	**dic·ta·tor**
diktionary	**dic·tion·ary**
dilay	**de·lay**
dilema	**di·lem·ma**
diletante	**dil·et·tante**

WRONG	RIGHT	WRONG	RIGHT
dilete	**de·lete**	dingy	**din·ghy** *(boat)*
diliberation	**de·lib·er·a·tion**	dinial	**de·ni·al**
dilicious	**de·li·cious**	dining	**din·ning**
dilight	**de·light**		*(repeating noisily)*
dilinquency	**de·lin·quen·cy**	dinner	**din·er** *(small restaurant)*
dilirious	**de·lir·i·ous**	dinning	**din·ing** *(eating)*
diliver	**de·liv·er**	dinomination	
dillapidated	**di·lap·i·dat·ed**		**de·nom·i·na·tion**
dillema	**di·lem·ma**	dinominator	**de·nom·i·na·tor**
dilletante	**dil·et·tante**	dinosor	**di·no·saur**
dilligence	**dil·i·gence**	dinote	**de·note**
dillusion	**de·lu·sion**	dinounce	**de·nounce**
dillute	**di·lute**	dint	**dent**
dilude	**de·lude**	dinunciation	**de·nun·ci·a·tion**
diluxe	**de·luxe**	diosese	**di·o·cese**
dimand	**de·mand** *(order)*	dipart	**de·part**
dimeanor	**de·mean·or**	dipendable	**de·pend·a·ble**
dimented	**de·ment·ed**	diper	**di·a·per**
dimention	**di·men·sion**	diplamat	**dip·lo·mat**
dimise	**de·mise**	diplete	**de·plete**
dimminish	**di·min·ish**	diplomasy	**di·plo·ma·cy**
dimolish	**de·mol·ish**	diplorable	**de·plor·a·ble**
dimond	**di·a·mond** *(gem)*	dipresant	**de·pres·sant**
dimoralize	**de·mor·al·ize**	diptheria	**diph·the·ria**
dimur	**de·mur** *(object)*	diranged	**de·ranged**
dimure	**de·mure** *(coy)*	direck	**di·rect**
dinamic	**dy·nam·ic**	directer	**di·rec·tor**
dinamite	**dy·na·mite**	directery	**di·rec·to·ry**
dinasaur	**di·no·saur**	dirigable	**dir·i·gi·ble**
dinasty	**dy·nas·ty**	dirisive	**de·ri·sive**
diner	**din·ner** *(meal)*	dirth	**dearth**
dinghy	**din·gy** *(grimy)*	disagrement	**dis·a·gree·ment**

WRONG	RIGHT	WRONG	RIGHT
disallusion	**dis·il·lu·sion**	diseminate	**dis·sem·i·nate**
disapear	**dis·ap·pear**	disenfectant	**dis·in·fect·ant**
disapointment	**dis·ap·point·ment**	disengagment	**dis·en·gage·ment**
disaray	**dis·ar·ray**	disent	**dis·sent** (disagreement)
disarmement	**dis·ar·ma·ment**	disentery	**dys·en·tery**
disasterous	**dis·as·trous**	disert	**de·sert** (abandon)
disatisfied	**dis·sat·is·fied**	disesed	**dis·eased** (ill)
disbeleif	**dis·be·lief**	disfigurment	**dis·fig·ure·ment**
disberse	**dis·burse** (pay out)	disgise	**dis·guise**
disburse	**dis·perse** (scatter)	disgrase	**dis·grace**
discapline	**dis·ci·pline**	disign	**de·sign**
discendant	**de·scend·ant**	disilusion	**dis·il·lu·sion**
discipal	**dis·ci·ple**	disimbark	**dis·em·bark**
disclozure	**dis·clo·sure**	disimilar	**dis·sim·i·lar**
discourageing	**dis·cour·ag·ing**	disinfectent	**dis·in·fect·ant**
discovry	**dis·cov·ery**	disintagrate	**dis·in·te·grate**
discreet	**dis·crete** (separate)	disipate	**dis·si·pate**
discression	**dis·cre·tion**	disiple	**dis·ci·ple**
discrete	**dis·creet** (prudent)	disipline	**dis·ci·pline**
discribe	**de·scribe**	dislexia	**dys·lex·ia**
discrimanation	**dis·crim·i·na·tion**	dismantel	**dis·man·tle**
discription	**de·scrip·tion**	dismissle	**dis·miss·al**
discus	**dis·cuss** (talk about)	disobediance	**dis·o·be·di·ence**
discusion	**dis·cus·sion**	disolve	**dis·solve**
discuss	**dis·cus** (heavy disk)	disonant	**dis·so·nant**
disdaneful	**dis·dain·ful**	disonest	**dis·hon·est**
disdressed	**dis·tressed**	disorderley	**dis·or·der·ly**
dise	**dice**	dispach	**dis·patch**
disect	**dis·sect**	dispair	**de·spair**
		disparate	**des·per·ate** (hopeless)

WRONG	RIGHT	WRONG	RIGHT
dispensible	**dis·pen·sa·ble**	distence	**dis·tance**
disperaging	**dis·par·ag·ing**	disterb	**dis·turb**
disperate	**dis·pa·rate**	distinguash	**dis·tin·guish**
	(not alike)	distink	**dis·tinct**
disperse	**dis·burse** *(pay out)*	distrabution	**dis·tri·bu·tion**
dispicable	**des·pi·ca·ble**	distrack	**dis·tract**
dispise	**de·spise**	distraut	**dis·traught**
dispite	**de·spite**	districk	**dis·trict**
dispondent	**de·spond·ent**	distrophy	**dys·tro·phy**
disposible	**dis·pos·a·ble**	distroy	**de·stroy**
dispurse	**dis·perse** *(scatter)*	disuade	**dis·suade**
disreguard	**dis·re·gard**	ditergent	**de·ter·gent**
disreputible	**dis·rep·u·ta·ble**	ditermine	**de·ter·mine**
dissagree	**dis·a·gree**	dity	**dit·ty**
dissapate	**dis·si·pate**	divadend	**div·i·dend**
dissappear	**dis·ap·pear**	divaluation	**de·val·u·a·tion**
dissappointment		divelopment	**de·vel·op·ment**
	dis·ap·point·ment	divergance	**di·ver·gence**
dissarmament		diversafy	**di·ver·si·fy**
	dis·ar·ma·ment	diversaty	**di·ver·si·ty**
disscord	**dis·cord**	divinety	**di·vin·i·ty**
disscount	**dis·count**	divisable	**di·vis·i·ble**
dissemanate	**dis·sem·i·nate**		*(dividable)*
dissent	**de·cent** *(proper)*	divizion	**di·vi·sion**
dissent	**de·scent** *(going down)*	divoid	**de·void**
dissert	**des·sert** *(food)*	divorse	**di·vorce**
disserts	**de·serts** *(rewards)*	divour	**de·vour**
dissinfectant	**dis·in·fect·ant**	divout	**de·vout**
dissintegrate	**dis·in·te·grate**	dizalve	**dis·solve**
dissmay	**dis·may**	dob	**daub**
dissonent	**dis·so·nant**	dochshund	**dachs·hund**
disstiled	**dis·tilled**	docter	**doc·tor**

WRONG	RIGHT	WRONG	RIGHT
doctran	**doc·trine**	drible	**drib·ble**
doctrinare	**doc·tri·naire**	driping	**drip·ping**
documentery	**doc·u·men·ta·ry**	driveing	**driv·ing**
dodle	**daw·dle**	drousy	**drow·sy**
doe	**dough** (flour)	drout	**drought**
doller	**dol·lar**	drowsey	**drow·sy**
dolphen	**dol·phin**	drugery	**drudg·ery**
domane	**do·main**	drugist	**drug·gist**
dominent	**dom·i·nant**	dual	**du·el** (fight)
dominoe	**dom·i·no**	dubble	**dou·ble**
domminate	**dom·i·nate**	dubeous	**du·bi·ous**
doner	**do·nor**	due	**dew** (moisture)
donky	**don·key**	duece	**deuce**
dontless	**daunt·less**	duel	**du·al** (two)
doosh	**douche**	dum	**dumb**
dormatory	**dor·mi·to·ry**	dumbell	**dumb·bell**
dosege	**dos·age**	dunkey	**don·key**
dosn't	**doesn't**	duplacate	**du·pli·cate**
dotter	**daugh·ter**	durible	**du·ra·ble**
doury	**dow·ry**	durress	**du·ress**
doutful	**doubt·ful**	durring	**dur·ing**
dowdey	**dow·dy**	durth	**dearth**
dowery	**dow·ry**	dutyful	**du·ti·ful**
dragatory	**de·rog·a·to·ry**	dwindel	**dwin·dle**
draggon	**drag·on**	dworf	**dwarf**
drainege	**drain·age**	dye	**die** (stop living)
draipry	**drap·ery**	dyeing	**dy·ing** (not living)
drammatic	**dra·mat·ic**	dying	**dye·ing** (tinting)
draneage	**drain·age**	dynamec	**dy·nam·ic**
dredful	**dread·ful**	dynesty	**dy·nas·ty**
dreery	**dreary**	dynomite	**dy·na·mite**
		dysintery	**dys·en·tery**

E

WRONG	RIGHT
eagel	**ea·gle**
eal	**eel**
ean	**eon** *(time period)*
earake	**ear·ache**
earfull	**ear·ful**
earie	**ee·rie** *(weird)*
earing	**ear·ring**
earn	**urn** *(vase)*
easally	**eas·i·ly**
easle	**ea·sel**
eastword	**east·ward**
eather	**ei·ther** *(each)*
eatible	**eat·a·ble**
eau de colone	**eau de Co·logne**
eavening	**eve·ning**
eaves	**eves** *(nights)*
eb	**ebb**
ebbony	**eb·ony**
ebulient	**ebul·lient**
eccentrisity	**ec·cen·tric·i·ty**
eccleziastic	**ec·cle·si·as·tic**
ecco	**echo**
eccology	**ecol·o·gy**
ecconomic	**eco·nom·ic**
eccosystem	**eco·sys·tem**
eccumenical	**ec·u·men·i·cal**
eccumenism	**ec·u·men·ism**
ecentric	**ec·cen·tric**

WRONG	RIGHT
echellon	**ech·e·lon**
eching	**etch·ing**
echos	**ech·oes**
ecko	**echo**
eckoic	**echo·ic**
eclare	**éclair**
eclesiastic	**ec·cle·si·as·tic**
ecollogy	**ecol·o·gy**
econamy	**econ·o·my**
ecstacy	**ec·sta·sy**
ect.	**etc.**
ecumanism	**ec·u·men·ism**
Ecwador	**Ec·ua·dor**
eczama	**ec·ze·ma**
Edan	**Eden**
edator	**ed·i·tor**
eddable	**ed·i·ble**
eddie	**ed·dy**
eddification	**edi·fi·ca·tion**
eddit	**ed·it**
edducate	**ed·u·cate**
edefy	**ed·i·fy**
edelwise	**edel·weiss**
Edenburg	**Ed·in·burgh**
edifacation	**edi·fi·ca·tion**
Edinburo	**Ed·in·burgh**
Edipus	**Oed·i·pus**
editer	**ed·i·tor**
edition	**ad·di·tion** *(adding)*
educater	**ed·u·ca·tor**
eek	**eke**
eether	**ether** *(in chemistry)*

WRONG	*RIGHT*	*WRONG*	*RIGHT*
eface	**ef·face**	eggo	**ego**
efect	**ef·fect** *(result)*	eggregious	**egre·gious**
efective	**ef·fec·tive**	Egiptian	**Egyp·tian**
	(having effect)	egosentric	**ego·cen·tric**
efectually	**ef·fec·tu·al·ly**	egrit	**egret**
efectuate	**ef·fec·tu·ate**	egzaggerate	**ex·ag·ger·ate**
efemminate	**ef·fem·i·nate**	egzamine	**ex·am·ine** *(test)*
efervescent	**ef·fer·ves·cent**	egzema	**ec·ze·ma**
efete	**ef·fete**	eightyith	**eight·i·eth**
effase	**ef·face**	eigth	**eighth**
effecacious	**ef·fi·ca·cious**	eirie	**ee·rie** *(weird)*
effect	**af·fect** *(to influence)*	eisel	**ea·sel**
effective	**af·fec·tive**	either	**ether** *(in chemistry)*
	(emotional)	ejakulate	**ejac·u·late**
effectualy	**ef·fec·tu·al·ly**	ejeck	**eject**
effegy	**ef·fi·gy**	ekanomic	**eco·nom·ic**
effemeral	**ephem·er·al**	eklair	**éclair**
effert	**ef·fort**	eklectic	**ec·lec·tic**
effervesent	**ef·fer·ves·cent**	eklesiastic	**ec·cle·si·as·tic**
efficiancy	**ef·fi·cien·cy**	eklipse	**eclipse**
effluent	**af·flu·ent** *(rich)*	eksentric	**ec·cen·tric**
effrontary	**ef·fron·tery**	ekstasy	**ec·sta·sy**
eficatious	**ef·fi·ca·cious**	ekumenical	**ec·u·men·i·cal**
eficiency	**ef·fi·cien·cy**	elaberate	**elab·o·rate**
efigy	**ef·fi·gy**	elagence	**el·e·gance**
efluent	**ef·flu·ent** *(flowing)*	elament	**el·e·ment**
efort	**ef·fort**	elamentary	**ele·men·ta·ry**
efrontery	**ef·fron·tery**		*(basic)*
efusive	**ef·fu·sive**	elavate	**el·e·vate**
egaletarian	**egal·i·tar·i·an**	elboe	**el·bow**
eger	**ea·ger**	eleck	**elect**
eggalitarian	**egal·i·tar·i·an**	elecktric	**elec·tric**

electer .... **elec·tor**

electracardiogram ....

.... **elec·tro·car·di·o·gram**

electral .... **elec·tor·al**

electramagnetic ....

.... **elec·tro·mag·net·ic**

electrefy .... **elec·tri·fy**

electricly .... **elec·tri·cal·ly**

electricute .... **elec·tro·cute**

electrisity .... **elec·tric·i·ty**

electrokardiogram ....

.... **elec·tro·car·di·o·gram**

electrollysis ...... **elec·trol·y·sis**

electronnic .... **elec·tron·ic**

election .... **el·o·cu·tion**

elektron .... **elec·tron**

elementary .... **ali·men·ta·ry**

(nourishing)

elementery .... **ele·men·ta·ry**

(basic)

elevan .... **elev·en**

elevater .... **el·e·va·tor**

elfs .... **elves**

eligable .... **el·i·gi·ble**

eligy .... **el·e·gy**

elimanate .... **elim·i·nate**

elimentary .... **ele·men·ta·ry**

(basic)

eliphant .... **el·e·phant**

elipse .... **el·lipse**

eliptical .... **el·lip·ti·cal**

elixer .... **elix·ir**

ellaborate .... **elab·o·rate**

ellastic .... **elas·tic**

ellate .... **elate**

ellder .... **eld·er**

ellect .... **elect**

ellecteral .... **elec·tor·al**

ellection .... **elec·tion**

ellectric .... **elec·tric**

ellectrolysis ...... **elec·trol·y·sis**

ellectron .... **elec·tron**

ellectronic .... **elec·tron·ic**

ellegance .... **el·e·gance**

ellegy .... **el·e·gy**

ellement .... **el·e·ment**

ellephant .... **el·e·phant**

ellevate .... **el·e·vate**

elleven .... **elev·en**

ellicit .... **elic·it** *(evoke)*

ellicit ...... **il·lic·it** *(unlawful)*

elligible .... **el·i·gi·ble**

elliminate .... **elim·i·nate**

ellipticle .... **el·lip·ti·cal**

ellite .... **elite** *(best)*

ellixir .... **elix·ir**

ellocution .... **el·o·cu·tion**

ellongation .... **elon·ga·tion**

elloquent .... **el·o·quent**

ellucidate .... **elu·ci·date**

ellude .... **elude** *(escape)*

ellusion .... **elu·sion** *(an escape)*

ellusive .... **elu·sive**

(hard to grasp)

eloquant	**el·o·quent**	emigrate	**im·mi·grate** *(arrive)*
El Salvidor	**El Sal·va·dor**	eminate	**em·a·nate**
elsewere	**else·where**	eminent	**im·mi·nent**
elucedate	**elu·ci·date**		*(impending)*
elude	**al·lude** *(refer to)*	emissery	**em·is·sary**
elusive	**al·lu·sive** *(referring to)*	emmancipate	**eman·ci·pate**
elusive	**il·lu·sive** *(deceptive)*	emmense	**im·mense**
emanent	**em·i·nent**	emmigrant	**em·i·grant**
	(prominent)		*(one who leaves)*
emansipate	**eman·ci·pate**	emmigrate	**em·i·grate** *(leave)*
emashiate	**ema·ci·ate**	emmisary	**em·is·sary**
emaskulate	**emas·cu·late**	emmission	**emis·sion**
embarass	**em·bar·rass**	emmulate	**em·u·late**
embass	**em·boss**	emnity	**en·mi·ty**
embasy	**em·bas·sy**	emolient	**emol·li·ent** *(softener)*
embelish	**em·bel·lish**	emollument	**emol·u·ment**
emberrass	**em·bar·rass**		*(wages)*
embezle	**em·bez·zle**	empair	**im·pair**
emblam	**em·blem**	empending	**im·pend·ing**
embom	**em·balm**	emperer	**em·per·or**
embrase	**em·brace**	emphases	**em·pha·sis** *(sing.)*
embrio	**em·bryo**	emphasis	**em·pha·ses** *(pl.)*
embroidary	**em·broi·dery**	empireal	**im·pe·ri·al**
emend	**amend** *(revise)*		*(sovereign)*
emergancy	**emer·gen·cy**	empithy	**em·pa·thy**
emerge	**im·merge** *(plunge)*	employible	**em·ploy·a·ble**
emerritus	**emer·i·tus**	emporer	**em·per·or**
emersion	**im·mer·sion**	emrald	**em·er·ald**
	(plunging)	emrey	**em·ery**
emfasis	**em·pha·sis** *(sing.)*	enamy	**en·e·my**
emigrant	**im·mi·grant**	enbankment	**em·bank·ment**
	(one who arrives)	encapsalate	**en·cap·su·late**

WRONG	RIGHT	WRONG	RIGHT
encefalitis	**en·ceph·a·li·tis**	entanglment ..	**en·tan·gle·ment**
encinderator	**in·cin·er·a·tor**	enterprize	**en·ter·prise**
encrimanate	**in·crim·i·nate**	entertaned	**en·ter·tained**
encumbrence ..	**en·cum·brance**	enthusiasticly	
encuragement		....	**en·thu·si·as·ti·cal·ly**
....	**en·cour·age·ment**	entirty	**en·tire·ty**
encyclepedia ..	**en·cy·clo·pe·dia**	entise	**en·tice**
endevor	**en·deav·or**	entomollogy	**en·to·mol·o·gy**
endorsment	**en·dorse·ment**		*(insect study)*
endurence	**en·dur·ance**	entomology	**et·y·mol·o·gy**
endurible	**en·dur·a·ble**		*(word study)*
engeneer	**en·gi·neer**	entoorage	**en·tou·rage**
engenue	**in·gé·nue**	entrales	**en·trails**
engenuity	**in·ge·nu·i·ty**	entre	**en·tree**
engrosing	**en·gross·ing**	entrepeneur ...	**en·tre·pre·neur**
enhanse	**en·hance**	enuff	**enough**
enima	**en·e·ma**	enummerate	**enu·mer·ate**
enjoyible	**en·joy·a·ble**	enunciate	**an·nun·ci·ate**
enlargment	**en·large·ment**		*(announce)*
enmaty	**en·mi·ty**	enurgy	**en·er·gy**
ennable	**en·a·ble**	envalope	**en·ve·lope** *(n.)*
ennamel	**en·am·el**	envelope	**en·vel·op** *(v.)*
ennema	**en·e·ma**	enveous	**en·vi·ous**
ennigma	**enig·ma**	envirement	**en·vi·ron·ment**
ennumerate	**enu·mer·ate**	envoke	**in·voke** *(put into use)*
enoble	**en·no·ble**	enzime	**en·zyme**
enormaty	**enor·mi·ty**	eon	**ion** *(atom)*
ensamble	**en·sem·ble**	epademic	**ep·i·dem·ic**
ensephalitis	**en·ceph·a·li·tis**	epagram	**ep·i·gram**
ensew	**en·sue**	epalepsy	**ep·i·lep·sy**
ensine	**en·sign**	epalog	**ep·i·logue**
entale	**en·tail**	epataph	**ep·i·taph**

WRONG	RIGHT	WRONG	RIGHT
epegraph	**ep·i·graph**	erasure	**eras·er**
epesode	**ep·i·sode**		*(something that erases)*
ephemmeral	**ephem·er·al**	eratic	**er·rat·ic** *(irregular)*
epic	**ep·och** *(era)*	erge	**urge**
epicurian	**ep·i·cu·re·an**	erid	**ar·id**
epifany	**epiph·a·ny**	eriudite	**er·u·dite**
epillepsy	**ep·i·lep·sy**	erksome	**irk·some**
Episcapalian	**Epis·co·pa·li·an**	erl	**earl**
episle	**epis·tle**	erly	**ear·ly**
epitaf	**ep·i·taph**	ermin	**er·mine**
epitomy	**epit·o·me**	ern	**earn** *(deserve)*
epoch	**ep·ic** *(poem)*	ern	**urn** *(vase)*
epoxey	**ep·oxy**	ernest	**ear·nest**
eppigram	**ep·i·gram**	eroneous	**er·ro·ne·ous**
equalibrium	**equi·lib·ri·um**	erotic	**er·rat·ic** *(irregular)*
equallity	**equal·i·ty**	erratic	**erot·ic** *(amatory)*
equasion	**equa·tion**	errection	**erec·tion**
equater	**equa·tor**	errend	**er·rand**
equestrien	**eques·tri·an**	errent	**er·rant**
equety	**eq·ui·ty**	errode	**erode**
equillateral	**equi·lat·er·al**	erronious	**er·ro·ne·ous**
equillibrium	**equi·lib·ri·um**	errotic	**erot·ic** *(amatory)*
equiped	**equipped**	erruption	**erup·tion**
equipmant	**equip·ment**	esaphogus	**esoph·a·gus**
equitible	**eq·ui·ta·ble**	esay	**es·say** *(try; composition)*
equivelance	**equiv·a·lence**	escalater	**es·ca·la·tor**
equivical	**equiv·o·cal**	escallate	**es·ca·late**
eradecate	**erad·i·cate**	eschuary	**es·tu·ary**
erant	**er·rant**	esence	**es·sence**
erascible	**iras·ci·ble**	esential	**es·sen·tial**
eraser	**era·sure**	eshelon	**ech·e·lon**
	(something erased)	Eskemo	**Es·ki·mo**

WRONG	RIGHT
esofagus	**esoph·a·gus**
especally	**espe·cial·ly**
espeonage	**es·pi·o·nage**
espouze	**es·pouse**
espreso	**es·pres·so**
essance	**es·sence**
essay	**as·say** *(analyze)*
essentricity	**ec·cen·tric·i·ty**
essoteric	**es·o·ter·ic**
estemation	**esti·ma·tion**
estimible	**es·ti·ma·ble**
estragen	**es·tro·gen**
estrangment	**es·trange·ment**
estuery	**es·tu·ary**
etaquette	**et·i·quette**
et cetara	**et cet·era**
eternaly	**eter·nal·ly**
eternaty	**eter·ni·ty**
ethel	**eth·yl**
Etheopia	**Ethi·o·pia**
ether	**ei·ther** *(each)*
etherial	**ethe·re·al**
ethicly	**eth·i·cal·ly**
ethireal	**ethe·re·al**
ethnik	**eth·nic**
etible	**ed·i·ble**
ettiquete	**et·i·quette**
ettymology	**et·y·mol·o·gy** *(word study)*
eturnally	**eter·nal·ly**
etymology	**en·to·mol·o·gy** *(insect study)*

WRONG	RIGHT
eucher	**eu·chre**
Eucherist	**Eu·cha·rist**
eu de cologne	**eau de Co·logne**
eufemism	**eu·phe·mism**
Eukarist	**Eu·cha·rist**
eukre	**eu·chre**
eullogy	**eu·lo·gy**
euphamism	**eu·phe·mism**
Eurapean	**Eu·ro·pe·an**
euthenasia	**eu·tha·na·sia**
evacative	**evoc·a·tive**
evaccuate	**evac·u·ate**
evacive	**eva·sive**
evadently	**ev·i·dent·ly**
evalluate	**eval·u·ate**
evally	**evil·ly**
evalution	**ev·o·lu·tion**
evangalist	**evan·gel·ist**
evangellical	**evan·gel·i·cal**
evaperate	**evap·o·rate**
evassive	**eva·sive**
evedence	**ev·i·dence**
evengelical	**evan·gel·i·cal**
eventially	**even·tu·al·ly**
everywere	**ev·ery·where**
eves	**eaves** *(roof edge)*
evesdrop	**eaves·drop**
evidance	**ev·i·dence**
evidentally	**ev·i·dent·ly**
evily	**evil·ly**
evning	**eve·ning**

WRONG	RIGHT
evoke	**in·voke** (put into use)
evry	**ev·ery**
exackly	**ex·act·ly**
exacution	**ex·e·cu·tion**
exagerrate	**ex·ag·ger·ate**
exagesis	**ex·e·ge·sis**
exalltation	**ex·al·ta·tion** (rapture)
exaltation	**ex·ul·ta·tion** (rejoicing)
examanation	**ex·am·i·na·tion**
examin	**ex·am·ine** (test)
examinor	**ex·am·in·er**
exampel	**ex·am·ple**
examplery	**ex·em·pla·ry**
examplify	**ex·em·pli·fy**
exasparate	**ex·as·per·ate**
exassperate	**ex·as·per·ate**
exatic	**ex·ot·ic**
exaust	**ex·haust**
exaustion	**ex·haus·tion**
excallence	**ex·cel·lence**
excavater	**ex·ca·va·tor**
excede	**ex·ceed** (surpass)
exceed	**ac·cede** (agree)
exceled	**ex·celled**
excelency	**ex·cel·len·cy**
excelent	**ex·cel·lent**
excell	**ex·cel**
excellancy	**ex·cel·len·cy**
excellant	**ex·cel·lent**
except	**ac·cept** (receive)

WRONG	RIGHT
excepted	**ac·cept·ed** (approved)
exceptionly	**ex·cep·tion·al·ly**
excercise	**ex·er·cise** (use)
excercism	**ex·or·cism**
excerp	**ex·cerpt**
excess	**ac·cess** (approach)
excevate	**ex·ca·vate**
excitible	**ex·cit·a·ble**
excitment	**ex·cite·ment**
excize	**ex·cise**
exclame	**ex·claim**
exclimation	**ex·cla·ma·tion**
exclusave	**ex·clu·sive**
exclussion	**ex·clu·sion**
excomunnicate	**ex·com·mu·ni·cate**
excreet	**ex·crete**
excriment	**ex·cre·ment**
excrushiating	**ex·cru·ci·at·ing**
excurzion	**ex·cur·sion**
excusible	**ex·cus·a·ble**
execcutive	**ex·ec·u·tive**
executionor	**ex·e·cu·tion·er**
exemplafy	**ex·em·pli·fy**
exemtion	**ex·emp·tion**
exentricity	**ec·cen·tric·i·ty**
exercise	**ex·or·cise** (drive out)
exercism	**ex·or·cism**
exerpt	**ex·cerpt**
exersize	**ex·er·cise** (use)

exestential	**ex·is·ten·tial**	expertese	**ex·pert·ise**
exhabition	**ex·hi·bi·tion**	explacate	**ex·pli·cate**
exhail	**ex·hale**	explane	**ex·plain**
exhertation	**ex·hor·ta·tion**	explination	**ex·pla·na·tion**
exhillarate	**ex·hil·a·rate**	explisit	**ex·plic·it**
exhorbitant	**ex·or·bi·tant**	explocive	**ex·plo·sive**
exibit	**ex·hib·it**	explotation	**ex·ploi·ta·tion**
exibition	**ex·hi·bi·tion**	exponant	**ex·po·nent**
exidus	**ex·o·dus**	exposer	**ex·po·sure**
exilarate	**ex·hil·a·rate**	expossitory	**ex·pos·i·to·ry**
existance	**ex·ist·ence**	expozier	**ex·po·sure**
exitement	**ex·cite·ment**	expresion	**ex·pres·sion**
exonnerate	**ex·on·er·ate**	expresive	**ex·pres·sive**
exorbatent	**ex·or·bi·tant**	expressable	**ex·press·i·ble**
exortation	**ex·hor·ta·tion**	expresso	**es·pres·so**
expadition	**ex·pe·di·tion**	expullsion	**ex·pul·sion**
expance	**ex·panse**	exruciating	**ex·cru·ci·at·ing**
expancion	**ex·pan·sion**	exsale	**ex·hale**
expantion	**ex·pan·sion**	exseed	**ex·ceed** *(surpass)*
expatriot	**ex·pa·tri·ate**	exselled	**ex·celled**
expec	**ex·pect**	exsept	**ex·cept** *(omit)*
expecially	**espe·cial·ly**	exsepted	**ex·cept·ed** *(left out)*
expectent	**ex·pect·ant**	exseptionally	
expecterant	**ex·pec·to·rant**		**ex·cep·tion·al·ly**
expediant	**ex·pe·di·ent**	exsess	**ex·cess** *(surplus)*
expell	**ex·pel**	exsile	**ex·ile**
expencive	**ex·pen·sive**	exsitement	**ex·cite·ment**
expendature	**ex·pend·i·ture**	exsize	**ex·cise**
expendible	**ex·pend·a·ble**	exspanse	**ex·panse**
experament	**ex·per·i·ment**	exspect	**ex·pect**
expergate	**ex·pur·gate**	exspell	**ex·pel**
experiance	**ex·pe·ri·ence**	exspendable	**ex·pend·a·ble**

WRONG	RIGHT
exspenditure	**ex·pend·i·ture**
exspire	**ex·pire**
exsponge	**ex·punge**
exsport	**ex·port**
exstinguish	**ex·tin·guish**
exsume	**ex·hume**
extant	**ex·tent** (degree)
exteerior	**ex·te·ri·or**
extennuating	**ex·ten·u·at·ing**
extent	**ex·tant** (existing)
extercate	**ex·tri·cate**
extercurricular	**ex·tra·cur·ric·u·lar**
exterier	**ex·te·ri·or**
exterminater	**ex·ter·mi·na·tor**
extervert	**ex·tro·vert**
extinc	**ex·tinct**
extordinary	**ex·traor·di·nary**
extracate	**ex·tri·cate**
extracktion	**ex·trac·tion**
extracuricullar	**ex·tra·cur·ric·u·lar**
extrapellate	**ex·trap·o·late**
extravegant	**ex·trav·a·gant**
extravert	**ex·tro·vert**
extreemly	**ex·treme·ly**
extremast	**ex·trem·ist**
extrematy	**ex·trem·i·ty**
extrordinary	**ex·traor·di·nary**
exuberence	**ex·u·ber·ance**
exulltation	**ex·ul·ta·tion** (rejoicing)

WRONG	RIGHT
exultation	**ex·al·ta·tion** (rapture)
exultent	**ex·ult·ant**
exume	**ex·hume**
exxodus	**ex·o·dus**
exzotic	**ex·ot·ic**
exzuberance	**ex·u·ber·ance**
eyelet	**is·let** (small island)
eylet	**eye·let** (small hole)

F

WRONG	RIGHT
fabrecate	**fab·ri·cate**
fabulus	**fab·u·lous**
facalty	**fac·ul·ty**
faccade	**fa·çade**
faceal	**fa·cial**
facesious	**fa·ce·tious**
facillitate	**facil·i·tate**
facillity	**fa·cil·i·ty**
facinate	**fas·ci·nate**
facist	**fas·cist**
facsimilies	**fac·sim·i·les**
facsion	**fac·tion**
facter	**fac·tor**
factery	**fac·to·ry**
factitious	**fic·ti·tious** (imaginary)
factry	**fac·to·ry**
factsimile	**fac·sim·i·le**
factule	**fac·tu·al**
Fahrenhite	**Fahr·en·heit**

WRONG	RIGHT
faillure	**fail·ure**
fain	**feign** *(pretend)*
faint	**feint** *(pretense)*
fair	**fare** *(fee)*
fairie	**fairy** *(elf)*
fairwell	**fare·well**
fairy	**fer·ry** *(boat)*
faithfull	**faith·ful**
faker	**fa·kir** *(Muslim beggar)*
fakir	**fak·er** *(fraud)*
faksimile	**fac·sim·i·le**
falacy	**fal·la·cy**
falcan	**fal·con**
falible	**fal·li·ble**
falicitous	**felic·i·tous**
faliure	**fail·ure**
fallable	**fal·li·ble**
fallecy	**fal·la·cy**
falloe	**fal·low** *(inactive)*
fallsetto	**fal·set·to**
fallter	**fal·ter**
falonious	**fe·lo·ni·ous**
Faloppian	**Fal·lo·pi·an**
falout	**fall·out**
falow	**fal·low** *(inactive)*
falsefy	**fal·si·fy**
falseto	**fal·set·to**
falsety	**fal·si·ty**
falsly	**false·ly**
falt	**fault**
famely	**fam·i·ly**
fameous	**fa·mous**

WRONG	RIGHT
familier	**fa·mil·iar**
familierity	**famil·i·ar·i·ty**
familliarize	**famil·iar·ize**
fammine	**fam·ine**
fancey	**fan·cy**
fancifull	**fan·ci·ful**
fane	**feign** *(pretend)*
fanfair	**fan·fare**
fannatic	**fa·nat·ic**
fantastik	**fan·tas·tic**
fantem	**phan·tom**
fantesy	**fan·ta·sy**
farcicle	**far·ci·cal**
fare	**fair** *(lovely; bazaar)*
farena	**fa·ri·na**
Farenheit	**Fahr·en·heit**
farensic	**fo·ren·sic**
farewel	**fare·well**
farfeched	**far–fetched**
farmacy	**phar·ma·cy**
farmasuitical	**phar·ma·ceu·ti·cal**
Faro	**Phar·aoh** *(Egyptian ruler)*
farse	**farce**
farsical	**far·ci·cal**
fasade	**fa·çade**
fascenate	**fas·ci·nate**
fasetious	**fa·ce·tious**
fashien	**fash·ion**
fashionible	**fash·ion·a·ble**
fashist	**fas·cist**
fasile	**fac·ile**

WRONG	RIGHT	WRONG	RIGHT
fasilitate	**facil·i·tate**	feasco	**fi·as·co**
fasinate	**fas·ci·nate**	feat	**feet** (pl. of foot)
fassen	**fas·ten**	featurless	**fea·ture·less**
fassenation	**fas·ci·na·tion**	Febuary	**Feb·ru·ary**
fassion	**fash·ion**	feching	**fetch·ing**
fastenner	**fas·ten·er**	fedaration	**fed·er·a·tion**
faston	**fas·ten**	fedral	**fed·er·al**
fatallistic	**fa·tal·is·tic**	feeline	**fe·line**
fatallity	**fa·tal·i·ty**	feend	**fiend**
fataly	**fa·tal·ly**	feesible	**fea·si·ble**
fateague	**fa·tigue**	feet	**feat** (deed)
fatefull	**fate·ful**	feild	**field**
fatel	**fa·tal**	fein	**feign** (pretend)
faten	**fat·ten**	feind	**fiend**
fathem	**fath·om**	feint	**faint** (weak)
fatige	**fa·tigue**	feirce	**fierce**
faught	**fought**	felany	**fel·o·ny**
faukon	**fal·con**	felisity	**fe·lic·i·ty**
faun ...	**fawn** (deer; act servilely)	fellicitous	**felic·i·tous**
faver	**fa·vor**	fellonious	**fe·lo·ni·ous**
faverite	**fa·vor·ite**	fellony	**fel·o·ny**
favorible	**fa·vor·a·ble**	Fellopian	**Fal·lo·pi·an**
fawcet	**fau·cet**	felow	**fel·low**
fawna	**fau·na**	feminity	**fem·i·nin·i·ty**
fax paus	**faux pas**	femminine	**fem·i·nine**
faze	**phase** (stage)	fendish	**fiend·ish**
feable	**fee·ble**	feotus	**fe·tus**
feancé	**fi·an·cé** (m.)	ferce	**fierce**
feancé	**fi·an·cée** (f.)	feret	**fer·ret**
fearfull	**fear·ful**	feric	**fer·ric**
feasable	**fea·si·ble**	ferina	**fa·ri·na**
feasant	**pheas·ant**	ferl	**furl**

| --- | --- | --- | --- |
ferlough	**fur·lough**	fiancé	**fi·an·cée** *(f.)*
fermament	**fir·ma·ment**	fiancée	**fi·an·cé** *(m.)*
fernace	**fur·nace**	fiassco	**fi·as·co**
ferniture	**fur·ni·ture**	fibreglass	**fi·ber·glass**
feror	**fu·ror**	fickel	**fick·le**
ferous	**fer·rous**	ficktion	**fic·tion**
ferrat	**fer·ret**	fictitious	**fac·ti·tious** *(artificial)*
ferrier	**fur·ri·er**	fictitous	**fic·ti·tious**
ferris	**fer·rous**		*(imaginary)*
ferrocious	**fe·ro·cious**	fiddeler	**fid·dler**
ferry	**fairy** *(elf)*	fidellity	**fi·del·i·ty**
ferther	**fur·ther**	fiftyeth	**fif·ti·eth**
ferthermore	**fur·ther·more**	figarine	**fig·u·rine**
fertillize	**fer·til·ize**	figerative	**fig·u·ra·tive**
fertive	**fur·tive**	figget	**fidg·et**
fertle	**fer·tile**	figgure	**fig·ure**
fervant	**fer·vent**	figmant	**fig·ment**
ferved	**fer·vid**	figureen	**fig·u·rine**
ferver	**fer·vor**	figuretive	**fig·u·ra·tive**
festeval	**fes·ti·val**	figurhead	**fig·ure·head**
festivaty	**fes·tiv·i·ty**	fiksation	**fix·a·tion**
festor	**fes·ter**	filement	**fil·a·ment**
fether	**feath·er**	filet minion	**fi·let mi·gnon**
fetis	**fe·tus**	filharmonic	**phil·har·mon·ic**
fettid	**fet·id**	fillament	**fil·a·ment**
fettish	**fet·ish**	fillbert	**fil·bert**
feudal	**fu·tile** *(useless)*	fillial	**fil·i·al**
feudallism	**feu·dal·ism**	fillie	**fil·ly**
feugitive	**fu·gi·tive**	fillter	**fil·ter**
feul	**fu·el**	filthally	**filth·i·ly**
fewd	**feud**	finalle	**fi·na·le**
fewdalism	**feu·dal·ism**	finallity	**fi·nal·i·ty**

finallize	**fi·nal·ize**	flabbie	**flab·by**
finaly	**fi·nal·ly** *(in conclusion)*	flabergast	**flab·ber·gast**
financeer	**fin·an·cier**	flacid	**flac·cid**
financialy	**finan·cial·ly**	fladdery	**flat·tery**
finantial	**fi·nan·cial**	flaged	**flagged**
finely	**fi·nal·ly** *(in conclusion)*	flaggon	**flag·on**
finerie	**fin·ery**	flagrent	**fla·grant**
fingerring	**fin·ger·ing**	flair	**flare** *(blaze)*
finnale	**fi·na·le**	flakey	**flaky**
finnaly	**fi·nal·ly** *(in conclusion)*	flaks	**flax**
finnancial	**fi·nan·cial**	flale	**flail**
finnesse	**fi·nesse** *(skill)*	flamable	**flam·ma·ble**
finnicky	**fin·icky**	flamboyent	**flam·boy·ant**
finnish	**fin·ish**	flamenco	**fla·min·go** *(bird)*
fintch	**finch**	flamingo	**fla·men·co** *(dance)*
fir	**fur** *(hair)*	flanel	**flan·nel**
firewerks	**fire·works**	flaped	**flapped**
firey	**fi·ery**	flare	**flair** *(knack)*
firmentation	**fer·men·ta·tion**	flashey	**flashy**
firn	**fern** *(plant)*	flashlite	**flash·light**
first ade	**first aid**	flassid	**flac·cid**
fiscaly	**fis·cal·ly**	flatery	**flat·tery**
fishion	**fis·sion**	flavering	**fla·vor·ing**
fishure	**fis·sure**	flavorfull	**fla·vor·ful**
fiskle	**fis·cal**	flea	**flee** *(run)*
fistacuffs	**fist·i·cuffs**	fleace	**fleece**
fistfull	**fist·ful**	flee	**flea** *(insect)*
fitfull	**fit·ful**	fleecey	**fleecy**
fixcher	**fix·ture**	fleese	**fleece**
fixible	**fix·a·ble**	flegeling	**fledg·ling**
fizle	**fiz·zle**	flegmatic	**phleg·mat·ic**
fizzion	**fis·sion**	flemm	**phlegm**

WRONG	RIGHT	WRONG	RIGHT
flertatious	**flir·ta·tious**	florrid	**flor·id**
fleshey	**fleshy**	florrist	**flo·rist**
fleur–de–lee	**fleur–de–lis**	flosed	**flossed**
flew	**flu** (influenza)	flour	**flow·er** (part of plant)
flew	**flue** (pipe)	flow	**floe** (ice)
flexable	**flex·i·ble**	flower	**flour** (grain)
flimsey	**flim·sy**	flownder	**floun·der**
flipancy	**flip·pan·cy**	flowt	**flout**
fliped	**flipped**	flu	**flue** (pipe)
flippency	**flip·pan·cy**	fluancy	**flu·en·cy**
flirtacious	**flir·ta·tious**	fluchuate	**fluc·tu·ate**
flite	**flight** (air travel)	flue	**flew** (pt. of fly)
flitey	**flighty**	flue	**flu** (influenza)
flo	**floe** (ice)	flued	**flu·id**
flo	**flow** (glide)	fluidety	**flu·id·i·ty**
flod	**flood**	fluoresent	**flu·o·res·cent**
floe	**flow** (glide)		(giving light)
floged	**flogged**	fluoresent	**flo·res·cent**
floidity	**flu·id·i·ty**		(blooming)
flont	**flaunt**	fluorish	**flour·ish**
flook	**fluke**	fluorride	**flu·o·ride**
floped	**flopped**	flur–de–lis	**fleur–de–lis**
floppie	**flop·py**	flurrie	**flur·ry**
Floreda	**Flor·i·da**	fo	**foe**
florel	**flo·ral**	foamey	**foamy**
florescent	**flu·o·res·cent**	fobia	**pho·bia**
	(giving light)	focallize	**fo·cal·ize**
floresent	**flo·res·cent**	focas	**fo·cus**
	(blooming)	foe pas	**faux pas**
floride	**flu·o·ride**	foggey	**fo·gy**
florish	**flour·ish**		(conservative person)
florral	**flo·ral**	fogy	**fog·gy** (misty)

71

WRONG	RIGHT
foibal	**foi·ble**
fokus	**fo·cus**
folage	**fo·li·age**
fole	**foal**
folksey	**folk·sy**
follacle	**fol·li·cle**
follder	**fold·er**
folley	**fol·ly**
folliage	**fo·li·age**
follio	**fo·lio**
folowing	**fol·low·ing**
folter	**fal·ter**
fon	**fawn** (deer; act servilely)
fondoo	**fon·due**
foney	**pho·ny**
foolhardie	**fool·har·dy**
foose	**fuse**
for	**fore** (golf cry)
for	**four** (number)
foram	**fo·rum**
forarm	**fore·arm**
forbear	**fore·bear** (ancestor)
forbearence	**for·bear·ance**
forbiding	**for·bid·ding** (dangerous looking)
forboding	**fore·bod·ing** (foretelling)
forcast	**fore·cast**
forcefull	**force·ful**
forclose	**fore·close**
fore	**four** (number)
forebear	**for·bear** (refrain)

WRONG	RIGHT
forebearance	**for·bear·ance**
forebearer	**fore·bear** (ancestor)
foreboding	**for·bid·ding** (dangerous looking)
foreceps	**for·ceps**
forelorn	**for·lorn**
foremula	**for·mu·la**
foresake	**for·sake**
foresite	**fore·sight**
foretitude	**for·ti·tude**
forety	**for·ty**
foreward	**fore·word** (preface)
foreward	**for·ward** (to the front)
forfather	**fore·fa·ther**
forfiet	**for·feit**
forfinger	**fore·fin·ger**
forfront	**fore·front**
forgary	**for·gery**
forgetfull	**for·get·ful**
forgeting	**for·get·ting**
forgo	**fore·go** (precede)
forgone	**fore·gone** (unavoidable)
forgoten	**for·got·ten**
forground	**fore·ground**
forhand	**fore·hand**
forhead	**fore·head**
foriegn	**for·eign**
formalldehyde	**form·al·de·hyde**

WRONG	RIGHT	WRONG	RIGHT
formallity	**for·mal·i·ty**	fortatude	**for·ti·tude**
formallize	**for·mal·ize**	forte	**fort** *(fortified place)*
formally	**for·mer·ly**	forteen	**four·teen**
	(in the past)	fortefy	**for·ti·fy**
formaly	**for·mal·ly** *(of form)*	forteith	**for·ti·eth**
forman	**fore·man**	fortell	**fore·tell**
formel	**for·mal**	forth	**fourth** *(number)*
formelize	**for·mal·ize**	fortifecation	**for·ti·fi·ca·tion**
formely	**for·mer·ly**	fortouitous	**for·tu·i·tous**
	(in the past)	forward	**fore·word** *(preface)*
formerly	**for·mal·ly** *(of form)*	forword	**for·ward** *(to the front)*
formidible	**for·mi·da·ble**	forword	**fore·word** *(preface)*
formost	**fore·most**	fosfate	**phos·phate**
formulla	**for·mu·la**	fosil	**fos·sil**
formullate	**for·mu·late**	fossillize	**fos·sil·ize**
fornecation	**for·ni·ca·tion**	fostor	**fos·ter**
forocious	**fe·ro·cious**	fotocopy	**pho·to·copy**
forrage	**for·age**	fotoelectric	**pho·to·e·lec·tric**
forray	**for·ay**	fotogenic	**pho·to·gen·ic**
forreign	**for·eign**	fotos	**pho·tos**
forrensic	**fo·ren·sic**	fotosynthesis	
forrest	**for·est**		**pho·to·syn·the·sis**
forrum	**fo·rum**	foul	**fowl** *(bird)*
forruner	**for·eign·er** *(stranger)*	foundery	**found·ry**
forrunner	**fore·run·ner**	founten	**foun·tain**
	(herald)	fourfinger	**fore·fin·ger**
forsee	**fore·see**	fourth	**forth** *(forward)*
forseps	**for·ceps**	fourty	**for·ty**
forsight	**fore·sight**	fowl	**foul** *(filthy)*
forsithia	**for·syth·ia**	fowndation	**foun·da·tion**
forstall	**fore·stall**	fowndry	**found·ry**
fort	**forte** *(skill)*	foyble	**foi·ble**

frachure	**frac·ture**	freese	**freeze** *(become ice)*
fractionallize	**frac·tion·al·ize**	freeweeling	**free·wheel·ing**
fracton	**frac·tion**	freind	**friend**
fradulent	**fraud·u·lent**	freize	**frieze** *(in architecture)*
fragill	**frag·ile**	frekle	**freck·le**
fragrent	**fra·grant**	frend	**friend**
fraight	**freight**	frenzie	**fren·zy**
fraighter	**freight·er**	frequant	**fre·quent**
fraktion	**frac·tion**	frequensy	**fre·quen·cy**
fralty	**frail·ty**	frescoe	**fres·co**
framewark	**frame·work**	fretfull	**fret·ful**
franc	**frank** *(honest)*	freting	**fret·ting**
Frances	**Fran·cis** *(m.)*	frett	**fret**
franchize	**fran·chise**	friccasee	**fric·as·see**
Francis	**Fran·ces** *(f.)*	frieght	**freight**
frank	**franc** *(coin)*	frieghter	**freight·er**
franticly	**fran·ti·cal·ly**	frier	**fri·ar** *(religious person)*
frase	**phrase**	frier	**fry·er** *(food)*
fraternaty	**fra·ter·ni·ty**	frieze	**freeze** *(become ice)*
fraturnal	**fra·ter·nal**	friggate	**frig·ate**
fraut	**fraught**	friggid	**frig·id**
frawd	**fraud**	frightning	**fright·en·ing**
frawdulent	**fraud·u·lent**	frigit	**frig·ate**
frazled	**fraz·zled**	friing	**fry·ing**
freckel	**freck·le**	frikassee	**fric·as·see**
freckeled	**freck·led**	friskey	**frisky**
fredom	**free·dom**	friter	**frit·ter**
freedum	**free·dom**	frivelous	**friv·o·lous**
freek	**freak**	frivollity	**fri·vol·i·ty**
freelanse	**free–lance**	Froidian	**Freud·i·an**
freeloder	**free·load·er**	frolicksome	**frol·ic·some**
freequency	**fre·quen·cy**	frollic	**frol·ic**

WRONG	RIGHT	WRONG	RIGHT
fronteer	**fron·tier**	functionnal	**func·tion·al**
frosbite	**frost·bite**	fundamently	
frostie	**frosty**		**fun·da·men·tal·ly**
frothey	**frothy**	fundation	**foun·da·tion**
frouning	**frown·ing**	fundimental	**fun·da·men·tal**
Fruedian	**Freud·i·an**	funel	**fun·nel**
frugel	**fru·gal**	funerial	**fu·ne·re·al**
fruitfull	**fruit·ful**	funerral	**fu·ner·al**
fruntier	**fron·tier**	fungases	**fun·gus·es**
frusstration	**frus·tra·tion**	fungecide	**fun·gi·cide**
fryed	**fried**	funireal	**fu·ne·re·al**
fuchia	**fuch·sia**	funktion	**func·tion**
fucilage	**fu·se·lage**	funneral	**fu·ner·al**
fudal	**feu·dal**	funtion	**func·tion**
fuge	**fugue**	fur	**fir** *(tree)*
fuge	**fudge**	fureous	**fu·ri·ous**
fugetive	**fu·gi·tive**	furier	**fur·ri·er**
fuise	**fuse**	furlow	**fur·lough**
fujative	**fu·gi·tive**	furmentation	**fer·men·ta·tion**
fulback	**full·back**	furn	**fern** *(plant)*
fulcram	**ful·crum**	furnature	**fur·ni·ture**
fule	**fu·el**	furnesh	**fur·nish**
fulfiled	**ful·filled**	furness	**fur·nace**
fullcrum	**ful·crum**	furow	**fur·row**
fullength	**full–length**	furrie	**fur·ry**
fullfil	**ful·fill**	furrious	**fu·ri·ous**
fullfilled	**ful·filled**	furror	**fu·ror**
fulness	**full·ness**	furtave	**fur·tive**
fumbeling	**fum·bling**	furthurmore	**fur·ther·more**
fumegate	**fu·mi·gate**	fushia	**fuch·sia**
fumey	**fumy**	fusilage	**fu·se·lage**
functionaly	**func·tion·al·ly**	fussally	**fuss·i·ly**

WRONG	RIGHT	WRONG	RIGHT
fusselage	**fu·se·lage**	gallavant	**gal·li·vant**
fussie	**fussy**	gallaxy	**gal·axy**
fussion	**fu·sion**	gallen	**gal·lon** *(liquid measure)*
futere	**fu·ture**	gallent	**gal·lant**
futeristic	**futur·is·tic**	galleyvant	**gal·li·vant**
futile	**feu·dal**	gallies	**gal·leys**
futill	**fu·tile** *(useless)*	gallore	**ga·lore**
futillity	**fu·til·i·ty**	galloshes	**ga·losh·es**
futurristic	**futur·is·tic**	gallup	**gal·lop**
		gallvanize	**gal·va·nize**
G		gally	**gal·ley**
		galon	**gal·lon** *(liquid measure)*
gabanzo	**gar·ban·zo**	galop	**gal·lop**
gabbardine	**gab·ar·dine**	galows	**gal·lows**
gabel	**ga·ble** *(roof)*	galvenize	**gal·va·nize**
gadgit	**gadg·et**	gama	**gam·ma**
gaety	**gai·e·ty**	gambet	**gam·bit**
gaff	**gaffe** *(mistake)*	gamble	**gam·bol** *(frolic)*
gaffe	**gaff** *(hook)*	gambleing	**gam·bling**
gage	**gauge** *(measure)*	gambol	**gam·ble** *(bet)*
gaget	**gadg·et**	gamet	**gam·ut**
gaging	**gag·ging** *(choking)*	gamey	**gamy**
gail	**gale** *(strong wind)*	gammut	**gam·ut**
gailey	**gai·ly**	gandola	**gon·do·la**
gait	**gate** *(opening)*	gandor	**gan·der**
gaje	**gauge** *(measure)*	gane	**gain**
galant	**gal·lant**	gangleing	**gan·gling**
galery	**gal·lery**	gangreen	**gan·grene**
galexy	**gal·axy**	ganre	**gen·re**
galey	**gal·ley**	gapeing	**gap·ing**
gallactic	**ga·lac·tic**	garanteeing	**guar·an·tee·ing**
gallary	**gal·lery**	garbege	**gar·bage**

WRONG	RIGHT	WRONG	RIGHT
gard	**guard**	gasslight	**gas·light**
gardian	**guard·i·an**	gassoline	**gas·o·line**
gardin	**gar·den**	gastly	**ghast·ly**
gardner	**gar·den·er**	gastrick	**gas·tric**
garet	**gar·ret**	gate	**gait** *(walk)*
garganchuan	**gar·gan·tu·an**	gaudey	**gaudy**
gargleing	**gar·gling**	gauk	**gawk**
gargoil	**gar·goyle**	gaul	**gall**
garilla	**guer·ril·la** *(soldier)*	gauranteeing	**guar·an·tee·ing**
garilla	**go·ril·la** *(ape)*	gaurd	**guard**
garison	**gar·ri·son**	gaurdian	**guard·i·an**
garlend	**gar·land**	gaushe	**gauche**
garlick	**gar·lic**	gavle	**gav·el**
garmint	**gar·ment**	gawnt	**gaunt**
garnesh	**gar·nish**	gawntlet	**gaunt·let**
garrage	**ga·rage**	gawze	**gauze**
garralous	**gar·ru·lous**	gayety	**gai·e·ty**
garrason	**gar·ri·son**	gayla	**ga·la**
garrbled	**gar·bled**	gayze	**gaze**
garrish	**gar·ish**	gazele	**ga·zelle**
garrit	**gar·ret**	gazete	**ga·zette**
garrlic	**gar·lic**	gazibo	**ga·ze·bo**
garson	**gar·çon**	geagraphical	**ge·o·graph·i·cal**
garulous	**gar·ru·lous**	gealogy	**ge·ol·o·gy**
gasahol	**gas·o·hol**	geametric	**ge·o·met·ric**
gasaline	**gas·o·line**	gease	**geese**
gasha	**gei·sha**	geens	**genes** *(hereditary units)*
gasious	**gas·e·ous**	geer	**gear**
gaskit	**gas·ket**	gel	**jell** *(become jelly)*
gaslite	**gas·light**	gell	**gel** *(jelly-like substance)*
gassamer	**gos·sa·mer**	gellatin	**gel·a·tin**
gasseous	**gas·e·ous**	gellding	**geld·ing**

WRONG	RIGHT
gelly	**jel·ly**
Gemmini	**Gem·i·ni**
genasis	**gen·e·sis**
geneology	**ge·ne·al·o·gy**
generalaty	**gen·er·al·i·ty**
generaly	**gen·er·al·ly**
generater	**gen·er·a·tor**
generick	**ge·ner·ic**
generousity	**gen·er·os·i·ty**
generus	**gen·er·ous**
genes	**jeans** (trousers)
genetal	**gen·i·tal**
geneticly	**ge·net·i·cal·ly**
geneus	**ge·nius** (talent)
genger	**gin·ger**
geniel	**ge·nial**
genius	**ge·nus** (class)
genneration	**gen·er·a·tion**
genneric	**ge·ner·ic**
genoside	**gen·o·cide**
genrally	**gen·er·al·ly**
genrous	**gen·er·ous**
genteal	**gen·teel** (refined)
genteel	**gen·tile** (not Jewish)
gentile	**gen·tle** (not rough)
gentile	**gen·teel** (refined)
gentle	**gen·tile** (not Jewish)
gentley	**gen·tly**
genuen	**gen·u·ine**
genufleck	**gen·u·flect**
genus	**ge·nius** (talent)
geografical	**ge·o·graph·i·cal**

WRONG	RIGHT
geomettric	**ge·o·met·ric**
geraffe	**gi·raffe**
gerage	**ga·rage**
geraneum	**ge·ra·ni·um**
gerble	**ger·bil**
gereatrics	**ger·i·at·rics**
gerkin	**gher·kin**
germacide	**ger·mi·cide**
germain	**ger·mane**
germanate	**ger·mi·nate**
geschure	**ges·ture** (movement)
geshtalt	**ge·stalt**
gess	**guess** (surmise)
gest	**guest** (person)
gest	**jest**
gestickulate	**ges·tic·u·late**
gestolt	**ge·stalt**
geting	**get·ting**
getogether	**get–to·geth·er**
getto	**ghet·to**
geurilla	**guer·ril·la** (soldier)
geuss	**guess** (surmise)
gezebo	**ga·ze·bo**
gezelle	**ga·zelle**
gheto	**ghet·to**
ghool	**ghoul**
gibe	**jibe** (agree)
giberish	**gib·ber·ish**
giblit	**gib·let**
gidance	**guid·ance**
giddyness	**gid·di·ness**
gient	**gi·ant**

WRONG	RIGHT	WRONG	RIGHT
giesha	**gei·sha**	glanduler	**glan·du·lar**
gigalo	**gig·o·lo**	glareing	**glar·ing**
gigantick	**gi·gan·tic**	glashal	**gla·cial**
gigling	**gig·gling**	glasier	**gla·cier**
gileless	**guile·less**	glaukoma	**glau·co·ma**
gillotine	**guil·lo·tine**	gleem	**gleam**
gilt	**guilt** *(blame)*	gleen	**glean**
gimick	**gim·mick**	glibb	**glib**
gimlit	**gim·let**	glideing	**glid·ing**
gimnasium	**gym·na·si·um**	glimer	**glim·mer**
ginea pig	**guin·ea pig**	glimse	**glimpse**
ginecology	**gyn·e·col·o·gy**	glissen	**glis·ten**
gingam	**ging·ham**	glitery	**glit·tery**
ginnie	**jin·ni**	globel	**glob·al**
gipsum	**gyp·sum**	gloomey	**gloomy**
girafe	**gi·raffe**	glorafy	**glo·ri·fy**
giration	**gy·ra·tion**	glorius	**glo·ri·ous**
girm	**germ**	glossery	**glos·sa·ry**
giroscope	**gy·ro·scope**	glossey	**glossy**
gise	**guise** *(aspect)*	glote	**gloat**
giser	**gey·ser**	gloucoma	**glau·co·ma**
giss	**gist**	gluecose	**glu·cose**
gitar	**gui·tar**	glueing	**glu·ing**
giudance	**guid·ance**	glumy	**gloomy**
giveing	**giv·ing**	gluttenous	**glut·ton·ous**
gizzerd	**giz·zard**	glyserine	**glyc·er·in**
glaceir	**gla·cier**	gnarlled	**gnarled**
glaciel	**gla·cial**	gnawwing	**gnaw·ing**
gladeator	**glad·i·a·tor**	gnoam	**gnome**
gladeolas	**glad·i·o·lus**	gnoo	**gnu**
glamorus	**glam·or·ous**	gobbeling	**gob·bling**
glanceing	**glanc·ing**	goblen	**gob·lin**

79

WRONG	RIGHT	WRONG	RIGHT
gobling	**gob·bling**	gosip	**gos·sip**
goblit	**gob·let**	gosspel	**gos·pel**
goche	**gauche**	gossup	**gos·sip**
gock	**gawk**	gost	**ghost**
goddy	**gaudy**	goucho	**gau·cho**
gode	**goad**	goul	**ghoul**
godess	**god·dess**	gourmey	**gour·met**
gofer	**go·pher** (animal)	goverment	**gov·ern·ment**
gogles	**gog·gles**	governer	**gov·er·nor**
goldan	**gold·en**	govurn	**gov·ern**
golf	**gulf** (bay; gap)	gowge	**gouge**
goll	**gall**	gowt	**gout**
gollbladder	**gall·blad·der**	goyter	**goi·ter·**
gollden	**gold·en**	goz	**gauze**
gondala	**gon·do·la**	grabing	**grab·bing**
gondoleer	**gon·do·lier**	gracius	**gra·cious**
gonorrea	**gon·or·rhea**	grackel	**grack·le**
gont	**gaunt**	gradiant	**gra·di·ent**
gontlet	**gaunt·let**	gradiation	**gra·da·tion**
goofey	**goofy**	gradualy	**grad·u·al·ly**
goolash	**gou·lash**	graduit	**grad·u·ate**
gopher	**go·fer** (errand runner)	graff	**graft**
gophor	**go·pher** (animal)	graff	**graph**
gord	**gourd**	grafic	**graph·ic**
gorey	**gory**	grafite	**graph·ite**
gorgous	**gor·geous**	grafitti	**graf·fi·ti**
gorila	**go·ril·la** (ape)	gragarious	**gre·gar·i·ous**
gorilla	**guer·ril·la** (soldier)	grainary	**gran·a·ry**
gorjeous	**gor·geous**	gram	**gra·ham** (flour)
gormet	**gour·met**	gramaticly	**gram·mat·i·cal·ly**
gorrila	**go·ril·la** (ape)	grammer	**gram·mar**
gosamer	**gos·sa·mer**	granade	**gre·nade**

WRONG	RIGHT	WRONG	RIGHT
grandaughter		gravetate .... **grav·i·tate**	
.... **grand·daugh·ter**		gravety .... **grav·i·ty**	
grandeose .... **gran·di·ose**		gravey .... **gra·vy**	
grandure .... **gran·deur**		gravill .... **grav·el**	
(grandness)		gravstone .... **grave·stone**	
granery .... **gran·a·ry**		gravvity .... **grav·i·ty**	
granet .... **gran·ite** *(stone)*		gravyard .... **grave·yard**	
granite .... **grant·ed** *(pt. of grant)*		grazeing .... **graz·ing**	
grannola .... **gran·o·la**		Greace .... **Greece**	
grannular .... **gran·u·lar**		greasey .... **greasy**	
granstand .... **grand·stand**		great .... **greet** *(meet)*	
granted .... **gran·ite** *(stone)*		great .... **grate** *(scrape)*	
granuler .... **gran·u·ler**		greatfull .... **grate·ful**	
grapfruit .... **grape·fruit**		greedally .... **greed·i·ly**	
graphick .... **graph·ic**		greenary .... **green·ery**	
grapling .... **grap·pling**		greenkeeper ... **greens·keep·er**	
grappel .... **grap·ple**		Greenwhich .... **Green·wich**	
grapvine .... **grape·vine**		Greese .... **Greece**	
grase .... **grace**		greesy .... **greasy**	
grassey .... **grassy**		gregarrious .... **gre·gar·i·ous**	
grasshoper .... **grass·hop·per**		greif .... **grief**	
grate .... **great** *(large)*		greivance .... **griev·ance**	
gratefull .... **grate·ful**		greiving .... **griev·ing**	
gratefy .... **grat·i·fy**		greivous .... **griev·ous**	
grateing .... **grat·ing**		gremlen .... **grem·lin**	
gratetude .... **grat·i·tude**		grenery .... **green·ery**	
gratious .... **gra·cious**		grennade .... **gre·nade**	
grattitude .... **grat·i·tude**		grennadine .... **gren·a·dine**	
gratuetous .... **gra·tu·i·tous**		Grennich .... **Green·wich**	
gravelly .... **grave·ly** *(soberly)*		griddiron .... **grid·i·ron**	
gravely .... **grav·el·ly**		gridle .... **grid·dle**	
(full of gravel)		grieveing .... **griev·ing**	

WRONG	RIGHT	WRONG	RIGHT
grievence	**griev·ance**	grouseing	**grous·ing**
grievius	**griev·ous**	grovell	**grov·el**
griffiti	**graf·fi·ti**	growchy	**grouchy**
griling	**grill·ing**	growel	**growl**
grimey	**grimy**	groweth	**growth**
grimmace	**gri·mace**	grown	**groan** *(moan)*
grimmly	**grim·ly**	growsing	**grous·ing**
grined	**grind**	growt	**grout**
grinestone	**grind·stone**	growwing	**grow·ing**
grining	**grin·ning**	groyn	**groin**
griping	**grip·ping** *(holding)*	grubing	**grub·bing**
gripping	**grip·ing**	gruby	**grub·by**
	(complaining)	grudgeingly	**grudg·ing·ly**
grissle	**gris·tle**	gruesum	**grue·some**
grizzely	**griz·zly** *(bear)*	gruge	**grudge**
grizzly	**gris·ly** *(horrible)*	grugingly	**grudg·ing·ly**
groan	**grown** *(mature)*	gruling	**gru·el·ing**
grogy	**grog·gy**	grumbleing	**grum·bling**
groing	**grow·ing**	grungey	**grun·gy**
grone	**grown** *(mature)*	grusome	**grue·some**
grone	**groan** *(moan)*	gruvel	**grov·el**
grool	**gru·el**	gruwel	**gru·el**
grooling	**gru·el·ing**	guacomole	**gua·ca·mo·le**
groosome	**grue·some**	guage	**gauge** *(measure)*
gropeing	**grop·ing**	guaranteing	**guar·an·tee·ing**
grose	**gross**	guardean	**guard·i·an**
grosery	**gro·cery**	guerila	**guer·ril·la** *(soldier)*
grotesk	**gro·tesque**	guerilla	**go·ril·la** *(ape)*
groth	**growth**	gues	**guest** *(person)*
groto	**grot·to**	gufaw	**guf·faw**
grouchey	**grouchy**	guideing	**guid·ing**
groupy	**group·ie**	guidence	**guid·ance**

WRONG	RIGHT	WRONG	RIGHT
guilless	**guile·less**		
guilotine	**guil·lo·tine**	**H**	
guilt	**gilt** (coated)	habbitation	**hab·i·ta·tion**
guinnea pig	**guin·ea pig**	habbitual	**ha·bit·u·al**
guittar	**gui·tar**	habet	**hab·it**
gulet	**gul·let**	habetation	**hab·i·ta·tion**
gulf	**golf** (game)	habitible	**hab·it·a·ble**
gullable	**gul·li·ble**	hachery	**hatch·ery**
gulley	**gul·ly**	hachet	**hatch·et**
gullit	**gul·let**	haching	**hatch·ing**
gultch	**gulch**	hachway	**hatch·way**
gumtion	**gump·tion**	hacknied	**hack·neyed**
gumy	**gum·my**	hadock	**had·dock**
guning	**gun·ning**	haf	**half** (n.)
guocamole	**gua·ca·mo·le**	haggerd	**hag·gard**
gurdle	**gir·dle**	hagle	**hag·gle**
gurgleing	**gur·gling**	haikoo	**hai·ku**
gurth	**girth**	hail	**hale** (healthy; force)
guset	**gus·set**	hainous	**hei·nous**
gussto	**gus·to**	hair	**heir** (inheritor)
guter	**gut·ter**	hair	**hare** (rabbit)
gutteral	**gut·tur·al**	hairbrained	**hare·brained**
guvernatorial		hairey	**hairy** (hair–covered)
	guber·na·to·ri·al	hairlip	**hare·lip**
guvernment	**gov·ern·ment**	hairloom	**heir·loom**
guvnor	**gov·er·nor**	hairpeace	**hair·piece**
guys	**guise** (aspect)	hairy	**har·ry** (harass)
guyser	**gey·ser**	haiven	**ha·ven**
gymnaseum	**gym·na·si·um**	haize	**haze**
gynacology	**gyn·e·col·o·gy**	haizel	**ha·zel**
gypsom	**gyp·sum**	hakneyed	**hack·neyed**
gyrascope	**gy·ro·scope**	hale	**hail** (ice; call)

WRONG	RIGHT	WRONG	RIGHT
halebut	**hal·i·but**	handeling	**han·dling**
halelujah	**hal·le·lu·jah**	handfull	**hand·ful**
half	**halve** (v.)	handicaped	**hand·i·capped**
hall	**haul** (pull)	handiman	**hand·y·man**
hallibut	**hal·i·but**	handkercheif	**hand·ker·chief**
hallo	**ha·lo** (ring of light)	handlely	**hand·i·ly**
hallowed	**hol·lowed**	handriting	**hand·writ·ing**
	(made empty inside)	handsome	**han·som** (carriage)
hallucenation		handsomly	**hand·some·ly**
	hal·lu·ci·na·tion	handsum	**hand·some**
hallucenogenic			(good–looking)
	hal·lu·ci·no·gen·ic	handwriten	**hand·writ·ten**
halmark	**hall·mark**	handycraft	**hand·i·craft**
halow	**hal·low** (venerate)	handywork	**hand·i·work**
halow	**ha·lo** (ring of light)	hangar	**hang·er**
halowed	**hal·lowed**		(garment holder)
	(venerated)	hangcuff	**hand·cuff**
Haloween	**Hal·low·een**	hanger	**hang·ar** (aircraft shed)
halsyon	**hal·cy·on**	hankerchief	**hand·ker·chief**
halucinnation		hansome	**han·som** (carriage)
	hal·lu·ci·na·tion	hansome	**hand·some**
halucinogenic			(good–looking)
	hal·lu·ci·no·gen·ic	hapened	**hap·pened**
halve	**half** (n.)	haphazerd	**hap·haz·ard**
hamberger	**ham·burg·er**	haram	**ha·rem**
hamering	**ham·mer·ing**	harang	**ha·rangue**
hammuck	**ham·mock**	harbenger	**har·bin·ger**
hanbook	**hand·book**	harber	**har·bor**
handcuf	**hand·cuff**	hardwear	**hard·ware**
handecapped	**hand·i·capped**	hardy	**hearty** (wholehearted)
handecraft	**hand·i·craft**	hardyness	**har·di·ness**
handelbar	**han·dle·bar**		(boldness)

WRONG	RIGHT
hare	**hair** *(fur)*
haresy	**her·e·sy**
harey	**har·ry** *(harass)*
harlekin	**har·le·quin**
harlet	**har·lot**
harliquin	**har·le·quin**
harmanic	**har·mon·ic**
harmfull	**harm·ful**
harmoneca	**har·mon·i·ca**
harmoneous	**har·mo·ni·ous**
harmoney	**har·mo·ny**
harmonicly	**har·mon·i·cal·ly**
harmonnic	**har·mon·ic**
harnes	**har·ness**
harowing	**har·row·ing**
harpsicord	**harp·si·chord**
harrangue	**ha·rangue**
harrassment	**har·ass·ment**
harrem	**ha·rem**
harry	**hairy** *(hair–covered)*
hart	**heart** *(organ)*
hartache	**heart·ache**
harth	**hearth**
harty	**hearty** *(wholehearted)*
harvister	**har·vest·er**
hasheesh	**hash·ish**
hassen	**has·ten**
hassuck	**has·sock**
hast	**haste**
hastey	**hasty**
hatable	**hate·a·ble**
hatchary	**hatch·ery**

WRONG	RIGHT
hatchit	**hatch·et**
hatefull	**hate·ful**
hater	**hat·ter** *(hat–maker)*
hatrid	**ha·tred**
hatter	**hat·er** *(one who hates)*
hauk	**hawk**
hauthorn	**haw·thorn**
hauture	**hau·teur**
hauty	**haugh·ty**
havan	**ha·ven**
Havanna	**Ha·vana**
havec	**hav·oc**
haveing	**hav·ing**
havock	**hav·oc**
Hawai	**Ha·waii**
Hawaien	**Ha·wai·ian**
hawl	**haul** *(pull)*
hawnch	**haunch** *(hindquarter)*
hawnted	**haunt·ed**
hawteur	**hau·teur**
hawthorne	**haw·thorn**
hawty	**haugh·ty**
haxsaw	**hack·saw**
hay	**hey** *(interj.)*
hazally	**ha·zi·ly**
hazerd	**haz·ard**
hazerdous	**haz·ard·ous**
hazey	**ha·zy**
hazle	**ha·zel**
hazzard	**haz·ard**
head	**heed** *(attend to)*
headake	**head·ache**

headfone	**head·phone**	hedache	**head·ache**
headquorters	**head·quar·ters**	hedanist	**he·do·nist**
headress	**head·dress**	heddress	**head·dress**
heal	**heel** *(part of foot)*	hede	**heed** *(attend to)*
healler	**heal·er**	hedgeing	**hedg·ing**
healthfull	**health·ful**	hedgrow	**hedge·row**
hear	**here** *(on this place)*	hedonnist	**he·do·nist**
hearafter	**here·af·ter**	hedquarters	**head·quar·ters**
hearby	**here·by**	heel	**heal** *(cure)*
heard	**herd** *(group)*	heelium	**he·li·um**
heart	**hart** *(deer)*	heelix	**he·lix**
heartake	**heart·ache**	heep	**heap**
heartally	**heart·i·ly**	heeth	**heath**
heartbeet	**heart·beat**	heeve	**heave**
heartbern	**heart·burn**	heffer	**heif·er**
heartbraking	**heart·break·ing**	heffty	**hefty**
heartiness	**har·di·ness**	hege	**hedge**
	(boldness)	hegehog	**hedge·hog**
heartrendering		hegerow	**hedge·row**
	heart–rend·ing	heightan	**height·en**
hearty	**har·dy** *(bold)*	heinious	**hei·nous**
heathan	**hea·then**	heirarchy	**hi·er·ar·chy**
heathe	**heath**	heires	**heir·ess**
heavilly	**heav·i·ly**	heiroglyphics	
heavin	**heav·en**		**hi·er·o·glyph·ics**
heavinly	**heav·en·ly**	he'l	**he'll** *(he will)*
heaviset	**heavy·set**	helecopter	**hel·i·cop·ter**
Hebrue	**He·brew**	Helenistic	**Hel·len·is·tic**
heckel	**heck·le**	heleum	**he·li·um**
heckeler	**heck·ler**	hell	**he'll** *(he will)*
hecks	**hex**	hellash	**hell·ish**
hectac	**hec·tic**	hellicopter	**hel·i·cop·ter**

WRONG	RIGHT	WRONG	RIGHT
hellium	**he·li·um**	heresay	**hear·say**
hellix	**he·lix**	heretige	**her·it·age**
helmit	**hel·met**	hering	**her·ring**
helpfull	**help·ful**	heritic	**her·e·tic**
helth	**health**	herkulean	**her·cu·le·an**
helthful	**health·ful**	herloom	**heir·loom**
helthy	**healthy**	hermatage	**her·mit·age**
hemaglobin	**he·mo·glo·bin**	hermet	**her·mit**
hemarroid	**hem·or·rhoid**	hermitege	**her·mit·age**
hemed	**hemmed**	hernea	**her·nia**
hemlok	**hem·lock**	heroe	**he·ro** (sing.)
hemmisphere	**hem·i·sphere**	heroin	**her·o·ine** (f.; hero)
hemmorage	**hem·or·rhage**	heroine	**her·o·in** (narcotic)
hemmroid	**hem·or·rhoid**	herold	**her·ald**
hemogloben	**he·mo·glo·bin**	heros	**he·roes** (pl.)
hemorrage	**hem·or·rhage**	herpez	**her·pes**
hemorroid	**hem·or·rhoid**	herrald	**her·ald**
hencforth	**hence·forth**	herreditary	**he·red·i·tary**
henpek	**hen·peck**	herresy	**her·e·sy**
hense	**hence**	herretic	**her·e·tic**
hensforth	**hence·forth**	herritage	**her·it·age**
hentchman	**hench·man**	herroic	**he·ro·ic**
herafter	**here·af·ter**	herroin	**her·o·in** (narcotic)
heram	**ha·rem**	herroine	**her·o·ine** (f.; hero)
herasy	**her·e·sy**	herron	**her·on**
herbacide	**her·bi·cide**	herrowing	**har·row·ing**
herbel	**herb·al**	her's	**hers**
herby	**here·by**	herse	**hearse**
herculian	**her·cu·le·an**	herth	**hearth**
herd	**heard** (pt. of hear)	hesetancy	**hes·i·tan·cy**
here	**hear** (listen)	hesetate	**hes·i·tate**
hereditery	**he·red·i·tary**	hesitasion	**hes·i·ta·tion**

WRONG	RIGHT
hesitency	**hes·i·tan·cy**
heterogeneous	
	het·er·og·e·nous
	(of different origin)
heterrosexual	
	het·er·o·sex·u·al
hethen	**hea·then**
hether	**heath·er**
hetrogenius	
	het·er·o·ge·ne·ous
	(of different origin)
hevally	**heav·i·ly**
heven	**heav·en**
hevy	**heavy**
hevyweight	**heavy·weight**
hew	**hue** *(color)*
hey	**hay** *(dried grass)*
heywire	**hay·wire**
hi alai	**jai alai**
hiararchy	**hi·er·ar·chy**
hiasinth	**hy·a·cinth**
hiatas	**hi·a·tus**
hibrid	**hy·brid**
hiburnate	**hi·ber·nate**
hichair	**high·chair**
hichhike	**hitch·hike**
hickery	**hick·o·ry**
hickup	**hic·cup**
hiddeous	**hid·e·ous**
hidrant	**hy·drant**
hidraulic	**hy·drau·lic**
hidrochloric	**hy·dro·chlo·ric**

WRONG	RIGHT
hidroelectric	**hy·dro·e·lec·tric**
hidrogen	**hy·dro·gen**
hieena	**hy·e·na**
hiefer	**heif·er**
hieght	**height**
hienous	**hei·nous**
hier	**heir** *(inheritor)*
hierchy	**hi·er·ar·chy**
hieress	**heir·ess**
hierloom	**heir·loom**
hierogliphics	**hi·er·o·glyph·ics**
hietus	**hi·a·tus**
higiene	**hy·giene**
hijact	**hi·jack**
hikory	**hick·o·ry**
hiku	**hai·ku**
hilaraty	**hi·lar·i·ty**
hilarrious	**hi·lar·i·ous**
hilbilly	**hill·bil·ly**
hilight	**high·light**
hillarious	**hi·lar·i·ous**
hillarity	**hi·lar·i·ty**
hillbillie	**hill·bil·ly**
hiltop	**hill·top**
Himilayas	**Hi·ma·la·yas**
himn	**hymn** *(song)*
hinderance	**hin·drance**
hinesight	**hind·sight**
hingeing	**hing·ing**
hiperbola	**hy·per·bo·la** *(curve)*
hiperbole	**hy·per·bo·le**
	(exaggeration)

88

WRONG	RIGHT	WRONG	RIGHT
hipertension ...	**hy·per·ten·sion**	historecal	**his·tor·i·cal**
	(high blood pressure)	historrian	**his·to·ri·an**
hiperventilation		histreonic	**his·tri·on·ic**
....	**hy·per·ven·ti·la·tion**	hitchike	**hitch·hike**
hiphen	**hy·phen**	hiway	**high·way**
hipnosis	**hyp·no·sis** *(sing.)*	hoan	**hone**
hipochondriac		hoar	**whore**
....	**hy·po·chon·dri·ac**	hoard	**horde** *(crowd)*
hipocrisy	**hy·poc·ri·sy**	hoarie	**hoary**
hipodermic	**hy·po·der·mic**	hobbeling	**hob·bling**
hipopotamus		hobbie	**hob·by**
....	**hip·po·pot·a·mus**	hobgoblen	**hob·gob·lin**
hipotension	**hy·po·ten·sion**	hobknob	**hob·nob**
	(low blood pressure)	hocky	**hock·ey**
hipothesis	**hy·poth·e·sis**	hoged	**hogged**
	(sing.)	hogepoge	**hodge·podge**
hipothetical	**hy·po·thet·i·cal**	holacaust	**hol·o·caust**
hipparcritical ..	**hyp·o·crit·i·cal**	Holand	**Hol·land**
	(deceitful)	hole	**whole** *(entire)*
Hippocritic	**Hip·po·crat·ic**	holeday	**hol·i·day**
	(of Hippocrates)	holesale	**whole·sale**
hirarchy	**hi·er·ar·chy**	holey	**ho·ly** *(sacred)*
hi–rise	**high–rise**	holey	**whol·ly** *(totally)*
hiroglyphics ..	**hi·er·o·glyph·ics**	hollandase	**hol·lan·daise**
Hispannic	**His·pan·ic**	Hollend	**Hol·land**
hisself	**him·self**	hollendaise	**hol·lan·daise**
histemine	**his·ta·mine**	holliday	**hol·i·day**
histerectomy		hollie	**hol·ly** *(plant)*
....	**hys·ter·ec·to·my**	hollistic	**ho·lis·tic**
histeria	**hys·te·ria**	hollocaust	**hol·o·caust**
histerical	**hys·ter·i·cal**	hollograph	**hol·o·graph**
histery	**his·to·ry**	hollow	**hal·low** *(venerate)*

WRONG	RIGHT	WRONG	RIGHT
hollowed	**hal·lowed** *(venerated)*	honnesty	**hon·es·ty**
		honney	**hon·ey**
Holloween	**Hal·low·een**	honnorable	**hon·or·a·ble**
hollster	**hol·ster**	Honoloolu	**Hon·o·lu·lu**
holly	**ho·ly** *(sacred)*	honorible	**hon·or·a·ble**
holocost	**hol·o·caust**	honted	**haunt·ed**
holy	**hol·ly** *(plant)*	hony	**hon·ey**
holy	**holey** *(with holes)*	honycomb	**hon·ey·comb**
holy	**whol·ly** *(totally)*	honymoon	**hon·ey·moon**
Holywood	**Hol·ly·wood**	honysuckle	**hon·ey·suck·le**
homacidal	**hom·i·ci·dal**	hoodlem	**hood·lum**
homage	**hom·mage** *(tribute)*	hoola	**hu·la**
homaly	**hom·i·ly**	hopefull	**hope·ful**
homanym	**hom·o·nym**	hopfully	**hope·ful·ly**
hombray	**hom·bre**	hoping	**hop·ping** *(bouncing)*
homested	**home·stead**	hopping	**hop·ing** *(wanting)*
homeword	**home·ward**	hopskotch	**hop·scotch**
homisidal	**hom·i·ci·dal**	horascope	**hor·o·scope**
homley	**home·ly**	horde	**hoard** *(reserve)*
hommage	**hom·age** *(reverence)*	hor dourve	**hors d'oeu·vre**
		hore	**hoar** *(frost)*
hommicidal	**hom·i·ci·dal**	hore	**whore**
hommily	**hom·i·ly**	horemone	**hor·mone**
hommogenize	**ho·mog·e·nize**	horendous	**hor·ren·dous**
hommonym	**hom·o·nym**	horezontal	**hor·i·zon·tal**
homogenious	**ho·mo·ge·ne·ous**	horible	**hor·ri·ble**
		horify	**hor·ri·fy**
homoginize	**ho·mog·e·nize**	horison	**ho·ri·zon**
homosexule	**ho·mo·sex·u·al**	horizontel	**hor·i·zon·tal**
Honalulu	**Hon·o·lu·lu**	hornit	**hor·net**
honering	**hon·or·ing**	horor	**hor·ror**
honeysukle	**hon·ey·suck·le**	horrable	**hor·ri·ble**

WRONG	RIGHT
horrably	hor·ri·bly
horred	hor·rid
horrefy	hor·ri·fy
horrer	hor·ror
horrescope	hor·o·scope
horrizen	ho·ri·zon
horrizontal	hor·i·zon·tal
hors derve	hors d'oeu·vre
horse	hoarse *(harsh)*
horshoe	horse·shoe
hortaculture	hor·ti·cul·ture
hosery	ho·siery
hospess	hos·pice
hospetable	hos·pi·ta·ble
hospetal	hos·pi·tal
hospetality	hos·pi·tal·i·ty
hospiece	hos·pice
hospitallity	hos·pi·tal·i·ty
hospitallization	hos·pi·tal·i·za·tion
hospitible	hos·pi·ta·ble
hostege	hos·tage
hostel	hos·tile *(unfriendly)*
hostes	host·ess
hostile	hos·tel *(inn)*
hostillity	hos·til·i·ty
hottel	ho·tel
houling	howl·ing
houskeeper	house·keep·er
houswife	house·wife
hovvel	hov·el
hovver	hov·er

WRONG	RIGHT
howlling	howl·ing
hownd	hound
hoxe	hoax
hoziery	ho·siery
huch	hutch
huddeling	hud·dling
hue	hew *(chop)*
huged	hugged
hukster	huck·ster
hulla	hu·la
human	hu·mane *(kind)*
humane	hu·man *(person)*
humaniterian	human·i·tar·i·an
humannity	hu·man·i·ty
humbelest	hum·blest
humbley	hum·bly
humed	hu·mid
humen	hu·man *(person)*
humenism	hu·man·ism
humer	hu·mor
humerous	hu·mer·us *(bone)*
humerous	hu·mor·ous *(funny)*
humidefier	humid·i·fi·er
humidety	hu·mid·i·ty
humilliation	humil·i·a·tion
humilllity	hu·mil·i·ty
humingbird	hum·ming·bird
hummanity	hu·man·i·ty
hummidifier	humid·i·fi·er
hummiliation	humil·i·a·tion
hummility	hu·mil·i·ty

91

WRONG	RIGHT	WRONG	RIGHT
humorous	**hu·mer·us** *(bone)*	hyacenth	**hy·a·cinth**
humous	**hu·mus**	hybred	**hy·brid**
hunch	**haunch** *(hindquarter)*	hydergen	**hy·dro·gen**
hunderd	**hun·dred**	hydracarbon	**hy·dro·car·bon**
hundreth	**hun·dredth**	hydrachloric	**hy·dro·chlo·ric**
hungerly	**hun·gri·ly**	hydraelectric	
hungery	**hun·gry**		**hy·dro·e·lec·tric**
Hungery	**Hun·ga·ry**	hydrafoil	**hy·dro·foil**
hungrilly	**hun·gri·ly**	hydragen	**hy·dro·gen**
hunny	**hon·ey**	hydraphobia	**hy·dro·pho·bia**
huntch	**hunch**	hydraullic	**hy·drau·lic**
hurbol	**herb·al**	hydrent	**hy·drant**
hurdel	**hur·dle** *(barrier)*	hydrocarben	**hy·dro·car·bon**
hurdeling	**hur·dling**	hydrocloric	**hy·dro·chlo·ric**
hurdle	**hur·tle** *(rush)*	hydrofobia	**hy·dro·pho·bia**
huricane	**hur·ri·cane**	hydrolic	**hy·drau·lic**
hurnia	**her·nia**	hyecinth	**hy·a·cinth**
hurpes	**her·pes**	hyeena	**hy·e·na**
hurrecane	**hur·ri·cane**	hyfen	**hy·phen**
hurrey	**hur·ry**	hygeinic	**hy·gi·en·ic**
hurring	**hur·ry·ing**	hygene	**hy·giene**
hurse	**hearse**	hym	**hymn** *(song)*
hurtel	**hur·tle** *(rush)*	hymnel	**hym·nal**
hurtfull	**hurt·ful**	hypacondriac	
hurtle	**hur·dle** *(barrier)*		**hy·po·chon·dri·ac**
husbandery	**hus·band·ry**	hypadermic	**hy·po·der·mic**
husbend	**hus·band**	hypatension	**hy·po·ten·sion**
huskie	**husky**		*(low blood pressure)*
hussie	**hus·sy**	hypathetical	**hy·po·thet·i·cal**
hussle	**hus·tle**	hyperbola	**hy·per·bo·le**
huvel	**hov·el**		*(exaggeration)*
huver	**hov·er**	hyperbole	**hy·per·bo·la** *(curve)*

WRONG	RIGHT	WRONG	RIGHT

hypercritical .... **hyp·o·crit·i·cal**
(deceitful)
hyperdermic ..... **hy·po·der·mic**
hypertension ... **hy·po·ten·sion**
(low blood pressure)
hypertention .. **hy·per·ten·sion**
(high blood pressure)
hyperventillation ....
.... **hy·per·ven·ti·la·tion**
hyphan .... **hy·phen**
hyphennate .... **hy·phen·ate**
hypnatism .... **hyp·no·tism**
hypnoses ...... **hyp·no·sis** *(sing.)*
hypnosis .... **hyp·no·ses** *(pl.)*
hypnottic .... **hyp·not·ic**
hypocrasy .... **hy·poc·ri·sy**
Hypocratic .... **Hip·po·crat·ic**
(of Hippocrates)
hypocrit .... **hyp·o·crite**
hypocritical .... **hy·per·crit·i·cal**
(too critical)
hypotension .... **hy·per·ten·sion**
(high blood pressure)
hypothalmus ....
.... **hy·po·thal·a·mus**
hypotheses .... **hy·poth·e·sis**
(sing.)
hypothesis .. **hy·poth·e·ses** *(pl.)*
hypothetacal .. **hy·po·thet·i·cal**
hypothurmia ... **hy·po·ther·mia**
hypottenuse ..... **hy·pot·e·nuse**
hyppacrisy .... **hy·poc·ri·sy**

hyppochondriac ....
.... **hy·po·chon·dri·ac**
hyppothalamus ....
.... **hy·po·thal·a·mus**
hyppothesis .... **hy·poth·e·sis**
(sing.)
hysterrectomy ....
.... **hys·ter·ec·to·my**
hysterria .... **hys·te·ria**
hysterrical .... **hys·ter·i·cal**

I

iadine .... **io·dine**
ian .... **ion** *(atom)*
iceburg .... **ice·berg**
iceing .... **ic·ing**
icey .... **icy**
icickle .... **ici·cle**
icilly .... **ici·ly**
iconnoclast .... **icon·o·clast**
icycle .... **ici·cle**
iddiocy .... **id·i·o·cy**
idealisticly ..... **ide·al·is·ti·cal·ly**
ideallism .... **ide·al·ism**
idealogical .... **ide·o·log·i·cal**
idealy .... **ide·al·ly**
idee .... **idea**
ideel .... **ide·al**
ideelism .... **ide·al·ism**
ideelistically ... **ide·al·is·ti·cal·ly**
ideelly .... **ide·al·ly**

93

WRONG	RIGHT	WRONG	RIGHT
idel	**idyll** (short poem)	idyllick	**idyl·lic**
idel	**idol** (object of worship)	iglue	**ig·loo**
idel	**idle** (inactive)	ignaramus	**ig·no·ra·mus**
identafy	**iden·ti·fy**	ignerance	**ig·no·rance**
identefication		igneus	**ig·ne·ous**
	iden·ti·fi·ca·tion	ignight	**ig·nite**
identety	**iden·ti·ty**	igmiminious	**ig·no·min·i·ous**
identicly	**iden·ti·cal·ly**	ignious	**ig·ne·ous**
ideologecal	**ide·o·log·i·cal**	ignomineous	**ig·no·min·i·ous**
ideom	**id·i·om**	ignoreing	**ig·nor·ing**
ideomatic	**id·i·o·mat·ic**	ignorence	**ig·no·rance**
ideosyncrasy	**id·i·o·syn·cra·sy**	igregious	**egre·gious**
ideot	**id·i·ot**	iguanna	**igua·na**
iderdown	**ei·der·down**	igwana	**igua·na**
idia	**idea**	ikonoclast	**icon·o·clast**
idiacy	**id·i·o·cy**	iland	**is·land**
idiam	**id·i·om**	Ilead	**Il·i·ad**
idiat	**id·i·ot**	ilegal	**il·le·gal**
idillic	**idyl·lic**	ilegible	**il·leg·i·ble**
idiosincrasy	**id·i·o·syn·cra·sy**	ilegitimate	**il·le·git·i·mate**
idle	**idol** (object of worship)	ilet	**is·let** (small island)
idle	**idyll** (short poem)	ilicit	**il·lic·it** (unlawful)
idleing	**idling**	Ilinois	**Il·li·nois**
idol	**idle** (inactive)	iliteracy	**il·lit·er·a·cy**
idollatrous	**idol·a·trous**	iliterate	**il·lit·er·ate**
idollatry	**idol·a·try**	Illanois	**Il·li·nois**
idollize	**idol·ize**	illate	**elate**
idological	**ide·o·log·i·cal**	illegable	**il·leg·i·ble**
idolotrous	**idol·a·trous**	illegle	**il·le·gal**
idolotry	**idol·a·try**	Illiad	**Il·i·ad**
idyll	**idol** (object of worship)	illicit	**elic·it** (evoke)
idyll	**idle** (inactive)	illigitimate	**il·le·git·i·mate**

WRONG	RIGHT	WRONG	RIGHT
Illinoi	**Il·li·nois**	imbarras	**em·bar·rass**
illisit	**il·lic·it** *(unlawful)*	imbellish	**em·bel·lish**
illitteracy	**il·lit·er·a·cy**	imbesile	**im·be·cile**
illogecal	**il·log·i·cal**	imbew	**im·bue**
illucidate	**elu·ci·date**	imbezzle	**em·bez·zle**
illude	**elude** *(escape)*	imbodiment	**em·bod·i·ment**
illumenation	**il·lu·mi·na·tion**	imboss	**em·boss**
illusion	**al·lu·sion** *(reference)*	imbrace	**em·brace**
illusion	**elu·sion** *(an escape)*	imbroider	**em·broi·der**
illusive	**elu·sive**	imediacy	**im·me·di·a·cy**
	(hard to grasp)	imediately	**im·me·di·ate·ly**
illustrater	**il·lus·tra·tor**	imemorial	**im·me·mo·ri·al**
illustrius	**il·lus·tri·ous**	imense	**im·mense**
ilogical	**il·log·i·cal**	imensity	**im·men·si·ty**
ilumination	**il·lu·mi·na·tion**	imeritus	**emer·i·tus**
ilusion	**il·lu·sion** *(false idea)*	imersible	**im·mers·i·ble**
ilustration	**il·lus·tra·tion**	imige	**im·age**
ilustrator	**il·lus·tra·tor**	imigrant	**im·mi·grant**
ilustrious	**il·lus·tri·ous**		*(one who arrives)*
imaciate	**ema·ci·ate**	imigrate	**im·mi·grate** *(arrive)*
imaculate	**im·mac·u·late**	iminent	**im·mi·nent**
imaganation	**imag·i·na·tion**		*(impending)*
imagenary	**imag·i·nary**	imission	**emis·sion**
imaginible	**imag·i·na·ble**	immaculate	**im·mac·u·late**
imanent	**im·ma·nent** *(inherent)*	immage	**im·age**
imasculate	**emas·cu·late**	immaginable	**imag·i·na·ble**
imatate	**im·i·tate**	immaginary	**imag·i·nary**
imaterial	**im·ma·te·ri·al**	immagination	**imag·i·na·tion**
imature	**im·ma·ture**	immanent	**im·mi·nent**
imbalm	**em·balm**		*(impending)*
imbargo	**em·bar·go**	immatereal	**im·ma·te·ri·al**
imbark	**em·bark**	immedeacy	**im·me·di·a·cy**

WRONG	*RIGHT*
immediatly	**im·me·di·ate·ly**
immerge	**emerge** *(come out)*
immersable	**im·mers·i·ble**
immersion	**emer·sion**
	(emerging)
immigrant	**em·i·grant**
	(one who leaves)
immigrate	**em·i·grate** *(leave)*
immigrent	**im·mi·grant**
	(one who arrives)
imminent	**em·i·nent**
	(prominent)
imminent	**im·ma·nent**
	(inherent)
immitate	**im·i·tate**
immoble	**im·mo·bile**
immolument	**emol·u·ment**
	(wages)
immorallity	**im·mo·ral·i·ty**
immortallize	**im·mor·tal·ize**
immortel	**im·mor·tal**
immovible	**im·mov·a·ble**
immunety	**im·mu·ni·ty**
immutible	**im·mu·ta·ble**
imobile	**im·mo·bile**
imoderate	**im·mod·er·ate**
imodest	**im·mod·est**
imolate	**im·mo·late**
imoral	**im·mor·al**
imorality	**im·mo·ral·i·ty**
imortal	**im·mor·tal**
imotional	**emo·tion·al**

WRONG	*RIGHT*
impack	**im·pact**
impare	**im·pair**
imparment	**im·pair·ment**
impasioned	**im·pas·sioned**
impasition	**im·po·si·tion**
impass	**im·passe**
impassable	**im·pas·si·ble**
	(cannot feel pain)
impassible	**im·pass·a·ble**
	(cannot be passed)
impateince	**im·pa·tience**
impeccible	**im·pec·ca·ble**
impedement	**im·ped·i·ment**
impeech	**im·peach**
impeed	**im·pede**
impeling	**im·pel·ling**
impell	**im·pel**
impenatrable	
	im·pen·e·tra·ble
impenge	**im·pinge**
imperceptable	
	im·per·cep·ti·ble
imperetive	**im·per·a·tive**
impermiable	**im·per·me·a·ble**
imperseptible	
	im·per·cep·ti·ble
impersonnate	**im·per·son·ate**
impersonnel	**im·per·son·al**
impertinance	**im·per·ti·nence**
impervius	**im·per·vi·ous**
impetence	**im·po·tence**
impettuous	**im·pet·u·ous**

impettus	**im·pe·tus**	impunaty	**im·pu·ni·ty**
impireal	**im·pe·ri·al**	impune	**im·pugn**
	(sovereign)	impuraty	**im·pu·ri·ty**
impirical	**em·pir·i·cal**	impurmeable	**im·per·me·a·ble**
implacible	**im·plac·a·ble**	impurvious	**im·per·vi·ous**
implecation	**im·pli·ca·tion**	imulsion	**emul·sion**
impliment	**im·ple·ment**	imunity	**im·mu·ni·ty**
implisit	**im·plic·it**	imutable	**im·mu·ta·ble**
imployee	**em·ploy·ee**	inable	**en·a·ble**
implyed	**im·plied**	inaccessable	**in·ac·ces·si·ble**
impollite	**im·po·lite**	inacurate	**in·ac·cu·rate**
importence	**im·por·tance**	inadvertantly	
imposeing	**im·pos·ing**		**in·ad·vert·ent·ly**
imposibility	**im·pos·si·bil·i·ty**	inagural	**in·au·gu·ral**
imposter	**im·pos·tor**	inallienable	**in·al·ien·a·ble**
	(deceiver)	inamel	**en·am·el**
impostor	**im·pos·ture**	inanamate	**in·an·i·mate**
	(deception)	inapropriate	**in·ap·pro·pri·ate**
impotant	**im·po·tent**	inapt	**in·ept** *(clumsy)*
impovrish	**im·pov·er·ish**	inate	**in·nate**
impracticle	**im·prac·ti·cal**	inaugral	**in·au·gu·ral**
impregnible	**im·preg·na·ble**	inbalance	**im·bal·ance**
impresion	**im·pres·sion**	inbibe	**im·bibe**
imprisise	**im·pre·cise**	incalcuble	**in·cal·cu·la·ble**
improbible	**im·prob·a·ble**	incandessent	**in·can·des·cent**
impromtu	**im·promp·tu**	incapasitate	**in·ca·pac·i·tate**
impropriaty	**im·pro·pri·e·ty**	incarserate	**in·car·cer·ate**
improvasation		incedence	**in·ci·dence**
	im·prov·i·sa·tion	incence	**in·cense**
improvment	**im·prove·ment**	incendery	**in·cen·di·ary**
impudance	**im·pu·dence**	incephalitis	**en·ceph·a·li·tis**
impullsive	**im·pul·sive**	incersion	**in·cur·sion**

WRONG	RIGHT
incessent	**in·ces·sant**
incestus	**in·ces·tu·ous**
incidently	**in·ci·den·tal·ly**
incinerater	**in·cin·er·a·tor**
incipiant	**in·cip·i·ent**
inciser	**in·ci·sor**
inclemment	**in·clem·ent**
inclinnation	**in·cli·na·tion**
inclusave	**in·clu·sive**
incode	**en·code**
incogneto	**in·cog·ni·to**
incoherance	**in·co·her·ence**
incombency	**in·cum·ben·cy**
incomeing	**in·com·ing**
incompareable	**in·com·pa·ra·ble**
incompatable	**in·com·pat·i·ble**
incompatent	**in·com·pe·tent**
incomperhensible	**in·com·pre·hen·si·ble**
incompettent	**in·com·pe·tent**
incomprable	**in·com·pa·ra·ble**
incomprehensable	**in·com·pre·hen·si·ble**
incomunicado	**in·com·mu·ni·ca·do**
inconceivible	**in·con·ceiv·a·ble**
incongrous	**in·con·gru·ous**
incongruant	**in·con·gru·ent**
inconsievable	**in·con·ceiv·a·ble**

WRONG	RIGHT
inconspickuous	**in·con·spic·u·ous**
incontrovertable	**in·con·tro·vert·i·ble**
inconveneince	**in·con·ven·ience**
incoppacitate	**in·ca·pac·i·tate**
incorigible	**in·cor·ri·gi·ble**
incorperate	**in·cor·po·rate**
incorruptable	**in·cor·rupt·i·ble**
incrament	**in·cre·ment**
increaseingly	**in·creas·ing·ly**
incredable	**in·cred·i·ble**
incredulus	**in·cred·u·lous**
increese	**in·crease**
incrimminate	**in·crim·i·nate**
incroach	**en·croach**
incubater	**in·cu·ba·tor**
incumbincy	**in·cum·ben·cy**
incureable	**in·cur·a·ble**
incurr	**in·cur**
incurzion	**in·cur·sion**
incyclopedia	**en·cy·clo·pe·dia**
indacate	**in·di·cate**
indanger	**en·dan·ger**
indead	**in·deed**
indecks	**in·dex**
indefinitly	**in·def·i·nite·ly**
indegence	**in·di·gence** *(poverty)*
indellible	**in·del·i·ble**

WRONG	RIGHT
indemmify	**in·dem·ni·fy**
indemnaty	**in·dem·ni·ty**
indenchured	**in·den·tured**
independant	**in·de·pend·ent**
indescribeable	
	in·de·scrib·a·ble
indesent	**in·de·cent**
indespensable	
	in·dis·pen·sa·ble
indestructable	
	in·de·struct·i·ble
indetted	**in·debt·ed**
indevidual	**in·di·vid·u·al**
indicater	**in·di·ca·tor**
Indien	**In·di·an**
indiffrence	**in·dif·fer·ence**
indigence	**in·di·gents**
	(poor persons)
indigense	**in·di·gence**
	(poverty)
indiginous	**in·dig·e·nous**
indignaty	**in·dig·ni·ty**
indignent	**in·dig·nant**
indipendent	**in·de·pend·ent**
indireck	**in·di·rect**
indiscrimanate	
	in·dis·crim·i·nate
indispensible	
	in·dis·pen·sa·ble
indisscretion	**in·dis·cre·tion**
inditment	**in·dict·ment**
	(formal charge)

WRONG	RIGHT
individal	**in·di·vid·u·al**
individuallity	
	in·di·vid·u·al·i·ty
indoctranate	**in·doc·tri·nate**
indollent	**in·do·lent**
indommitable	**in·dom·i·ta·ble**
indorsment	**en·dorse·ment**
indubbitably	**in·du·bi·ta·bly**
inducktion	**in·duc·tion**
inducment	**in·duce·ment**
indulgance	**in·dul·gence**
indurance	**en·dur·ance**
indusement	**in·duce·ment**
industralize	**in·dus·tri·al·ize**
industreal	**in·dus·tri·al**
industrey	**in·dus·try**
industriallize	**in·dus·tri·al·ize**
inebreated	**in·e·bri·at·ed**
inedable	**in·ed·i·ble**
ineficient	**in·ef·fi·cient**
inelligible	**in·el·i·gi·ble**
inemical	**in·im·i·cal**
inepp	**in·ept** *(clumsy)*
inept	**in·apt** *(not apt)*
inequity	**in·iq·ui·ty**
	(wickedness)
inevatible	**in·ev·i·ta·ble**
infallable	**in·fal·li·ble**
infaltrate	**in·fil·trate**
infamus	**in·fa·mous**
infantsy	**in·fan·cy**
infattuation	**in·fat·u·a·tion**

WRONG	RIGHT	WRONG	RIGHT
infecktion	in·fec·tion	infrequint	in·fre·quent
infectuous	in·fec·tious	infringeing	in·fring·ing
infedelity	in·fi·del·i·ty	infurnal	in·fer·nal
infency	in·fan·cy	infurno	in·fer·no
infenite	in·fi·nite	infuryate	in·fu·ri·ate
infenitesimal	in·fin·i·tes·i·mal	ingagement	en·gage·ment
infenitive	in·fin·i·tive	ingenius	in·gen·ious
infentry	in·fan·try	ingenuety	in·ge·nu·i·ty
inferance	in·fer·ence	ingit	in·got
inferier	in·fe·ri·or	ingraciate	in·gra·ti·ate
infermation	in·for·ma·tion	ingraned	in·grained
inferr	in·fer	ingrave	en·grave
infidellity	in·fi·del·i·ty	ingrediant	in·gre·di·ent
infilltrate	in·fil·trate	ingrossing	en·gross·ing
infinetesimal	in·fin·i·tes·i·mal	inhabbitable	in·hab·it·a·ble
infinetive	in·fin·i·tive	inhabitent	in·hab·it·ant
infinety	in·fin·i·ty	inharent	in·her·ent
infinnite	in·fi·nite	inheret	in·her·it
infirior	in·fe·ri·or	inheritence	in·her·it·ance
infirmry	in·fir·ma·ry	inhibbition	in·hi·bi·tion
inflamable	in·flam·ma·ble	inhibiter	in·hib·i·tor
inflamation	in·flam·ma·tion	inhirent	in·her·ent
inflateing	in·flat·ing	inhospittable	in·hos·pi·ta·ble
inflatible	in·flat·a·ble	inibition	in·hi·bi·tion
inflationery	in·fla·tion·ary	ining	in·ning
inflexable	in·flex·i·ble	iniquity	in·eq·ui·ty (unfairness)
inflick	in·flict	inititive	in·i·ti·a·tive
influance	in·flu·ence	injeck	in·ject
influencial	in·flu·en·tial	injenue	in·gé·nue
influinza	in·flu·en·za	injenuity	in·ge·nu·i·ty
informallity	in·for·mal·i·ty	injenuous	in·gen·u·ous
informent	in·form·ant	injery	in·ju·ry

WRONG	RIGHT	WRONG	RIGHT
injest	**in·gest**	innerupt	**in·ter·rupt**
injoin	**en·join**	innerval	**in·ter·val**
injunktion	**in·junc·tion**	innervene	**in·ter·vene**
injurius	**in·ju·ri·ous**	innervention	**in·ter·ven·tion**
inkandescent	**in·can·des·cent**	innerview	**in·ter·view**
inkey	**inky**	innimical	**in·im·i·cal**
inkubation	**in·cu·ba·tion**	innitial	**in·i·tial**
inlayed	**in·laid**	innitiate	**in·i·ti·ate**
innacence	**in·no·cence**	innitiative	**in·i·ti·a·tive**
innane	**in·ane**	innoccuous	**in·noc·u·ous**
innanimate	**in·an·i·mate**	innoculation	**in·oc·u·la·tion**
innapt	**in·apt** *(not apt)*	innordinate	**in·or·di·nate**
innavation	**in·no·va·tion**	innosense	**in·no·cence**
innebriated	**in·e·bri·at·ed**	innundate	**in·un·date**
inneresting	**in·ter·est·ing**	innure	**in·ure**
innerject	**in·ter·ject**	inoble	**ig·no·ble**
innerlude	**in·ter·lude**	inocculation	**in·oc·u·la·tion**
innermediary		inocence	**in·no·cence**
	in·ter·me·di·ary	inocent	**in·no·cent**
innermediate	**in·ter·me·di·ate**	inocuous	**in·noc·u·ous**
innermission	**in·ter·mis·sion**	inordenate	**in·or·di·nate**
innermittent	**in·ter·mit·tent**	inormous	**enor·mous**
innernational		inovation	**in·no·va·tion**
	in·ter·na·tion·al	inpacted	**im·pact·ed**
innerogative	**in·ter·rog·a·tive**	inpale	**im·pale**
innerpersonal		inpartial	**im·par·tial**
	in·ter·per·son·al	inpeach	**im·peach**
innerracial	**in·ter·ra·cial**	inpending	**im·pend·ing**
innersect	**in·ter·sect**	inpersonal	**im·per·son·al**
innersection	**in·ter·sec·tion**	inpersonate	**im·per·son·ate**
innersperse	**in·ter·sperse**	inpractical	**im·prac·ti·cal**
innertia	**in·er·tia**	inprecise	**im·pre·cise**

WRONG	RIGHT	WRONG	RIGHT
inprint	**im·print**	insisive	**in·ci·sive**
inpromptu	**im·promp·tu**	insisor	**in·ci·sor**
inpropriety	**im·pro·pri·e·ty**	insistance	**in·sist·ence**
inquery	**in·quiry**	insite	**in·sight** *(understanding)*
inquireing	**in·quir·ing**	insite	**in·cite** *(rouse)*
inquisative	**in·quis·i·tive**	insollent	**in·so·lent**
inrage	**en·rage**	insomnea	**in·som·nia**
insalation	**in·su·la·tion**	inspeck	**in·spect**
insamnia	**in·som·nia**	inspecter	**in·spec·tor**
insanety	**in·san·i·ty**	insperation	**in·spi·ra·tion**
inseck	**in·sect**	instagate	**in·sti·gate**
insectecide	**in·sec·ti·cide**	instalation	**in·stal·la·tion**
insemanation		instance	**in·stants** *(moments)*
	in·sem·i·na·tion	instantaneus	
insendiary	**in·cen·di·ary**		**in·stan·ta·ne·ous**
insense	**in·cense**	instants	**in·stance** *(occasion)*
insentive	**in·cen·tive**	instatution	**in·sti·tu·tion**
inseperable	**in·sep·a·ra·ble**	insted	**in·stead**
insergence	**in·sur·gence**	insterment	**in·stru·ment**
inserrection	**in·sur·rec·tion**	instince	**in·stance** *(occasion)*
insessant	**in·ces·sant**	instinctave	**in·stinc·tive**
insestuous	**in·ces·tu·ous**	instink	**in·stinct**
insicure	**in·se·cure**	instrament	**in·stru·ment**
insidence	**in·ci·dence**	instruck	**in·struct**
insideous	**in·sid·i·ous**	instructer	**in·struc·tor**
insight	**in·cite** *(rouse)*	insue	**en·sue**
insignea	**in·sig·nia**	insuffrable	**in·suf·fer·a·ble**
insinerator	**in·cin·er·a·tor**	insulater	**in·su·la·tor**
insinnuate	**in·sin·u·ate**	insulen	**in·su·lin**
insiped	**in·sip·id**	insuler	**in·su·lar**
insipient	**in·cip·i·ent**	insullation	**in·su·la·tion**
insision	**in·ci·sion**	insurection	**in·sur·rec·tion**

WRONG	RIGHT	WRONG	RIGHT
insurence	in·sur·ance	interlood	in·ter·lude
insurjence	in·sur·gence	intermedeary	in·ter·me·di·ary
insurt	in·sert	intermision	in·ter·mis·sion
intail	en·tail	intermitent	in·ter·mit·tent
intamet	in·ti·mate	intermural	in·tra·mu·ral
intanation	in·to·na·tion	internationel	in·ter·na·tion·al
intangable	in·tan·gi·ble	internel	in·ter·nal
inteference	in·ter·fer·ence	interogate	in·ter·ro·gate
integrel	in·te·gral	interogative	in·ter·rog·a·tive
integrety	in·teg·ri·ty	interpersonnal	
intelectual	in·tel·lec·tu·al		in·ter·per·son·al
inteligence	in·tel·li·gence	interpetation	
inteligible	in·tel·li·gi·ble		in·ter·pre·ta·tion
intence	in·tense	interpollate	in·ter·po·late
intensefy	in·ten·si·fy		*(insert; estimate)*
intensety	in·ten·si·ty	interseck	in·ter·sect
intentionly	in·ten·tion·al·ly	intersecktion	in·ter·sec·tion
interacial	in·ter·ra·cial	intersede	in·ter·cede
interceed	in·ter·cede	intersept	in·ter·cept
interchangable		intersession	in·ter·ces·sion
	in·ter·change·a·ble		*(an interceding)*
interdisiplinary		interspurse	in·ter·sperse
	in·ter·dis·ci·pli·nary	interupt	in·ter·rupt
interductory	in·tro·duc·to·ry	interveiw	in·ter·view
interem	in·ter·im	intervel	in·ter·val
interferance	in·ter·fer·ence	intervenous	in·tra·ve·nous
interger	in·te·ger	intervension	in·ter·ven·tion
intergral	in·te·gral	intervine	in·ter·vene
intergrate	in·te·grate	intestenal	in·tes·tin·al
intergration	in·te·gra·tion	intice	en·tice
interier	in·te·ri·or	intiger	in·te·ger
interjeck	in·ter·ject	intigrate	in·te·grate

WRONG	RIGHT	WRONG	RIGHT
intimadate	**in·tim·i·date**	inturn	**in·tern**
intimmacy	**in·ti·ma·cy**	inuendo	**in·nu·en·do**
intimmate	**in·ti·mate**	inumerable	**in·nu·mer·a·ble**
intirety	**en·tire·ty**	inunciate	**enun·ci·ate**
intirior	**in·te·ri·or**		*(pronounce)*
intolerence	**in·tol·er·ance**	inurtia	**in·er·tia**
intollerable	**in·tol·er·a·ble**	invacation	**in·vo·ca·tion**
intoxacate	**in·tox·i·cate**	invadeing	**in·vad·ing**
intracacy	**in·tri·ca·cy**	invagle	**in·vei·gle**
intraduce	**in·tro·duce**	invallid	**in·va·lid**
intraductory	**in·tro·duc·to·ry**	invalluable	**in·val·u·a·ble**
intramurral	**in·tra·mu·ral**	invantory	**in·ven·to·ry**
intransagent	**in·tran·si·gent**	invaribly	**in·var·i·a·bly**
intransative	**in·tran·si·tive**	invatation	**in·vi·ta·tion**
intravenus	**in·tra·ve·nous**	invay	**in·veigh**
intraverted	**in·tro·vert·ed**	invazion	**in·va·sion**
intreeg	**in·trigue**	invecktive	**in·vec·tive**
intreging	**in·trigu·ing**	inventer	**in·ven·tor**
intrensic	**in·trin·sic**	investagate	**in·ves·ti·gate**
intreppid	**in·trep·id**	investature	**in·ves·ti·ture**
intresting	**in·ter·est·ing**	invetarate	**in·vet·er·ate**
intricasy	**in·tri·ca·cy**	inviegh	**in·veigh**
intrige	**in·trigue**	inviegle	**in·vei·gle**
intrigueing	**in·trigu·ing**	invigerate	**in·vig·or·ate**
intrinsick	**in·trin·sic**	invinsible	**in·vin·ci·ble**
introductry	**in·tro·duc·to·ry**	invisable	**in·vis·i·ble**
introduse	**in·tro·duce**	involuntery	**in·vol·un·tary**
introvurted	**in·tro·vert·ed**	invurse	**in·verse**
intrust	**en·trust**	inyure	**in·ure**
intruzion	**in·tru·sion**	ion	**eon** *(time period)*
intuative	**in·tu·i·tive**	iphemeral	**ephem·er·al**
intuision	**in·tu·i·tion**	iradiate	**ir·ra·di·ate**

WRONG	RIGHT	WRONG	RIGHT
irassible	**iras·ci·ble**	irreguler	**ir·reg·u·lar**
irational	**ir·ra·tion·al**	irrelavent	**ir·rel·e·vant**
irection	**erec·tion**	irrepairable	**ir·rep·a·ra·ble**
ireducible	**ir·re·duc·i·ble**	irresistable	**ir·re·sist·i·ble**
irefutable	**ir·ref·u·ta·ble**	irresponsable	**ir·re·spon·si·ble**
iregular	**ir·reg·u·lar**	irretreivable	**ir·re·triev·a·ble**
irellevant	**ir·rel·e·vant**	irreverance	**ir·rev·er·ence**
iren	**iron**	irreversable	**ir·re·vers·i·ble**
ireny	**iro·ny**	irrevokable	**ir·rev·o·ca·ble**
ireplaceable	**ir·re·place·a·ble**	irridescent	**ir·i·des·cent**
irepparable	**ir·rep·a·ra·ble**	irritent	**ir·ri·tant**
irepressible	**ir·re·press·i·ble**	irritible	**ir·ri·ta·ble**
ires	**iris**	irronical	**iron·i·cal**
iresistible	**ir·re·sist·i·ble**	isalate	**iso·late**
iresponsible	**ir·re·spon·si·ble**	isametrics	**iso·met·rics**
iretrievable	**ir·re·triev·a·ble**	isatope	**iso·tope**
ireverence	**ir·rev·er·ence**	ishue	**is·sue**
ireversible	**ir·re·vers·i·ble**	isle	**aisle** *(passage)*
irevocable	**ir·rev·o·ca·ble**	Islem	**Is·lam**
iridessent	**ir·i·des·cent**	islet	**eye·let** *(small hole)*
irie	**aer·ie** *(nest)*	ismus	**isth·mus**
irigate	**ir·ri·gate**	isometricks	**iso·met·rics**
iritable	**ir·ri·ta·ble**	Isreal	**Is·ra·el**
iritation	**ir·ri·ta·tion**	isshue	**is·sue**
irksum	**irk·some**	issolate	**iso·late**
irode	**erode**	issometrics	**iso·met·rics**
ironicle	**iron·i·cal**	isue	**is·sue**
irradicate	**erad·i·cate**	Itallian	**Ital·ian**
irragate	**ir·ri·gate**	itallics	**ital·ics**
irratation	**ir·ri·ta·tion**	itchey	**itchy**
irreduceable	**ir·re·duc·i·ble**	itinnerary	**itin·er·ary**
irrefutible	**ir·ref·u·ta·ble**		

WRONG	RIGHT	WRONG	RIGHT
its	**it's** (it is; it has)	Jappanese	**Jap·a·nese**
it's	**its** (poss.)	jared	**jarred**
itsself	**it·self**	jargen	**jar·gon**
ivasion	**eva·sion**	jasmen	**jas·mine**
ivery	**ivo·ry**	jaundes	**jaun·dice**
ivey	**ivy**	jauntey	**jaun·ty**
ivoke	**evoke** (draw forth)	javellin	**jav·e·lin**
ivolve	**evolve**	jawl	**jowl**
		jawnt	**jaunt**
J		jax	**jacks**
		jazmine	**jas·mine**
jackel	**jack·al**	jeallous	**jeal·ous**
jackit	**jack·et**	jealoussy	**jeal·ousy**
jacknife	**jack·knife**	jealousy	**jal·ou·sie** (shade)
jaged	**jag·ged**	jeans	**genes** (hereditary units)
jagwire	**jag·uar**	jeapardy	**jeop·ardy**
Jahovah	**Je·ho·vah**	jear	**jeer**
jaid	**jade**	jeens	**jeans** (trousers)
jai lai	**jai alai**	Jehoveh	**Je·ho·vah**
jailbrake	**jail·break**	jejoon	**je·june**
jailler	**jail·er**	jelatin	**gel·a·tin**
jalousy	**jeal·ousy**	jell	**gel** (jelly–like substance)
jalousy	**jal·ou·sie** (shade)	jelley	**jel·ly**
jam	**jamb** (side post)	jellyed	**jel·lied**
Jamaca	**Ja·mai·ca**	jelous	**jeal·ous**
jamb	**jam** (jelly)	jem	**gem**
jamberee	**jam·bo·ree**	jender	**gen·der**
jamed	**jammed**	jenealogy	**ge·ne·al·o·gy**
jangeled	**jan·gled**	jenetically	**ge·net·i·cal·ly**
janiter	**jan·i·tor**	jenial	**ge·nial**
Jannuary	**Jan·u·ary**	jenie	**jin·ni**
janquil	**jon·quil**	jenital	**gen·i·tal**

WRONG	RIGHT	WRONG	RIGHT
jenius	**ge·nius** *(talent)*	jifey	**jif·fy**
jenre	**gen·re**	jigalo	**gig·o·lo**
jentry	**gen·try**	jiger	**jig·ger**
jepardy	**jeop·ardy**	jiggsaw	**jig·saw**
jeranium	**ge·ra·ni·um**	jigled	**jig·gled**
jerbil	**ger·bil**	jijune	**je·june**
jeriatrics	**ger·i·at·rics**	jimied	**jim·mied**
jerkey	**jerky**	jin	**gin**
jernalism	**jour·nal·ism**	jingley	**jin·gly**
jersies	**jer·seys**	jinks	**jinx**
Jeruselam	**Je·ru·sa·lem**	jinny	**jin·ni**
Jessuit	**Jes·u·it**	jipsum	**gyp·sum**
jestation	**ges·ta·tion**	jist	**gist**
jester	**ges·ture** *(movement)*	jive	**gibe** *(taunt)*
jesticulate	**ges·tic·u·late**	jocand	**joc·und**
jestor	**jest·er** *(clown)*	jockular	**joc·u·lar**
jetisson	**jet·ti·son**	jocky	**jock·ey**
jeuse	**juice**	joger	**jog·ger**
Jewash	**Jew·ish**	johnquil	**jon·quil**
Jewery	**Jew·ry**	joinning	**join·ing**
jewjitsu	**ju·jit·su**	jokeing	**jok·ing**
jewl	**jew·el**	jokund	**joc·und**
jewler	**jew·el·er**	jondice	**jaun·dice**
jewlery	**jew·el·ry**	jonquill	**jon·quil**
jewlip	**ju·lep**	jont	**jaunt**
jewvenile	**ju·ven·ile**	jontey	**jaun·ty**
ji ali	**jai alai**	joobilation	**ju·bi·la·tion**
jiant	**gi·ant**	Jordon	**Jor·dan**
jibbrish	**gib·ber·ish**	jornalism	**jour·nal·ism**
jibe	**gibe** *(taunt)*	jossle	**jos·tle**
jibe	**jive** *(nonsense)*	joted	**jot·ted**
jiblet	**gib·let**	joul	**jowl**

WRONG	RIGHT	WRONG	RIGHT
journallism	**jour·nal·ism**	juiniper	**ju·ni·per**
journel	**jour·nal**	juise	**juice**
journied	**jour·neyed**	jule	**jew·el**
journy	**jour·ney**	julien	**ju·li·enne**
jovvial	**jo·vi·al**	julip	**ju·lep**
joyfullness	**joy·ful·ness**	jullienne	**ju·li·enne**
jubalee	**ju·bi·lee**	juncsure	**junc·ture**
jubelation	**ju·bi·la·tion**	jungel	**jun·gle**
jubillant	**ju·bi·lant**	junier	**jun·ior**
jubillation	**ju·bi·la·tion**	junipar	**ju·ni·per**
jubillee	**ju·bi·lee**	junkit	**jun·ket**
juce	**juice**	junktion	**junc·tion**
juddicious	**ju·di·cious**	junkture	**junc·ture**
Judeism	**Ju·da·ism**	juornal	**jour·nal**
judgemint	**judg·ment**	Jupeter	**Ju·pi·ter**
judiciery	**ju·di·ci·ary**	jurasdiction	**ju·ris·dic·tion**
judicous	**ju·di·cious**	jurasprudence	
judishal	**ju·di·cial**		**ju·ris·pru·dence**
juggeler	**jug·u·lar**	jurer	**ju·ror**
	(of the throat)	jurey	**ju·ry**
juggeler	**jug·gler** *(performer)*	jurisdiksion	**ju·ris·dic·tion**
juggeling	**jug·gling**	jurisprudance	
juggement	**judg·ment**		**ju·ris·pru·dence**
juggler	**jug·u·lar** *(of the throat)*	jurk	**jerk**
jugitsu	**ju·jit·su**	jurnal	**jour·nal**
jugling	**jug·gling**	jurney	**jour·ney**
jugular	**jug·gler** *(performer)*	jurrisdiction	**ju·ris·dic·tion**
juguler	**jug·u·lar** *(of the throat)*	jurrisprudence	
juicey	**juicy**		**ju·ris·pru·dence**
juidicial	**ju·di·cial**	jurry	**ju·ry**
juidiciary	**ju·di·ci·ary**	jurseys	**jer·seys**
juidicious	**ju·di·cious**	justace	**jus·tice**

108

WRONG	RIGHT	WRONG	RIGHT
justafiable	**jus·ti·fi·a·ble**	kebob	**ke·bab**
justafication	**jus·ti·fi·ca·tion**	kechup	**ketch·up**
justafy	**jus·ti·fy**	keewee	**ki·wi**
justapose	**jux·ta·pose**	kelo	**ki·lo**
justfieble	**jus·ti·fi·a·ble**	kemp	**kempt**
justifacation	**jus·ti·fi·ca·tion**	ken	**kin** *(relatives)*
justise	**jus·tice**	kendle	**kin·dle**
juvanile	**ju·ven·ile**	kendling	**kin·dling**
juxtipose	**jux·ta·pose**	kendred	**kin·dred**
jymnasium	**gym·na·si·um**	kenetic	**ki·net·ic**
jyration	**gy·ra·tion**	kennal	**ken·nel**
		kenship	**kin·ship**
		Kentukey	**Ken·tucky**
K		keosk	**ki·osk**
		kerasene	**ker·o·sene**
kadre	**ca·dre**	kercheif	**ker·chief**
Kajun	**Ca·jun**	kernel	**colo·nel** *(officer)*
kakhi	**kha·ki**	kettel	**ket·tle**
kalleidoscope	**ka·lei·do·scope**	kewe	**ki·wi**
kalrabi	**kohl·ra·bi**	key	**quay** *(wharf)*
kamono	**ki·mo·no**	keybord	**key·board**
kangeroo	**kan·ga·roo**	keyestone	**key·stone**
kanine	**ca·nine**	kiak	**kay·ak**
kaos	**cha·os**	kibbutz	**kib·itz** *(meddle)*
karafe	**ca·rafe**	kibutz	**kib·butz** *(settlement)*
Karea	**Ko·rea**	kiche	**quiche**
karet	**car·at** *(gem weight)*	kichen	**kitch·en**
karrat	**kar·at** *(1/24)*	kidnies	**kid·neys**
karrate	**ka·ra·te**	kielbassa	**kiel·ba·sa**
kawala	**ko·a·la**	kilagram	**kil·o·gram**
Kawanis	**Ki·wa·nis**	kilameter	**ki·lo·me·ter**
keal	**keel**	kilawatt	**kil·o·watt**
kean	**keen**		

109

kilbasa	**kiel·ba·sa**	knicknack	**knick·knack**
killogram	**kil·o·gram**	knicks	**nix** *(disapprove of)*
killometer	**ki·lo·me·ter**	knifeing	**knif·ing**
killowatt	**kil·o·watt**	knifes	**knives** *(pl.)*
kimona	**ki·mo·no**	knikers	**knick·ers**
kin	**ken** *(understanding)*		*(short pants)*
kindel	**kin·dle**	knite	**knight** *(rank)*
kindeling	**kin·dling**	kniting	**knit·ting**
kinderd	**kin·dred**	knitwit	**nit·wit**
kindergarden	**kin·der·gar·ten**	knive	**knife** *(sing.)*
kinely	**kind·ly**	knoby	**knob·by**
kingdum	**king·dom**	knoted	**knot·ted**
kingley	**king·ly**	knowledgable	
kingpen	**king·pin**		**knowl·edge·a·ble**
kinkey	**kinky**	knowlege	**knowl·edge**
kinly	**kind·ly**	knuckel	**knuck·le**
kinnetic	**ki·net·ic**	koalla	**ko·a·la**
kitch	**kitsch**	koasher	**ko·sher**
kitchan	**kitch·en**	kolidoscope	**ka·lei·do·scope**
kitchenwear	**kitch·en·ware**	kolrabi	**kohl·ra·bi**
kiten	**kit·ten**	koochen	**ku·chen**
kleptomaneac		Koria	**Ko·rea**
	klep·to·ma·ni·ac	Korran	**Ko·ran**
kluts	**klutz**	Kremlen	**Krem·lin**
knackworst	**knack·wurst**	kuken	**ku·chen**
knak	**knack**	kumkwat	**kum·quat**
knapsak	**knap·sack**	kurchief	**ker·chief**
knave	**nave** *(part of a church)*	kurnel	**ker·nel** *(grain)*
knaveish	**knav·ish**	kuzoo	**ka·zoo**
knead	**need** *(require)*	kwafure	**coif·fure** *(hair style)*
kneal	**kneel**	kwagmire	**quag·mire**
kneed	**knead** *(work dough)*	kwagulate	**co·ag·u·late**

WRONG	RIGHT	WRONG	RIGHT
kwala	**ko·a·la**	lacsivious	**las·civ·i·ous**
kwell	**quell**	ladden	**lad·en**
kwintet	**quin·tet**	ladder	**lat·ter** *(more recent)*
kwixotic	**quix·ot·ic**	lade	**laid** *(pt. of lay)*
Kwonset	**Quon·set**	ladel	**la·dle**
kworum	**quo·rum**	ladeling	**la·dling**
kyudos	**ku·dos**	lader	**lad·der**
			(framework of steps)
		ladys	**la·dies** *(pl.)*
L		laety	**la·i·ty**
		laffable	**laugh·a·ble**
labarinth	**lab·y·rinth**	lafter	**laugh·ter**
labborious	**la·bo·ri·ous**	lager	**lag·ger** *(one who lags)*
laber	**la·bor**	lagger	**la·ger** *(beer)*
laberatory	**lab·o·ra·to·ry**	laggoon	**la·goon**
laberor	**la·bor·er**	laghable	**laugh·a·ble**
labirynth	**lab·y·rinth**	lagitemate	**legit·i·mate**
lable	**la·bel**	lai	**lei** *(wreath)*
laborrious	**la·bo·ri·ous**	laim	**lame** *(crippled)*
labratory	**lab·o·ra·to·ry**	lain	**lane** *(road)*
labrinth	**lab·y·rinth**	laing	**lay·ing**
lacerration	**lac·er·a·tion**	lair	**lay·er** *(stratum)*
lached	**latched**	laissay faire	**lais·sez faire**
lachkey	**latch·key**	laithe	**lathe** *(cutting machine)*
lacker	**lac·quer**	lakadaisical	**lack·a·dai·si·cal**
lackidaisical	**lack·a·dai·si·cal**	lakluster	**lack·lus·ter**
lackies	**lack·eys**	lam	**lamb** *(sheep)*
lacks	**lax** *(loose)*	lama	**lla·ma** *(animal)*
lacksative	**lax·a·tive**	lamay	**la·mé** *(fabric)*
lacktic	**lac·tic**	lamb	**lam** *(flight)*
lacluster	**lack·lus·ter**	lamenated	**lam·i·nat·ed**
lacquor	**lac·quer**	lamma	**la·ma** *(monk)*
lacross	**la·crosse**		

WRONG	RIGHT	WRONG	RIGHT
lamme	**la·mé** *(fabric)*	larseny	**lar·ce·ny**
lamment	**la·ment**	larve	**lar·va**
lamminated	**lam·i·nat·ed**	lasania	**la·sa·gna**
lamppoon	**lam·poon**	lasor	**la·ser**
lampray	**lam·prey**	lassagna	**la·sa·gna**
landow	**lan·dau**	lasseration	**lac·er·a·tion**
landscaipe	**land·scape**	lassivious	**las·civ·i·ous**
lane	**lain** *(pp. of lie)*	lassoo	**las·so**
lanelin	**lan·o·lin**	Las Vagas	**Las Ve·gas**
langauge	**lan·guage**	latant	**la·tent**
langerrie	**lin·ge·rie**	latecks	**la·tex**
langourous	**lan·guor·ous**	Laten	**Lat·in**
langwid	**lan·guid**	later	**lat·ter** *(more recent)*
langwish	**lan·guish**	laterrel	**lat·er·al**
lankey	**lanky**	latetude	**lat·i·tude**
lanlady	**land·la·dy**	lath	**lathe** *(cutting machine)*
lanlord	**land·lord**	lathargic	**le·thar·gic**
lannolin	**lan·o·lin**	lathe	**lath** *(wood strip)*
lanscape	**land·scape**	latice	**lat·tice**
lanturn	**lan·tern**	latreen	**la·trine**
laped	**lapped**	latter	**lad·der**
lappel	**la·pel**		*(framework of steps)*
laquer	**lac·quer**	latter	**lat·er** *(subsequently)*
larciny	**lar·ce·ny**	latteral	**lat·er·al**
lare	**lair** *(den)*	lattess	**lat·tice**
lareit	**lar·i·at**	lattex	**la·tex**
larengitis	**lar·yn·gi·tis**	lattitude	**lat·i·tude**
largly	**large·ly**	laudible	**laud·a·ble**
larinx	**lar·ynx**	laughible	**laugh·a·ble**
larriat	**lar·i·at**	laugter	**laugh·ter**
larryngitis	**lar·yn·gi·tis**	laundermat	**laun·dro·mat**
larrynx	**lar·ynx**	laundery	**laun·dry**

WRONG	RIGHT	WRONG	RIGHT
laurreate	**lau·re·ate**	leakedge	**leak·age**
laurrel	**lau·rel**	leakey	**leaky**
lauyer	**law·yer**	lean	**lien** (legal claim)
lavendar	**lav·en·der**	lear	**leer**
lavertory	**lav·a·to·ry**	leatard	**le·o·tard**
lavesh	**lav·ish**	leavenning	**leav·en·ing**
lavinder	**lav·en·der**	leaway	**lee·way**
lavitory	**lav·a·to·ry**	Lebinon	**Leb·a·non**
lavva	**la·va**	Lebra	**Li·bra**
lavvish	**lav·ish**	lechorous	**lech·er·ous**
lawd	**laud** (praise)	lectrolysis	**elec·trol·y·sis**
lawfull	**law·ful**	lecturn	**lec·tern**
lawsoot	**law·suit**	lecturor	**lec·tur·er**
lawwer	**law·yer**	led	**lead** (chemical; to guide)
lax	**lacks** (needs)	ledgend	**leg·end**
lax	**lox** (salmon)	ledgeslature	**leg·is·la·ture**
laxitive	**lax·a·tive**		(lawmaking body)
lay	**lei** (wreath)	ledgible	**leg·i·ble**
layed	**laid** (pt. of lay)	ledgor	**ledg·er**
layity	**la·i·ty**	leech	**leach** (filter)
lazally	**la·zi·ly**	leef	**leaf** (plant organ)
lazay faire	**lais·sez faire**	leegal	**le·gal**
lazer	**la·ser**	leegion	**le·gion**
lazey	**la·zy**	leek	**leak** (escape)
leach	**leech** (worm)	leen	**lean** (bend; thin)
leacherous	**lech·er·ous**	leep	**leap**
lead	**led** (pt. of lead)	leeves	**leaves**
leader	**li·ter** (metric unit)	leeword	**lee·ward**
leafey	**leafy**	leftenant	**lieu·ten·ant**
leage	**league**	legable	**leg·i·ble**
leaison	**li·ai·son**	legallity	**le·gal·i·ty**
leak	**leek** (vegetable)	legallization	**legal·i·za·tion**

legand	**leg·end**	leperosy	**lep·ro·sy**
legasy	**leg·a·cy**	leprachaun	**lep·re·chaun**
legel	**le·gal**	leprasy	**lep·ro·sy**
legeslation	**leg·is·la·tion**	lerch	**lurch**
leggacy	**leg·a·cy**	lerning	**learn·ing**
leggendary	**leg·end·ary**	lerynx	**lar·ynx**
legger	**ledg·er**	lese	**lease**
leggislation	**leg·is·la·tion**	lessen	**les·son** (instruction)
leggume	**leg·ume**	lesser	**les·sor** (landlord)
legian	**le·gion**	lesson	**less·en** (decrease)
legilazation	**legal·i·za·tion**	lessor	**less·er** (smaller)
legindary	**leg·end·ary**	lest	**least**
leging	**leg·ging**	lesure	**lei·sure**
legionaire	**legion·naire**	leter	**li·ter** (metric unit)
legislater	**leg·is·la·tor**	lethel	**le·thal**
	(lawmaker)	lether	**leath·er**
legislator	**leg·is·la·ture**	leting	**let·ting**
	(lawmaking body)	letrine	**la·trine**
legitamate	**legit·i·mate**	lettice	**let·tuce**
legoom	**leg·ume**	leud	**lewd**
lein	**lien** (legal claim)	leutenant	**lieu·ten·ant**
leisier	**lei·sure**	levarege	**lev·er·age**
leisurly	**lei·sure·ly**	leve	**leave**
leiu	**lieu**	levee	**levy** (tax)
leman	**lem·on** (fruit)	leven	**elev·en**
lemonaid	**lem·on·ade**	levening	**leav·en·ing**
leniant	**le·ni·ent**	levetation	**lev·i·ta·tion**
lentel	**len·til** (pea)	levie	**lev·ee** (embankment)
lenthen	**length·en**	levie	**levy** (tax)
lenthy	**lengthy**	levrage	**lev·er·age**
lentil	**lin·tel** (beam)	levy	**lev·ee** (embankment)
leoperd	**leop·ard**	ley	**lei** (wreath)

WRONG	RIGHT	WRONG	RIGHT
liabillity	li·a·bil·i·ty	lie	lye *(alkaline substance)*
liable	li·bel *(defame)*	lien	lean *(bend; thin)*
liannize	li·on·ize	liesure	lei·sure
liar	lyre *(harp)*	liesurely	lei·sure·ly
liason	li·ai·son	lieutenent	lieu·ten·ant
liballous	li·bel·ous	liggament	lig·a·ment
libarian	li·brar·i·an	lightening	light·ning
libary	li·brary		*(flash of light)*
libbelous	li·bel·ous	lightin	light·en
libberalize	lib·er·al·ize	lightning	light·en·ing
libberally	lib·er·al·ly		*(making less heavy)*
libberation	lib·er·a·tion	likelyhood	like·li·hood
libberty	lib·er·ty	likley	like·ly
libedo	li·bi·do	liklihood	like·li·hood
libel	li·a·ble *(likely)*	likness	like·ness
liberallize	lib·er·al·ize	lile	lisle
liberetto	li·bret·to	lillac	li·lac
liberration	lib·er·a·tion	lilly	lily
Libia	Lib·ya	lim	limb *(branch)*
libility	li·a·bil·i·ty	limb	limn *(draw)*
lible	li·bel *(defame)*	limboe	lim·bo
lible	li·a·ble *(likely)*	limetation	lim·i·ta·tion
libralize	lib·er·al·ize	limitting	lim·it·ing
librally	lib·er·al·ly	limmerick	lim·er·ick
librarean	li·brar·i·an	limmitation	lim·i·ta·tion
librery	li·brary	limmiting	lim·it·ing
libreto	li·bret·to	limosine	lim·ou·sine
licarice	lic·o·rice	limph	lymph
licence	li·cense	limrick	lim·er·ick
licencious	licen·tious	limstone	lime·stone
licker	liq·uor *(alcoholic drink)*	linament	lin·i·ment *(salve)*
licorish	lic·o·rice	linan	lin·en

WRONG	RIGHT	WRONG	RIGHT
linch	**lynch**	liquify	**liq·ue·fy**
lindseed	**lin·seed**	liquor ... **li·queur** *(flavored liquor)*	
lineament	**lin·i·ment** *(salve)*	lire	**li·ar** *(one who tells lies)*
linege	**lin·age**	lire	**lyre** *(harp)*
	(number of lines)	lirecal	**lyr·i·cal**
lineing	**lin·ing**	lisense	**li·cense**
lingeray	**lin·ge·rie**	lisentious	**licen·tious**
lingueenie	**lin·gui·ne**	listenning	**lis·ten·ing**
lingwistics	**lin·guis·tics**	litagation	**lit·i·ga·tion**
linier	**lin·e·ar**	litarel	**lit·er·al** *(actual)*
liniment ... **lin·e·a·ment** *(outline)*		litargy	**lit·ur·gy**
linjerie	**lin·ge·rie**	liteny	**lit·a·ny**
linkege	**link·age**	liter	**lit·ter** *(rubbish; young)*
links	**lynx** *(animal)*	literachure	**lit·er·a·ture**
linnament	**lin·i·ment** *(salve)*	literal ... **lit·to·ral** *(on the shore)*	
linneage	**lin·e·age** *(ancestry)*	literaly	**lit·er·al·ly**
linneament	**lin·e·a·ment**	literecy	**lit·er·a·cy**
	(outline)	literrary	**lit·er·ary**
linnear	**lin·e·ar**	lith	**lithe**
linnen	**lin·en**	litheum	**lith·i·um**
linnoleum	**li·no·le·um**	litmas	**lit·mus**
linsede	**lin·seed**	litning	**light·ning**
lintel	**len·til** *(pea)*		*(flash of light)*
lintil	**lin·tel** *(beam)*	litning	**light·en·ing**
linx	**links** *(golf course)*		*(making less heavy)*
linx	**lynx** *(animal)*	litoral ... **lit·to·ral** *(on the shore)*	
Lio	**Leo**	litrature	**lit·er·a·ture**
lionnize	**li·on·ize**	littany	**lit·a·ny**
lip–sink	**lip–sync**	littelest	**lit·tlest**
liqeur ... **li·queur** *(flavored liquor)*		litter	**li·ter** *(metric unit)*
liquadate	**liq·ui·date**	litteral	**lit·er·al** *(actual)*
liquer .... **liq·uor** *(alcoholic drink)*		litteral ... **lit·to·ral** *(on the shore)*	

WRONG	RIGHT	WRONG	RIGHT
litterary	**lit·er·ary**	lockit	**lock·et**
litterature	**lit·er·a·ture**	locks	**lox** (salmon)
littergy	**lit·ur·gy**	locus	**lo·cust** (grasshopper)
littigation	**lit·i·ga·tion**	lode	**load** (burden)
liutenant	**lieu·ten·ant**	lodge	**loge** (theater box)
livary	**liv·ery**	lodgeing	**lodg·ing**
liveable	**liv·a·ble**	lofer	**loaf·er**
livelyhood	**live·li·hood**	logarhythm	**log·a·rithm**
liverworst	**liv·er·wurst**	loge	**lodge** (house)
livley	**live·ly**	loger	**log·ger** (lumberjack)
livlihood	**live·li·hood**	logger	**la·ger** (beer)
livry	**liv·ery**	loggistics	**lo·gis·tics**
livver	**liv·er**	logicly	**log·i·cal·ly**
livvid	**liv·id**	logorithm	**log·a·rithm**
lizerd	**liz·ard**	loiterring	**loi·ter·ing**
llama	**la·ma** (monk)	lolypop	**lol·li·pop**
load	**lode** (ore)	lome	**loam**
loan	**lone** (solitary)	lone	**loan** (something lent)
loar	**lore**	lonelyness	**lone·li·ness**
loath	**loathe** (detest)	longetude	**lon·gi·tude**
loathe	**loath** (unwilling)	longevety	**lon·gev·i·ty**
loathesome	**loath·some**	lonliness	**lone·li·ness**
lobbie	**lob·by**	looau	**lu·au**
lobstar	**lob·ster**	loobricant	**lu·bri·cant**
local	**lo·cale** (place)	loocid	**lu·cid**
locale	**lo·cal** (of a district)	loominary	**lu·mi·nary**
locallity	**lo·cal·i·ty**	loored	**lu·rid** (startling)
locallize	**lo·cal·ize**	loose	**lose** (mislay)
localy	**lo·cal·ly**	loosing	**los·ing** (mislaying)
locamotive	**lo·co·mo·tive**	loot	**lute** (musical instrument)
loccation	**lo·ca·tion**	loped	**lopped** (cut)
loces	**lo·cus** (place)	loreate	**lau·re·ate**

117

WRONG	RIGHT	WRONG	RIGHT
lorel	**lau·rel**	lukemia	**leu·ke·mia**
lose	**loose** *(free)*	lukerative	**lu·cra·tive**
loseing	**los·ing** *(mislaying)*	lukwarm	**luke·warm**
lose–leaf	**loose–leaf**	lulaby	**lull·a·by**
losenge	**loz·enge**	lumanescent	**lumi·nes·cent**
lossed	**lost**	lumbar	**lum·ber** *(timber)*
Los Vegas	**Las Ve·gas**	lumbego	**lum·ba·go**
lotery	**lot·tery**	lumber	**lum·bar** *(of the loins)*
lotien	**lo·tion**	lumenous	**lu·mi·nous**
lotis	**lo·tus**	luminesent	**lumi·nes·cent**
lottary	**lot·tery**	lumminary	**lu·mi·nary**
lou	**lieu**	lunchen	**lunch·eon**
loud	**laud** *(praise)*	lunessy	**lu·na·cy**
loungeing	**loung·ing**	lung	**lunge** *(thrust)*
lousey	**lousy**	lunge	**lung** *(breathing organ)*
Lousiana	**Lou·i·si·ana**	lunnacy	**lu·na·cy**
lovliness	**love·li·ness**	luow	**lu·au**
lovly	**love·ly**	lured	**lu·rid** *(startling)*
lowse	**louse**	lushious	**lus·cious**
loyelty	**loy·al·ty**	lusid	**lu·cid**
loyer	**law·yer**	lustey	**lusty**
lubrecant	**lu·bri·cant**	lustfull	**lust·ful**
lubricater	**lubri·ca·tor**	lute	**loot** *(plunder)*
luced	**lu·cid**	Lutharen	**Lu·ther·an**
Lucefer	**Lu·ci·fer**	luxerious	**lux·u·ri·ous**
luckey	**lucky**	luxery	**lux·u·ry**
lucretive	**lu·cra·tive**	luxurient	**lux·u·ri·ant**
lucsious	**lus·cious**	lyrecs	**lyr·ics**
lude	**lewd**	lyrrical	**lyr·i·cal**
ludecrous	**lu·di·crous**		
luggege	**lug·gage**		
Luisiana	**Lou·i·si·ana**		

M

WRONG	RIGHT
mabbe	**may·be**
macabb	**ma·ca·bre**
macarroni	**mac·a·ro·ni**
macarroon	**mac·a·roon**
maccaroni	**mac·a·ro·ni**
maccaroon	**mac·a·roon**
macedamia	**mac·a·dam·ia**
macerel	**mack·er·el**
mach	**match** *(equal)*
machanation	**mach·i·na·tion**
machanic	**me·chan·ic**
machene	**ma·chine**
machesmo	**ma·chis·mo**
machette	**ma·che·te**
Machievellian	
	Mach·i·a·vel·li·an
machinary	**ma·chin·ery**
machinest	**ma·chin·ist**
mackaral	**mack·er·el**
mackaroni	**mac·a·ro·ni**
mackaroon	**mac·a·roon**
mackentosh	**mack·in·tosh**
	(coat)
mackerrel	**mack·er·el**
Mackiavellian	
	Mach·i·a·vel·li·an
mackination	**mach·i·na·tion**
mackintosh	**Mc·In·tosh**
	(apple)
mackrame	**mac·ra·mé**

WRONG	RIGHT
macobre	**ma·ca·bre**
macramay	**mac·ra·mé**
madam	**mad·ame** *(title)*
madame	**mad·am** *(lady)*
madamoiselle	
	made·moi·selle
maddam	**mad·am** *(lady)*
madder	**mat·ter** *(substance)*
made	**maid** *(servant)*
madem	**mad·am** *(lady)*
mademoizelle	
	made·moi·selle
maden	**maid·en**
mader	**mad·der** *(angrier)*
Madera	**Ma·deira**
madicinal	**me·dic·i·nal**
madley	**mad·ly**
madmaselle	**made·moi·selle**
madona	**ma·don·na**
magasine	**mag·a·zine**
magestic	**ma·jes·tic**
magesty	**maj·es·ty**
maggazine	**mag·a·zine**
maggic	**mag·ic**
maggit	**mag·got**
maggma	**mag·ma**
maggnolia	**mag·no·lia**
maggpie	**mag·pie**
magick	**mag·ic**
magickal	**mag·i·cal**
maginta	**ma·gen·ta**
magisian	**ma·gi·cian**

WRONG	RIGHT	WRONG	RIGHT
magistarial	**mag·is·te·ri·al**	magor	**ma·jor**
magistrait	**mag·is·trate**	magorette	**ma·jor·ette**
magizine	**mag·a·zine**	magot	**mag·got**
magna cum loude	**mag·na cum lau·de**	magpye	**mag·pie**
		mahagany	**ma·hog·a·ny**
magnafication	**mag·ni·fi·ca·tion**	mahem	**may·hem**
		mahogony	**ma·hog·a·ny**
magnanimaty	**mag·na·nim·i·ty**	maid	**made** *(prepared)*
		maidin	**maid·en**
magnanimus	**mag·nan·i·mous**	mail	**male** *(masculine)*
		main	**mane** *(hair)*
magnate	**mag·net** *(iron attracter)*	mainge	**mange**
		mainger	**man·ger**
magnatise	**mag·net·ize**	mainia	**ma·nia**
magnatude	**mag·ni·tude**	mainnaise	**may·on·naise**
magnesia	**mag·ne·si·um** *(element)*	maintane	**main·tain**
		maintenence	**main·te·nance**
magnesium	**mag·ne·sia** *(laxative)*	mair	**mare** *(female horse)*
		maitre dee	**mai·tre d'**
magnet	**mag·nate** *(important person)*	maize	**maze** *(labyrinth)*
		majarity	**ma·jor·i·ty**
magnetick	**mag·net·ic**	majenta	**ma·gen·ta**
magnettism	**mag·net·ism**	majer	**ma·jor**
magnezium	**mag·ne·si·um** *(element)*	majerette	**ma·jor·ette**
		majestick	**ma·jes·tic**
magnifficence	**mag·nif·i·cence**	majesticly	**ma·jes·ti·cal·ly**
magnificant	**mag·nif·i·cent**	majic	**mag·ic**
magnifisense	**mag·nif·i·cence**	majisterial	**mag·is·te·ri·al**
magnifyer	**mag·ni·fi·er**	majistrate	**mag·is·trate**
magninimity	**mag·na·nim·i·ty**	majisty	**maj·es·ty**
magnolya	**mag·no·lia**	majong	**mah–jongg**
		majoraty	**ma·jor·i·ty**

WRONG	RIGHT	WRONG	RIGHT
majoret	**ma·jor·ette**	malladjusted	**mal·ad·just·ed**
makadamia	**mac·a·dam·ia**	malladroit	**mal·a·droit**
makaw	**ma·caw**	mallady	**mal·a·dy**
makeing	**mak·ing**	mallapropism	
makismo	**ma·chis·mo**		**mal·a·prop·ism**
makup	**make·up**	mallaria	**ma·lar·ia**
malace	**mal·ice**	mallarkey	**ma·lar·key**
maladdy	**mal·a·dy**	mallcontent	**mal·con·tent**
maladroyt	**mal·a·droit**	mallerd	**mal·lard**
malaize	**ma·laise**	mallevolence	**malev·o·lence**
malaprapism	**mal·a·prop·ism**	mallevolent	**malev·o·lent**
malard	**mal·lard**	mallfeasance	**mal·fea·sance**
malasses	**mo·las·ses**	mallformation	
malatto	**mu·lat·to**		**mal·for·ma·tion**
malayse	**ma·laise**	mallfunction	**mal·func·tion**
malcantent	**mal·con·tent**	mallice	**mal·ice**
male	**mail** *(letters)*	mallicious	**ma·li·cious**
maleable	**mal·le·a·ble**	mallify	**mol·li·fy**
malee	**me·lee**	mallignant	**ma·lig·nant**
maleria	**ma·lar·ia**	mallinger	**ma·lin·ger**
malest	**mo·lest**	mallit	**mal·let**
malet	**mal·let**	mallnourished	
malevalence	**malev·o·lence**		**mal·nour·ished**
malevolant	**malev·o·lent**	mallnutrition	**mal·nu·tri·tion**
malfeesance	**mal·fea·sance**	mallodorous	**mal·o·dor·ous**
malicius	**ma·li·cious**	mallpractice	**mal·prac·tice**
malignansy	**ma·lig·nan·cy**	mallted	**malt·ed**
malignent	**ma·lig·nant**	malnurished	**mal·nour·ished**
maline	**ma·lign**	maloderous	**mal·o·dor·ous**
malise	**mal·ice**	mamal	**mam·mal**
mall	**maul** *(injure)*	mamary	**mam·ma·ry**
mallable	**mal·le·a·ble**	mame	**maim**

WRONG	RIGHT	WRONG	RIGHT
mammagraphy .... **mam·mog·ra·phy**		manea .... **ma·nia**	
		maneac .... **ma·ni·ac**	
mammel .... **mam·mal**		manefest .... **man·i·fest**	
mammery .... **mam·ma·ry**		manege .... **man·age** (control)	
mammeth .... **mam·moth**		maneger .... **man·ag·er**	
mammry .... **mam·ma·ry**		manequin .... **man·ne·quin**	
mamography .... **mam·mog·ra·phy**		maner .... **man·ner** (method)	
		manerism .... **man·ner·ism**	
mamoth .... **mam·moth**		manestery .... **mon·as·tery**	
mana .... **man·na**		manetain .... **main·tain**	
manacal .... **man·a·cle**		mangel .... **man·gle**	
manacotti .... **man·i·cot·ti**		mangey .... **man·gy**	
manacure .... **man·i·cure**		mangleing .... **man·gling**	
manafest .... **man·i·fest**		mangrel .... **mon·grel**	
manafesto .... **man·i·fes·to**		Manhatten .... **Man·hat·tan**	
manafold .... **man·i·fold**		maniack .... **ma·ni·ac**	
managable .... **man·age·a·ble**		maniacle .... **ma·ni·a·cal**	
manageing .... **man·ag·ing**		manicle .... **man·a·cle**	
managemint .... **man·age·ment**		manicurest .... **man·i·cur·ist**	
managerie .... **me·nag·er·ie**		manifess .... **man·i·fest**	
managment .... **man·age·ment**		manifessto .... **man·i·fes·to**	
managor .... **man·ag·er**		manilla .... **ma·nila**	
manarch .... **mon·arch**		manipalate .... **manip·u·late**	
manarchy .... **mon·ar·chy**		maniplative .... **manip·u·la·tive**	
mancion .... **man·sion**		manippulate .... **manip·u·late**	
mandable .... **man·di·ble**		manipulater ..... **manip·u·la·tor**	
mandalin .... **man·do·lin**		manitor .... **mon·i·tor**	
mander .... **maun·der**		manje .... **mange**	
manderin .... **man·da·rin**		manjer .... **man·ger**	
mandetory .... **man·da·to·ry**		mankine .... **man·kind**	
mandolen .... **man·do·lin**		manley .... **man·ly**	
mane .... **main** (important)		mannacle .... **man·a·cle**	

WRONG	RIGHT	WRONG	RIGHT
mannage	**man·age** (control)	manuer	**ma·nure**
mannaise	**may·on·naise**	manuever	**ma·neu·ver**
manndate	**man·date**	manufacter	**man·u·fac·ture**
mannekin	**man·ne·quin**	manuskript	**man·u·script**
manner	**man·or** (estate)	manuver	**ma·neu·ver**
manneuver	**ma·neu·ver**	manyascript	**man·u·script**
mannicure	**man·i·cure**	mapel	**ma·ple**
mannifest	**man·i·fest**	maping	**map·ping**
mannifesto	**man·i·fes·to**	marader	**ma·raud·er**
mannifold	**man·i·fold**	maragold	**mar·i·gold**
mannila	**ma·nila**	maranade	**mar·i·nade**
mannipulate	**manip·u·late**	maranara	**ma·ri·na·ra**
mannor	**man·ner** (method)	maranate	**mar·i·nate** (v.)
mannsion	**man·sion**	maraner	**mar·i·ner**
mannual	**man·u·al**	marascheno	**mar·a·schi·no**
mannufacture	**man·u·fac·ture**	maratal	**mar·i·tal** (of marriage)
mannure	**ma·nure**	maratime	**mar·i·time**
manocle	**mon·o·cle**	marbel	**mar·ble**
manogamy	**mo·nog·a·my**	marbleing	**mar·bling**
manologue	**mon·o·logue**	mare	**may·or** (official)
manopolize	**mo·nop·o·lize**	mareachi	**ma·ri·a·chi**
manopoly	**mo·nop·o·ly**	marejuana	**ma·ri·jua·na**
manotonous	**mo·not·o·nous**	marena	**ma·ri·na**
manslotter	**man·slaugh·ter**	marenate	**mar·i·nate** (v.)
mansoon	**mon·soon**	marene	**ma·rine**
manster	**mon·ster**	mareonette	**mar·i·o·nette**
manstrosity	**mon·stros·i·ty**	margen	**mar·gin**
mantal	**man·tel** (shelf)	margenalia	**mar·gi·na·lia**
mantel	**man·tle** (cloak)	margerine	**mar·ga·rine** (spread)
mantice	**man·tis**		
mantle	**man·tel** (shelf)	marginale	**mar·gin·al**
manuel	**man·u·al**	marginallia	**mar·gi·na·lia**

WRONG	RIGHT	WRONG	RIGHT
marginel	**mar·gin·al**	marraschino	**mar·a·schi·no**
margrin	**mar·ga·rine** *(spread)*	marrathon	**mar·a·thon**
mariage	**mar·riage**	marrble	**mar·ble**
marianette	**mar·i·o·nette**	marriachi	**ma·ri·a·chi**
maridian	**me·rid·i·an**	marriagable	**mar·riage·a·ble**
maried	**mar·ried**	marriege	**mar·riage**
maring	**mar·ring**	marrigold	**mar·i·gold**
maringue	**me·ringue**	marrijuana	**ma·ri·jua·na**
	(pie topping)	marrimba	**ma·rim·ba**
marinnara	**ma·ri·na·ra**	marrinade	**mar·i·nade**
marionet	**mar·i·o·nette**	marrinara	**ma·ri·na·ra**
marital	**mar·tial** *(military)*	marrinate	**mar·i·nate** *(v.)*
maritle	**mar·i·tal** *(of marriage)*	marrionette	**mar·i·o·nette**
mariuana	**ma·ri·jua·na**	marrital	**mar·i·tal** *(of marriage)*
marjeram	**mar·jo·ram** *(plant)*	marry	**mer·ry** *(happy)*
marjin	**mar·gin**	marryed	**mar·ried**
marjinalia	**mar·gi·na·lia**	marshal	**mar·tial** *(military)*
marjorine	**mar·ga·rine**	marshall	**mar·shal**
	(spread)		*(law officer)*
markee	**mar·quee**	Marshen	**Mar·tian** *(of Mars)*
marketible	**mar·ket·a·ble**	marshmellow	**marsh·mal·low**
marketting	**mar·ket·ing**	Marsian	**Mar·tian** *(of Mars)*
markidly	**mark·ed·ly**	marsipan	**mar·zi·pan**
markit	**mar·ket**	marsupeal	**mar·su·pi·al**
Marksism	**Marx·ism**	marten	**mar·tin** *(bird)*
marlen	**mar·lin** *(fish)*	martenet	**mar·ti·net**
marmelade	**mar·ma·lade**	martengale	**mar·tin·gale**
marow	**mar·row**	marteni	**mar·ti·ni**
marquey	**mar·quee**	marter	**mar·tyr**
marr	**mar**	martial	**mar·shal** *(law officer)*
marraca	**ma·ra·ca**	martial	**mar·i·tal** *(of marriage)*
marrage	**mar·riage**	martin	**mar·ten** *(mammal)*

Martin	**Mar·tian** (of Mars)	maskuline	**mas·cu·line**
martinette	**mar·ti·net**	masokism	**mas·och·ism**
martordom	**mar·tyr·dom**	masoleum	**mau·so·le·um**
marune	**ma·roon**	masonrey	**ma·son·ry**
marvalous	**mar·vel·ous**	masque	**mask** (cover)
marvell	**mar·vel**	masquito	**mos·qui·to**
marvelus	**mar·vel·ous**	masquorade	**mas·quer·ade**
marygold	**mar·i·gold**	massacer	**mas·sa·cre**
marzapan	**mar·zi·pan**	Massachusets	
masa	**me·sa**		**Mas·sa·chu·setts**
masachism	**mas·och·ism**	massage	**mes·sage**
Masachusetts			(communication)
	Mas·sa·chu·setts	massaje ... **mas·sage** (a rubbing)
masacre	**mas·sa·cre**	massakre	**mas·sa·cre**
masage ... **mas·sage** (a rubbing)		masscara	**mas·ca·ra**
masc	**mask** (cover)	massectomy	**mas·tec·to·my**
mascera	**mas·ca·ra**	masser	**mas·seur** (m.)
mascet	**mas·cot**	massiah	**mes·si·ah**
masculen	**mas·cu·line**	massochism	**mas·och·ism**
mase	**mace**	masson	**ma·son**
masen	**ma·son**	Massonic	**Ma·son·ic**
masenry	**ma·son·ry**	massquerade	**mas·quer·ade**
maseur	**mas·seur** (m.)	massticate	**mas·ti·cate**
maseuse	**mas·seuse** (f.)	masstiff	**mas·tiff**
mashete	**ma·che·te**	masstodon	**mas·to·don**
mashination	**mach·i·na·tion**	massuer	**mas·seur** (m.)
mashine	**ma·chine**	massuse	**mas·seuse** (f.)
masive	**mas·sive**	mastacate	**mas·ti·cate**
mask	**masque** (masked ball)	mastadon	**mas·to·don**
maskara	**mas·ca·ra**	mastead	**mast·head**
maskerade	**mas·quer·ade**	masterbate	**mas·tur·bate**
maskot	**mas·cot**	masterey	**mas·tery**

WRONG	RIGHT	WRONG	RIGHT

masterfull .... **mas·ter·ful**

masterley .... **mas·ter·ly**

mastermine .... **mas·ter·mind**

masterry .... **mas·tery**

mastro .... **ma·es·tro**

mat .... **matte** *(dull finish)*

matabolism ...... **me·tab·o·lism**

matallic .... **me·tal·lic**

matcher .... **ma·ture** *(full–grown)*

matchuration .... **mat·u·ra·tion**

mateing .... **mat·ing** *(joining)*

matenee .... **mat·i·nee**

mater de .... **mai·tre d'**

material ... **ma·te·ri·el** *(supplies)*

materiallism ..... **ma·te·ri·al·ism**

materiallize .... **ma·te·ri·al·ize**

materiel .... **ma·te·ri·al** *(cloth)*

maternaty .... **ma·ter·ni·ty**

maternel .... **ma·ter·nal**

math .... **moth**

mathamatical ....

.... **math·e·mat·i·cal**

mathematicks .. **math·e·mat·ics**

mathematitian ....

.... **math·e·ma·ti·cian**

mathmatical .. **math·e·mat·i·cal**

mathmatician ....

.... **math·e·ma·ti·cian**

mathmatics ..... **math·e·mat·ics**

maticulous .... **metic·u·lous**

matinay .... **mat·i·nee**

mating .. **mat·ting** *(interweaving)*

matirial .... **ma·te·ri·al** *(cloth)*

matiriel ... **ma·te·ri·el** *(supplies)*

matoor ...... **ma·ture** *(full–grown)*

matramonial ... **mat·ri·mo·ni·al**

matrearch .... **ma·tri·arch**

matre d' .... **mai·tre d'**

matren .... **ma·tron**

matress .... **mat·tress**

matriark .... **ma·tri·arch**

matricks .... **ma·trix**

matrickulate ...... **matric·u·late**

matriculateing ....

.... **matric·u·lat·ing**

matrimonal ..... **mat·ri·mo·ni·al**

matriside .... **mat·ri·cide**

mattador .... **mat·a·dor**

matte .... **mat** *(floor covering)*

matter .... **mad·der** *(angrier)*

mattinee .... **mat·i·nee**

matting .... **mat·ing** *(joining)*

mattled .... **mot·tled**

mattriculate .... **matric·u·late**

mattrimonial ... **mat·ri·mo·ni·al**

mattrimony ...... **mat·ri·mo·ny**

mattriss .... **mat·tress**

matturation ...... **mat·u·ra·tion**

maturaty .... **ma·tu·ri·ty**

maturnal .... **ma·ter·nal**

maturnity .... **ma·ter·ni·ty**

maudlen .... **maud·lin**

maukish .... **mawk·ish**

maul ...... **mall** *(shopping center)*

WRONG	RIGHT	WRONG	RIGHT
mausolium	**mau·so·le·um**	mechannic	**me·chan·ic**
mave	**mauve** *(purple)*	mechenism	**mech·a·nism**
mavrick	**mav·er·ick**	meckanic	**me·chan·ic**
maxamal	**max·i·mal**	meckanism	**mech·a·nism**
maxamize	**max·i·mize**	medacal	**med·i·cal**
maxamum	**max·i·mum**	medacation	**med·i·ca·tion**
maxem	**max·im**	medal	**med·dle** *(interfere)*
mayem	**may·hem**	medal	**met·al** *(iron, etc.)*
mayer	**may·or** *(official)*	medalion	**me·dal·lion**
mayme	**maim**	medatation	**med·i·ta·tion**
mayonaise	**may·on·naise**	Medaterranean	
mayorality	**may·or·al·ty**		**Med·i·ter·ra·ne·an**
maze	**maize** *(corn)*	meddallion	**me·dal·lion**
mcintosh	**mack·in·tosh** *(coat)*	meddication	**med·i·ca·tion**
meak	**meek**	Medditerranean	
mean	**mien** *(manner)*		**Med·i·ter·ra·ne·an**
meanial	**me·ni·al**	meddle	**med·al** *(award)*
meaningfull	**mean·ing·ful**	meddle	**met·tle** *(courage)*
meanning	**mean·ing**	meddlesum	**med·dle·some**
measels	**mea·sles**	medea	**me·dia**
measley	**mea·sly**	medean	**me·di·an**
measureable	**meas·ur·a·ble**	medecine	**med·i·cine**
measureing	**meas·ur·ing**	Medeira	**Ma·deira**
measurment	**meas·ure·ment**	medel	**med·al** *(award)*
meat	**meet** *(encounter)*	medelist	**med·al·ist**
meat	**mete** *(distribute)*	medeocre	**me·di·o·cre**
meatey	**meaty**	medeocrity	**me·di·oc·ri·ty**
meazles	**mea·sles**	medeum	**me·di·um**
meazure	**meas·ure**	medeval	**me·di·e·val**
mebbe	**may·be**	mediateing	**me·di·at·ing**
mecaw	**ma·caw**	mediater	**me·di·a·tor**
mechanicle	**me·chan·i·cal**	medicel	**med·i·cal**

WRONG	RIGHT
medick	**med·ic**
medievil	**me·di·e·val**
mediocer	**me·di·o·cre**
mediocraty	**me·di·oc·ri·ty**
mediokre	**me·di·o·cre**
medion	**me·di·an**
medisinal	**me·dic·i·nal**
medisine	**med·i·cine**
Mediteranean	**Med·i·ter·ra·ne·an**
medle	**med·dle** *(interfere)*
medlesome	**med·dle·some**
medly	**med·ley**
medow	**mead·ow**
meeger	**mea·ger**
meel	**meal**
meen	**mean** *(middle)*
meer	**mere**
meesles	**mea·sles**
meesly	**mea·sly**
meet	**meat** *(food)*
meet	**mete** *(distribute)*
meeting	**met·ing** *(distributing)*
meetting	**meet·ing** *(encountering)*
meggaphone	**meg·a·phone**
meggaton	**meg·a·ton**
meladic	**me·lod·ic**
meladrama	**mel·o·dra·ma**
melady	**mel·o·dy**
melaise	**ma·laise**
melan	**mel·on**

WRONG	RIGHT
melancolly	**mel·an·choly**
melaria	**ma·lar·ia**
melay	**me·lee**
meld	**melt** *(dissolve)*
melenoma	**mel·a·no·ma**
melinger	**ma·lin·ger**
melinkoly	**mel·an·choly**
melled	**meld** *(cards; blend)*
mellodic	**me·lod·ic**
mellodious	**me·lo·di·ous**
mellodrama	**mel·o·dra·ma**
mellody	**mel·o·dy**
mellon	**mel·on**
mellt	**melt** *(dissolve)*
melodick	**me·lod·ic**
melodius	**me·lo·di·ous**
melow	**mel·low**
melt	**meld** *(cards; blend)*
memarandum	**mem·o·ran·dum**
membor	**mem·ber**
membrain	**mem·brane**
memerabilia	**mem·o·ra·bil·ia**
memerize	**mem·o·rize**
memery	**mem·o·ry**
memior	**mem·oir**
memmorial	**me·mo·ri·al**
memmorize	**mem·o·rize**
memor	**mem·oir**
memorabillia	**mem·o·ra·bil·ia**
memorandom	**mem·o·ran·dum**

WRONG	RIGHT	WRONG	RIGHT
memoreal	**me·mo·ri·al**	mercyful	**mer·ci·ful**
memrable	**mem·o·ra·ble**	mercyless	**mer·ci·less**
memry	**mem·o·ry**	merder	**mur·der**
memwar	**mem·oir**	mere	**mare** (female horse)
menajerie	**me·nag·er·ie**	meret	**mer·it**
menapause	**men·o·pause**	meretorious	**mer·i·to·ri·ous**
menase	**men·ace**	meridean	**me·rid·i·an**
menastrate	**men·stru·ate**	merinade	**mar·i·nade**
mendacant	**men·di·cant**	merine	**ma·rine**
meneal	**me·ni·al**	meritorius	**mer·i·to·ri·ous**
menice	**men·ace**	merje	**merge**
mennopause	**men·o·pause**	merkantile	**mer·can·tile**
menshun	**men·tion**	merky	**murky**
menstrate	**men·stru·ate**	merly	**mere·ly**
menstrul	**men·stru·al**	mermade	**mer·maid**
ment	**meant** (pt. of mean)	mermur	**mur·mur**
ment	**mint**	merridian	**me·rid·i·an**
mentallity	**men·tal·i·ty**	merrimint	**mer·ri·ment**
mentaly	**men·tal·ly**	merrit	**mer·it**
mentel	**men·tal**	merritorious	**mer·i·to·ri·ous**
menthal	**men·thol**	merrow	**mar·row**
mently	**men·tal·ly**	merry	**mar·ry** (wed)
menue	**menu**	merryment	**mer·ri·ment**
merange	**me·ringue**	mersenary	**mer·ce·nary**
	(pie topping)	mersiful	**mer·ci·ful**
meraschino	**mar·a·schi·no**	mersiless	**mer·ci·less**
merathon	**mar·a·thon**	mersy	**mer·cy**
merauder	**ma·raud·er**	merth	**mirth**
mercanary	**mer·ce·nary**	mesage	**mes·sage**
merchendise	**mer·chan·dise**		(communication)
merchent	**mer·chant**	mesenger	**mes·sen·ger**
mercurey	**mer·cu·ry**	mesiah	**mes·si·ah**

message .. **mas·sage** *(a rubbing)*
messinger .... **mes·sen·ger**
mesure .... **meas·ure**
metabalism ...... **me·tab·o·lism**
metafor .... **met·a·phor**
metal .... **met·tle** *(courage)*
metal .... **med·al** *(award)*
metalic .... **me·tal·lic**
metalurgy .... **met·al·lur·gy**
metamorfosis ....
.... **met·a·mor·pho·sis** *(sing.)*
metamorphick ....
.... **met·a·mor·phic**
metamorphosis ....
.... **met·a·mor·pho·ses** *(pl.)*
mete .... **meet** *(encounter)*
mete .... **meat** *(food)*
metear .... **me·te·or**
metearology ... **mete·or·ol·o·gy**
meteing ... **met·ing** *(distributing)*
metellurgy .... **met·al·lur·gy**
meterology ..... **mete·or·ol·o·gy**
methadical .... **method·i·cal**
methadology .. **meth·od·ol·o·gy**
methed .... **meth·od**
metickulous .... **metic·u·lous**
meting .... **meet·ing**
                              (encountering)
metle .... **met·tle** *(courage)*
metomorphosis ....
.... **met·a·mor·pho·sis** *(sing.)*
metranome .... **met·ro·nome**

metrapolitan .. **met·ro·pol·i·tan**
metrick .... **met·ric**
metricle .... **met·ri·cal**
metropollitan ....
.... **met·ro·pol·i·tan**
mettabolism ..... **me·tab·o·lism**
mettal .... **met·al** *(iron, etc.)*
mettamorphic ....
.... **met·a·mor·phic**
mettamorphosis ....
.... **met·a·mor·pho·sis** *(sing.)*
mettaphor .... **met·a·phor**
metticulous .... **metic·u·lous**
mettronome ...... **met·ro·nome**
mettropolitan ....
.... **met·ro·pol·i·tan**
Mexaco .... **Mex·i·co**
mezanine .... **mez·za·nine**
mezmerize .... **mes·mer·ize**
Micheal .... **Mi·chael**
micraphone .... **mi·cro·phone**
micrascope .... **mi·cro·scope**
micrawave .... **mi·cro·wave**
microfeche .... **mi·cro·fiche**
microfone .... **mi·cro·phone**
microscopec ..... **mi·cro·scop·ic**
micsellanious ....
.... **mis·cel·la·ne·ous**
miday .... **mid·day**
middair .... **mid·air**
middel .... **mid·dle**
middleing .... **mid·dling**

WRONG	*RIGHT*
midgit	**midg·et**
midieval	**me·di·e·val**
midle	**mid·dle**
midling	**mid·dling**
midruff	**mid·riff**
mien	**mean** *(middle)*
miget	**midg·et**
might	**mite**
	(insect; small amount)
migrane	**mi·graine**
migrateing	**mi·grat·ing**
migrent	**mi·grant**
mika	**mi·ca**
mikrofiche	**mi·cro·fiche**
mikrofilm	**mi·cro·film**
milatary	**mil·i·tary**
mildley	**mild·ly**
mildue	**mil·dew**
mileiu	**mi·lieu**
milenium	**mil·len·ni·um**
milicia	**mi·li·tia**
miligram	**mil·li·gram**
milimeter	**mil·li·me·ter**
milinery	**mil·li·nery** *(hat shop)*
milion	**mil·lion**
milionaire	**mil·lion·aire**
militent	**mil·i·tant**
militery	**mil·i·tary**
miliue	**mi·lieu**
milktoast	**milque·toast**
	(timid person)
milkyness	**milk·i·ness**

WRONG	*RIGHT*
millagram	**mil·li·gram**
millameter	**mil·li·me·ter**
milldew	**mil·dew**
milleage	**mile·age**
millenary	**mil·li·nery**
	(hat shop)
millieu	**mi·lieu**
millinery	**mil·le·nary**
	(a thousand)
millinnium	**mil·len·ni·um**
millionare	**mil·lion·aire**
millit	**mil·let**
millitant	**mil·i·tant**
millitary	**mil·i·tary**
millitia	**mi·li·tia**
milliun	**mil·lion**
Millwaukee	**Mil·wau·kee**
mimeagraph	**mim·e·o·graph**
mimick	**mim·ic**
mimickry	**mim·ic·ry**
mimmeograph	
	mim·e·o·graph
mimmic	**mim·ic**
minamal	**min·i·mal**
minamum	**min·i·mum**
minarity	**mi·nor·i·ty**
minaster	**min·is·ter**
minasterial	**min·is·te·ri·al**
minastrone	**mine·strone**
minature	**min·i·a·ture**
minceing	**minc·ing**
mind	**mine** *(pron.)*

WRONG	RIGHT	WRONG	RIGHT
mine	**mind** (intellect)	miricle	**mir·a·cle**
miner	**mi·nor**	mirrage	**mi·rage**
	(underage person)	mirrer	**mir·ror**
minerel	**min·er·al**	mirrh	**myrrh**
Minesota	**Min·ne·so·ta**	mirtle	**myr·tle**
miniscule	**mi·nus·cule**	miscarrege	**mis·car·riage**
ministery	**min·is·try**	miscelaneous	
ministrone	**mine·strone**		**mis·cel·la·ne·ous**
minits	**min·utes**	mischeif	**mis·chief**
miniture	**min·i·a·ture**	mischevious	**mis·chie·vous**
Minnasota	**Min·ne·so·ta**	misconstrew	**mis·con·strue**
minneral	**min·er·al**	misdemeaner	
minnestrone	**mine·strone**		**mis·de·mean·or**
minniature	**min·i·a·ture**	mishapen	**mis·shap·en**
minnimal	**min·i·mal**	misile	**mis·sile**
minnimum	**min·i·mum**	mision	**mis·sion**
minnister	**min·is·ter**	misionary	**mis·sion·ary**
minnisterial	**min·is·te·ri·al**	Misissippi	**Mis·sis·sippi**
minor	**min·er** (mine worker)	Misouri	**Mis·souri**
minoraty	**mi·nor·i·ty**	mispell	**mis·spell**
minow	**min·now**	mispernounce	
minsing	**minc·ing**		**mis·pro·nounce**
mint	**meant** (pt. of mean)	misrable	**mis·er·a·ble**
mintion	**men·tion**	misrey	**mis·ery**
mintsmeat	**mince·meat**	missal	**mis·sile**
minuette	**min·u·et**	missap	**mis·hap**
minural	**min·er·al**	misscarriage	**mis·car·riage**
minuts	**min·utes**	misscellaneous	
miracel	**mir·a·cle**		**mis·cel·la·ne·ous**
mirackulous	**mirac·u·lous**	misschief	**mis·chief**
miraje	**mi·rage**	misschievous	**mis·chie·vous**
miriad	**myr·i·ad**	missconstrue	**mis·con·strue**

WRONG	RIGHT
missdemeanor	
.... **mis·de·mean·or**	
missellaneous	
.... **mis·cel·la·ne·ous**	
missfit .... **mis·fit**	
missfortune .... **mis·for·tune**	
missile .... **mis·sal** (book)	
missionery .... **mis·sion·ary**	
Missisippi .... **Mis·sis·sippi**	
missle .... **mis·sile**	
misslead .... **mis·lead**	
missletoe .... **mis·tle·toe**	
missplace .... **mis·place**	
misspronounce	
.... **mis·pro·nounce**	
missrepresent	
.... **mis·rep·re·sent**	
misstake .... **mis·take**	
misstress .... **mis·tress**	
misstrial .... **mis·tri·al**	
Missuri .... **Mis·souri**	
mist .... **midst** (middle)	
misterious .... **mys·te·ri·ous**	
mistey .... **misty**	
mistical .... **mys·ti·cal**	
misticism .... **mys·ti·cism**	
mistify .... **mys·ti·fy**	
mistique .... **mys·tique**	
mistriss .... **mis·tress**	
mistro .... **ma·es·tro**	
mitagate .... **mit·i·gate**	
mite .... **might** (aux.v.; power)	

WRONG	RIGHT
miten .... **mit·ten**
mithical .... **myth·i·cal**
mithological ... **myth·o·log·i·cal**
mithology .... **my·thol·o·gy**
mitst .... **midst** (middle)
mittigate .... **mit·i·gate**
mittin .... **mit·ten**
mixchure .... **mix·ture**
mizer .... **mi·ser**
mizerable .... **mis·er·a·ble**
mizery .... **mis·ery**
mnemonick .... **mne·mon·ic**
moan .... **mown** (pp. of mow)
moat .... **mote** (particle)
mobillize .... **mo·bi·lize**
moble .... **mo·bile**
mockasin .... **moc·ca·sin**
mockry .... **mock·ery**
modal .... **mod·el** (a copy)
modallity .... **mo·dal·i·ty**
modaration ...... **mod·er·a·tion**
moddern .... **mod·ern**
moddest .... **mod·est**
moddo .... **mot·to**
modecum .... **mod·i·cum**
modefier .... **mod·i·fi·er**
model .... **mod·al** (of a mode)
moderater .... **mod·er·a·tor**
modifecation ... **mod·i·fi·ca·tion**
modjule .... **mod·ule**
modlin .... **maud·lin**
modren .... **mod·ern**

moduler	**mod·u·lar**	monapoly	**mo·nop·o·ly**
mogel	**mo·gul**	monarcical	**mo·nar·chi·cal**
moing	**mow·ing**	monarcy	**mon·ar·chy**
moissen	**mois·ten**	monark	**mon·arch**
moister	**mois·ture** *(wetness)*	monasstic	**mo·nas·tic**
molacule	**mol·e·cule**	monastary	**mon·as·tery**
molases	**mo·las·ses**	monatone	**mon·o·tone**
moldey	**moldy**	monder	**maun·der**
moleculer	**mo·lec·u·lar**	mone	**moan** *(groan)*
moler	**mo·lar**	mone	**mown** *(pp. of mow)*
molesstation	**moles·ta·tion**	mongrul	**mon·grel**
molify	**mol·li·fy**	monimental	**mon·u·men·tal**
mollecular	**mo·lec·u·lar**	monitary	**mon·e·tary**
mollecule	**mol·e·cule**	moniter	**mon·i·tor**
mollesk	**mol·lusk**	monky	**mon·key**
mollest	**mo·lest**	monnarchical	**mo·nar·chi·cal**
mollestation	**moles·ta·tion**	monnetary	**mon·e·tary**
mollten	**mol·ten**	monney	**mon·ey**
molusk	**mol·lusk**	monnitor	**mon·i·tor**
momemtery	**mo·men·tary**	monnogram	**mon·o·gram**
momentem	**mo·men·tum**	monnolith	**mon·o·lith**
momenterily	**momen·tar·i·ly**	monnotny	**mo·not·o·ny**
momento	**me·men·to**	monnumental	**mon·u·men·tal**
momentus	**mo·men·tous**	mononukleosis	
momint	**mo·ment**		**mon·o·nu·cle·o·sis**
monacle	**mon·o·cle**	monoply	**mo·nop·o·ly**
monagamy	**mo·nog·a·my**	monopollize	**mo·nop·o·lize**
monagram	**mon·o·gram**	monostery	**mon·as·tery**
monagraph	**mon·o·graph**	monotany	**mo·not·o·ny**
monalith	**mon·o·lith**	monotnous	**mo·not·o·nous**
monalogue	**mon·o·logue**	Monseigneur	**Mon·si·gnor**
monapolize	**mo·nop·o·lize**		*(Catholic title)*

WRONG	RIGHT
Monsignor	**Mon·sei·gneur** *(French title)*
monstrosaty	**mon·stros·i·ty**
monstrus	**mon·strous**
monsune	**mon·soon**
montaj	**mon·tage**
monthley	**month·ly**
monumentel	**mon·u·men·tal**
mony	**mon·ey**
mooce	**moose**
moodey	**moody**
mool	**mule**
moor	**more** *(additional)*
moosse	**mousse** *(food)*
moping	**mop·ping** *(washing)*
mopping	**mop·ing** *(sulking)*
moral	**mo·rale** *(spirit)*
moralaty	**mo·ral·i·ty**
morale	**mor·al** *(ethical)*
morall	**mo·rale** *(spirit)*
morallistic	**mor·al·is·tic**
morallity	**mo·ral·i·ty**
moran	**mo·ron**
moratoreum	**mor·a·to·ri·um**
morays	**mo·res**
morbed	**mor·bid**
morbidety	**mor·bid·i·ty**
morchuary	**mor·tu·ary**
more	**moor** *(secure a ship)*
morel	**mor·al** *(ethical)*
morelistick	**mor·al·is·tic**
morfine	**mor·phine**

WRONG	RIGHT
morgage	**mort·gage**
morge	**morgue**
moring	**moor·ing**
moritorium	**mor·a·to·ri·um**
Morman	**Mor·mon**
morning	**mourn·ing** *(grieving)*
morover	**more·over**
morphene	**mor·phine**
morral	**mor·al** *(ethical)*
morrale	**mo·rale** *(spirit)*
morrass	**mo·rass**
morratorium	**mor·a·to·ri·um**
morron	**mo·ron**
morrose	**mo·rose**
morsle	**mor·sel**
mortafy	**mor·ti·fy**
mortallity	**mor·tal·i·ty**
mortarbord	**mor·tar·board**
mortel	**mor·tal**
morter	**mor·tar**
mortgege	**mort·gage**
mortitian	**mor·ti·cian**
mortle	**mor·tal**
mortuery	**mor·tu·ary**
mosaick	**mo·sa·ic**
mosion	**mo·tion**
mosk	**mosque**
moskito	**mos·qui·to**
mossoleum	**mau·so·le·um**
motavate	**mo·ti·vate**
mote	**moat** *(ditch)*
moteef	**mo·tif**

WRONG	RIGHT	WRONG	RIGHT
motell	**mo·tel**	mownt	**mount**
moter	**mo·tor**	mowse	**mouse** (rodent)
motercade	**mo·tor·cade**	mowthful	**mouth·ful**
motiff	**mo·tif**	mowwing	**mow·ing**
motled	**mot·tled**	moysture	**mois·ture** (wetness)
motly	**mot·ley**	mozaic	**mo·sa·ic**
moto	**mot·to**	mozarella	**moz·za·rella**
motorcaid	**mo·tor·cade**	muchually	**mu·tu·al·ly**
motorcross	**mo·to·cross**	mucous	**mu·cus** (n.)
motorcykle	**mo·tor·cy·cle**	mucsle	**mus·cle** (brawn)
motorest	**mo·tor·ist**	mucus	**mu·cous** (adj.)
motsarella	**moz·za·rella**	muddey	**mud·dy**
mottel	**mo·tel**	mudey	**moody**
mottivate	**mo·ti·vate**	mudled	**mud·dled**
mottley	**mot·ley**	muffen	**muf·fin**
mouce	**mouse** (rodent)	mufler	**muf·fler**
mounteneer	**moun·tain·eer**	muger	**mug·ger**
mountin	**moun·tain**	muggey	**mug·gy**
mountnous	**moun·tain·ous**	mukraker	**muck·rak·er**
mournfull	**mourn·ful**	mulato	**mu·lat·to**
mourning	**morn·ing**	mulet	**mul·let**
	(part of day)	mullberry	**mul·ber·ry**
mouse	**mousse** (food)	mullish	**mul·ish**
mouthfull	**mouth·ful**	mullit	**mul·let**
move	**mauve** (purple)	multafarious	**mul·ti·far·i·ous**
moveing	**mov·ing**	multaple	**mul·ti·ple**
movemint	**move·ment**	multaplication	
movey	**mov·ie**		**mul·ti·pli·ca·tion**
movible	**mov·a·ble**	multaplicity	**mul·ti·plic·i·ty**
movment	**move·ment**	multatude	**mul·ti·tude**
mown	**moan** (groan)	multatudinous	
mownd	**mound**		**mul·ti·tu·di·nous**

WRONG	RIGHT	WRONG	RIGHT
multch	**mulch**	muscet	**mus·ket**
multifairious	**mul·ti·far·i·ous**	muscle	**mus·sel** *(shellfish)*
multipal	**mul·ti·ple**	muscrat	**musk·rat**
multiplacation		musculer	**mus·cu·lar**
	mul·ti·pli·ca·tion	museing	**mus·ing**
multiplisity	**mul·ti·plic·i·ty**	mushmelon	**musk·mel·on**
multitudanous		mushrum	**mush·room**
	mul·ti·tu·di·nous	musicall	**mu·si·cale**
mumbleing	**mum·bling**		*(social affair)*
mummyfy	**mum·mi·fy**	musick	**mu·sic**
mundain	**mun·dane**	musicle	**mu·si·cal** *(of music)*
Munday	**Mon·day**	musitian	**mu·si·cian**
munger	**mon·ger**	musium	**mu·se·um**
municipallity	**mu·nic·i·pal·i·ty**	muskatel	**mus·ca·tel**
municiple	**mu·nic·i·pal**	muskey	**musky**
munifisent	**munif·i·cent**	muskit	**mus·ket**
munisipality	**mu·nic·i·pal·i·ty**	muskmellon	**musk·mel·on**
munk	**monk**	muslen	**mus·lin**
munkey	**mon·key**	mussey	**mussy**
munnitions	**mu·ni·tions**	mussle	**mus·sel** *(shellfish)*
munth	**month**	mussle	**mus·cle** *(brawn)*
murcantile	**mer·can·tile**	mussmelon	**musk·mel·on**
murcurial	**mer·cu·ri·al**	mussrat	**musk·rat**
murcury	**mer·cu·ry**	mustache	**mus·tache**
murcy	**mer·cy**	musterd	**mus·tard**
murderus	**mur·der·ous**	mutanous	**mu·ti·nous**
murel	**mu·ral**	mute	**moot** *(debatable)*
murge	**merge**	muteable	**mu·ta·ble**
murkey	**murky**	mutent	**mu·tant**
murmer	**mur·mur**	muteny	**mu·ti·ny**
murral	**mu·ral**	muther	**moth·er**
murtle	**myr·tle**	mutible	**mu·ta·ble**

WRONG	RIGHT	WRONG	RIGHT
mutillate	**mu·ti·late**	naghty	**naugh·ty**
mutinus	**mu·ti·nous**	nagotiate	**ne·go·ti·ate**
mutten	**mut·ton**	naigh	**neigh** *(whinny)*
muttilate	**mu·ti·late**	naivte	**na·ive·té**
mutualy	**mu·tu·al·ly**	namly	**name·ly**
muzeum	**mu·se·um**	namsake	**name·sake**
muzic	**mu·sic**	nannie	**nan·ny**
muzical	**mu·si·cal** *(of music)*	naped	**napped**
muzle	**muz·zle**	napken	**nap·kin**
muzlin	**mus·lin**	napsack	**knap·sack**
myread	**myr·i·ad**	naration	**nar·ra·tion**
myrh	**myrrh**	narative	**nar·ra·tive**
myrtel	**myr·tle**	narator	**nar·ra·tor**
mystefy	**mys·ti·fy**	narcisism	**nar·cis·sism**
mysteke	**mys·tique**	naritive	**nar·ra·tive**
mysterius	**mys·te·ri·ous**	narkotic	**nar·cot·ic**
mystickal	**mys·ti·cal**	narled	**gnarled**
mystirious	**mys·te·ri·ous**	narow	**nar·row**
mystisism	**mys·ti·cism**	narrater	**nar·ra·tor**
mystry	**mys·tery**	narretive	**nar·ra·tive**
mythalogical	**myth·o·log·i·cal**	narsicism	**nar·cis·sism**
mythalogy	**my·thol·o·gy**	nasallize	**na·sal·ize**
mythicel	**myth·i·cal**	Nasau	**Nas·sau**
		nasel	**na·sal**
		nashing	**gnash·ing**
N		Nassaw	**Nas·sau**
		nastey	**nas·ty**
Nabraska	**Ne·bras·ka**	nat	**gnat**
nachure	**na·ture**	natave	**na·tive**
nack	**knack**	natel	**na·tal**
nader	**na·dir**	naterallize	**nat·u·ral·ize**
naeve	**na·ive**	naterally	**nat·u·ral·ly**
naevete	**na·ive·té**		

natetorium	**nata·to·ri·um**	nawtical	**nau·ti·cal**
natianally	**nation·al·ly**	nay	**neigh** (whinny)
natily	**nat·ti·ly**	nay	**nee** (f.; born)
nationallistic	**nation·al·is·tic**	nazel	**na·sal**
nationallity	**nation·al·i·ty**	Nazereth	**Naz·a·reth**
nationallize	**nation·al·ize**	Nazie	**Na·zi**
nationaly	**nation·al·ly**	nead	**knead** (work dough)
nativety	**na·tiv·i·ty**	neaded	**need·ed** (required)
nattally	**nat·ti·ly**	nealism	**ni·hil·ism**
nattivity	**na·tiv·i·ty**	nean	**ne·on**
natur	**na·ture**	Neanderthol	**Nean·der·thal**
naturallize	**nat·u·ral·ize**	neaphyte	**ne·o·phyte**
naturely	**nat·u·ral·ly**	Neapollitan	**Nea·pol·i·tan**
naturralist	**nat·u·ral·ist**	neatenning	**neat·en·ing**
nausiate	**nau·se·ate**	nebulla	**neb·u·la**
nausious	**nau·seous**	nebullous	**neb·u·lous**
nauticle	**nau·ti·cal**	necesary	**nec·es·sary**
nauty	**naugh·ty**	necesity	**ne·ces·si·ty**
Navada	**Ne·vada**	necessarally	**nec·es·sar·i·ly**
navagation	**nav·i·ga·tion**	neckercheif	**neck·er·chief**
navagible	**nav·i·ga·ble**	neckless	**neck·lace**
naval	**na·vel** (umbilicus)	necktarine	**nec·tar·ine**
nave	**knave** (rogue)	necsesary	**nec·es·sary**
navegator	**nav·i·ga·tor**	necter	**nec·tar**
Naveho	**Nav·a·ho**	necterine	**nec·tar·ine**
navel	**na·val** (of a navy)	nee	**knee**
navery	**knav·ery**	nee	**né** (m.; born)
navice	**nov·ice**	need	**knead** (work dough)
navigater	**nav·i·ga·tor**	neel	**kneel**
navish	**knav·ish**	nefew	**neph·ew**
navvigation	**nav·i·ga·tion**	neggation	**ne·ga·tion**
nawing	**gnaw·ing**	neggative	**neg·a·tive**

WRONG	RIGHT	WRONG	RIGHT
neggotiate	**ne·go·ti·ate**	neted	**net·ted**
neghbor	**neigh·bor**	nether	**nei·ther** *(not either)*
negitive	**neg·a·tive**	Nethorlands	**Neth·er·lands**
neglagible	**neg·li·gi·ble**	netled	**net·tled**
negleck	**neg·lect**	netwark	**net·work**
neglectfull	**neg·lect·ful**	neuance	**nu·ance**
neglegee	**neg·li·gee**	neumatic	**pneu·mat·ic**
negligable	**neg·li·gi·ble**	neumonia	**pneu·mo·nia**
negligance	**neg·li·gence**	neurallgia	**neu·ral·gia**
neglige	**neg·li·gee**	neurollogy	**neu·rol·o·gy**
neice	**niece**	neuroses	**neu·ro·sis** *(sing.)*
neighber	**neigh·bor**	neurosis	**neu·ro·ses** *(pl.)*
neither	**neth·er** *(lower)*	neurottic	**neu·rot·ic**
neklace	**neck·lace**	neute	**newt**
nektar	**nec·tar**	neuteron	**neu·tron**
nell	**knell**	neutrallity	**neu·tral·i·ty**
nemeses	**nem·e·sis** *(sing.)*	neutrallize	**neu·tral·ize**
nemesis	**nem·e·ses** *(pl.)*	neutril	**neu·tral**
nemonic	**mne·mon·ic**	nevertheless	**nev·er·the·less**
neophite	**ne·o·phyte**	New Jersy	**New Jer·sey**
Neopolitan	**Nea·pol·i·tan**	newliwed	**new·ly·wed**
nepatism	**nep·o·tism**	New Orleens	**New Or·le·ans**
neralgia	**neu·ral·gia**	newral	**neu·ral**
neroses	**neu·ro·ses** *(pl.)*	newveau riche	**nou·veau riche**
nerration	**nar·ra·tion**		
nerture	**nur·ture**	New Zeeland	**New Zea·land**
nervana	**nir·va·na**	nexous	**nex·us**
nervey	**nervy**	ney	**nee** *(f.; born)*
nervus	**nerv·ous**	ney	**nay** *(no)*
nesesary	**nec·es·sary**	ney	**neigh** *(whinny)*
nesesity	**ne·ces·si·ty**	Niagera	**Ni·ag·a·ra**
nessle	**nes·tle**	nialism	**ni·hil·ism**

nibbeling	**nib·bling**	niped	**nipped**
nicatine	**nic·o·tine**	nippel	**nip·ple**
niceaty	**ni·ce·ty**	nitch	**niche**
Niceragua	**Nic·a·ra·gua**	nitragen	**ni·tro·gen**
nich	**niche**	nitraglycerin	**ni·tro·glyc·er·in**
nickers	**knick·ers** *(short pants)*	nitrait	**ni·trate**
nickknack	**knick·knack**	nitrick	**ni·tric**
nickle	**nick·el**	nitroglisserin	**ni·tro·glyc·er·in**
nickotine	**nic·o·tine**	nittie–grittie	**nit·ty–grit·ty**
nicks	**nix** *(disapprove of)*	nitting	**knit·ting**
nie	**nigh**	nittwit	**nit·wit**
nieghbor	**neigh·bor**	niusance	**nui·sance**
niese	**niece**	nives	**knives** *(pl.)*
niether	**nei·ther** *(not either)*	Noa	**No·ah**
nieve	**na·ive**	nobby	**knob·by**
nife	**knife** *(sing.)*	nobel	**no·ble**
nigation	**ne·ga·tion**	nobeler	**no·bler**
night	**knight** *(rank)*	nobelman	**no·ble·man**
nightengale	**night·in·gale**	nobillity	**no·bil·i·ty**
nightime	**night·time**	Noble	**No·bel**
nightmair	**night·mare**	nobley	**no·bly**
niglect	**neg·lect**	nock	**knock** *(rap)*
nihalism	**ni·hil·ism**	nockout	**knock·out**
nikname	**nick·name**	nockwurst	**knack·wurst**
nikotine	**nic·o·tine**	nocternal	**noc·tur·nal**
nilon	**ny·lon**	nodjule	**nod·ule**
nimbley	**nim·bly**	Noell	**No·el**
nimph	**nymph**	noisally	**nois·i·ly**
ninconpoop	**nin·com·poop**	noisey	**noisy**
ninteen	**nine·teen**	noissome	**noi·some**
nintieth	**nine·ti·eth**	nomanee	**nom·i·nee**
ninty	**nine·ty**	nome	**gnome**

nominaly	**nom·i·nal·ly**
nominnation	**nom·i·na·tion**
nommad	**no·mad**
nomminally	**nom·i·nal·ly**
nommination	**nom·i·na·tion**
nomminee	**nom·i·nee**
non	**none**
noncense	**non·sense**
nonchallance	**non·cha·lance**
noncomittal	**non·com·mit·tal**
nonconformest	**non·con·form·ist**
nondiscrept	**non·de·script**
nonpariel	**non·pa·reil**
nonpartesan	**non·par·ti·san**
nonpluss	**non·plus**
nonprofet	**non·prof·it**
nonsence	**non·sense**
nonsensecal	**non·sen·si·cal**
non sequiter	**non se·qui·tur**
nonshalance	**non·cha·lance**
nontheless	**none·the·less**
nonuclear	**non·nu·cle·ar**
noodel	**noo·dle**
noogat	**nou·gat** *(confection)*
nooter	**neu·ter**
nootrient	**nu·tri·ent**
nootritionally	**nutri·tion·al·ly**
nootritous	**nutri·tious**
Nordick	**Nor·dic**
norishment	**nour·ish·ment**
normallity	**nor·mal·i·ty**

normallize	**nor·mal·ize**
normalsy	**nor·mal·cy**
normelly	**nor·mal·ly**
northurn	**north·ern**
northword	**north·ward**
Norwejian	**Nor·we·gian**
nostallgia	**nos·tal·gia**
nostrel	**nos·tril**
notabley	**no·ta·bly**
notafication	**noti·fi·ca·tion**
notariety	**no·to·ri·e·ty**
notarrize	**no·ta·rize**
noteably	**no·ta·bly**
notefy	**no·ti·fy**
noteriety	**no·to·ri·e·ty**
noterize	**no·ta·rize**
notery	**no·ta·ry**
noticably	**notice·a·bly**
notical	**nau·ti·cal**
noticeing	**no·tic·ing**
notifacation	**noti·fi·ca·tion**
notoriaty	**no·to·ri·e·ty**
notorrious	**no·to·ri·ous**
notted	**knot·ted**
notworthy	**note·wor·thy**
nougat	**nug·get** *(lump)*
novellet	**nov·el·ette**
novellist	**nov·el·ist**
novilty	**nov·el·ty**
nowere	**no·where**
noxous	**nox·ious**
nozle	**noz·zle**

WRONG	RIGHT	WRONG	RIGHT
nu	**gnu**	nurishment	**nour·ish·ment**
nuckle	**knuck·le**	nuritis	**neu·ri·tis**
nucleas	**nu·cle·us**	nurology	**neu·rol·o·gy**
nucular	**nu·cle·ar**	nurrosis	**neu·ro·sis** *(sing.)*
nuculus	**nu·cle·us**	nurrotic	**neu·rot·ic**
nudety	**nu·di·ty**	nurseing	**nurs·ing**
nudgeing	**nudg·ing**	nursmaid	**nurse·maid**
nuence	**nu·ance**	nursrey	**nurs·ery**
nueral	**neu·ral**	nusance	**nui·sance**
nueron	**neu·ron**	nute	**newt**
nuerosis	**neu·ro·sis** *(sing.)*	nuter	**neu·ter**
nueter	**neu·ter**	nutreant	**nu·tri·ent**
nuetral	**neu·tral**	nutricious	**nutri·tious**
nuetron	**neu·tron**	nutritionaly	**nutri·tion·al·ly**
nugget	**nou·gat** *(confection)*	nuveau riche	**nou·veau riche**
nuggit	**nug·get** *(lump)*	nylong	**ny·lon**
nuging	**nudg·ing**	nymf	**nymph**
nuisence	**nui·sance**		
nukleer	**nu·cle·ar**		
nukleus	**nu·cle·us**	**O**	
nulify	**nul·li·fy**		
num	**numb**	oad	**ode**
numarel	**nu·mer·al**	oakan	**oak·en**
numbor	**num·ber**	oar	**ore** *(mineral)*
numerater	**nu·mer·a·tor**	oases	**oa·sis** *(sing.)*
numerrical	**nu·mer·i·cal**	oasis	**oa·ses** *(pl.)*
numerus	**nu·mer·ous**	oatmeel	**oat·meal**
nummeral	**nu·mer·al**	obalisk	**ob·e·lisk**
nummerical	**nu·mer·i·cal**	obasance	**obei·sance**
nummskull	**num·skull**	obay	**obey**
nuptual	**nup·tial**	obbelisk	**ob·e·lisk**
nurchure	**nur·ture**	obbese	**obese**
		obbituary	**obit·u·ary**

WRONG	RIGHT	WRONG	RIGHT
obbligatory	**ob·lig·a·to·ry**	observent	**ob·serv·ant**
obblivion	**ob·liv·i·on**	observible	**ob·serv·a·ble**
obece	**obese**	observitory	**ob·serv·a·to·ry**
obediance	**obe·di·ence**	obsesion	**ob·ses·sion**
obediant	**obe·di·ent**	obsesive	**ob·ses·sive**
obeisence	**obei·sance**	obsidean	**ob·sid·i·an**
obeyance	**abey·ance**	obsiquies	**ob·se·quies**
obeysance	**obei·sance**	obsolescense	**ob·so·les·cence**
obichuary	**obit·u·ary**	obsolessent	**ob·so·les·cent**
objeck	**ob·ject**	obstanately	**ob·sti·nate·ly**
objecktion	**ob·jec·tion**	obstatrician	**ob·ste·tri·cian**
objectionible	**ob·jec·tion·a·ble**	obstetricks	**ob·stet·rics**
objectivety	**ob·jec·tiv·i·ty**	obstickle	**ob·sta·cle**
oblagation	**ob·li·ga·tion**	obstinasy	**ob·sti·na·cy**
obleke	**ob·lique**	obstinatly	**ob·sti·nate·ly**
obligeing	**oblig·ing**	obstruck	**ob·struct**
obligetory	**ob·lig·a·to·ry**	obstrucktion	**ob·struc·tion**
oblije	**oblige**	obsurvation	**ob·ser·va·tion**
oblitterate	**ob·lit·er·ate**	obtane	**ob·tain**
obliveon	**ob·liv·i·on**	obtoose	**ob·tuse**
oblivious	**ob·liv·i·ous**	obtrussive	**ob·tru·sive**
obnoctious	**ob·nox·ious**	obveate	**ob·vi·ate**
obow	**oboe**	obveous	**ob·vi·ous**
obsalescent	**ob·so·les·cent**	obvurse	**ob·verse**
obsalete	**ob·so·lete**	obzervable	**ob·serv·a·ble**
obscenaty	**ob·scen·i·ty**	obzervation	**ob·ser·va·tion**
obscuraty	**ob·scu·ri·ty**	occasionly	**oc·ca·sion·al·ly**
obseckwies	**ob·se·quies**	occassion	**oc·ca·sion**
obsene	**ob·scene**	occelot	**oce·lot**
obsenity	**ob·scen·i·ty**	occidentel	**oc·ci·den·tal**
obsequius	**ob·se·qui·ous**	occular	**oc·u·lar**
observence	**ob·serv·ance**	occupansy	**oc·cu·pan·cy**

WRONG	RIGHT	WRONG	RIGHT
occupent	**oc·cu·pant**	o da cologne	**eau de Co·logne**
occupie	**oc·cu·py**		
occured	**oc·curred**	oddaty	**odd·i·ty**
occuring	**oc·cur·ring**	oddometer	**odom·e·ter**
occurrance	**oc·cur·rence**	oddyssey	**od·ys·sey**
oceanagraphy	**oce·an·og·ra·phy**	odeous	**odi·ous**
		oder	**odor**
oceanick	**oce·an·ic**	oderus	**odor·ous**
ocellot	**oce·lot**	Odisseus	**Odys·se·us**
ocian	**ocean**	odissey	**od·ys·sey**
ocktagon	**oc·ta·gon**	odity	**odd·i·ty**
ocktane	**oc·tane**	odius	**odi·ous**
Ocktober	**Oc·to·ber**	odrous	**odor·ous**
ocktopus	**oc·to·pus**	Odyseus	**Odys·se·us**
oclock	**o'clock**	odyssy	**od·ys·sey**
oclusion	**oc·clu·sion**	Oedapus	**Oed·i·pus**
ocra	**okra**	ofal	**of·fal**
ocsidental	**oc·ci·den·tal**	ofe	**oaf**
ocsillate	**os·cil·late**	ofend	**of·fend**
octain	**oc·tane**	ofense	**of·fense**
octapus	**oc·to·pus**	ofensive	**of·fen·sive**
octive	**oc·tave**	ofer	**of·fer**
octogon	**oc·ta·gon**	ofering	**of·fer·ing**
oculer	**oc·u·lar**	offace	**of·fice**
ocult	**oc·cult**	offel	**of·fal**
ocupancy	**oc·cu·pan·cy**	offen	**of·ten**
ocupant	**oc·cu·pant**	offerring	**of·fer·ing**
ocupational	**oc·cu·pa·tion·al**	officiery	**of·fi·ci·ary**
ocupy	**oc·cu·py**	officius	**of·fi·cious**
ocurred	**oc·curred**	offiser	**of·fi·cer**
ocurrence	**oc·cur·rence**	offishal	**of·fi·cial**
ocurring	**oc·cur·ring**	offishiary	**of·fi·ci·ary**

WRONG	RIGHT	WRONG	RIGHT
offishiate	**of·fi·ci·ate**	Olympicks	**Olym·pics**
oficer	**of·fi·cer**	ombudzman	**om·buds·man**
oficial	**of·fi·cial**	ome	**ohm**
oficiary	**of·fi·ci·ary**	omellet	**om·e·let**
oficiate	**of·fi·ci·ate**	omenous	**om·i·nous**
oficious	**of·fi·cious**	omin	**omen**
ofing	**off·ing**	omision	**omis·sion**
ofset	**off·set**	omiting	**omit·ting**
oftin	**of·ten**	omlet	**om·e·let**
oger	**ogre**	ommen	**omen**
oggled	**ogled**	omminous	**om·i·nous**
ohem	**ohm**	ommision	**omis·sion**
oiller	**oil·er**	omnabus	**om·ni·bus**
oilly	**oily**	omnipitence	**om·nip·o·tence**
ointmint	**oint·ment**	omnipotant	**om·nip·o·tent**
oister	**oys·ter**	omnisciance	**om·nis·cience**
oke	**oak** *(tree)*	omnisciant	**om·nis·cient**
oker	**ocher**	omniverous	**om·niv·o·rous**
okre	**okra**	onamatopoeia	
olagarchy	**ol·i·gar·chy**		**on·o·mat·o·poe·ia**
oldin	**old·en**	oncore	**en·core**
oleomargerine		one	**won** *(pt. of win)*
	ole·o·mar·ga·rine	onerus	**on·er·ous**
olfactry	**ol·fac·to·ry**	oness	**onus**
oligarky	**ol·i·gar·chy**	onesself	**one·self**
Olimpics	**Olym·pics**	onian	**on·ion**
oliomargarine		onix	**on·yx**
	ole·o·mar·ga·rine	onley	**on·ly**
ollfactory	**ol·fac·to·ry**	onomatapoeia	
olligarchy	**ol·i·gar·chy**		**on·o·mat·o·poe·ia**
ollive	**ol·ive**	onorous	**on·er·ous**
ol–timer	**old–tim·er**	on route	**en route**

WRONG	RIGHT	WRONG	RIGHT
onse	**once**	oportunism	**op·por·tun·ism**
onsemble	**en·sem·ble**	oportunity	**op·por·tu·ni·ty**
onslot	**on·slaught**	oposite	**op·po·site**
ontourage	**en·tou·rage**	opossition	**op·po·si·tion**
ontray	**en·tree**	opp	**opt**
onvoy	**en·voy**	oppalescent	**opal·es·cent**
onword	**on·ward**	oppaque	**opaque**
onyon	**on·ion**	oppen	**open**
oozo	**ou·zo**	oppera	**op·era**
opake	**opaque**	opperant	**op·er·ant**
opalessent	**opal·es·cent**	opperate	**op·er·ate**
opasity	**opac·i·ty**	opperational	**op·er·a·tion·al**
opeate	**opi·ate**	opperetta	**op·er·et·ta**
opel	**opal**	oppertune	**op·por·tune**
openner	**open·er**	oppertunity	**op·por·tu·ni·ty**
openning	**open·ing**	oppinion	**opin·ion**
operater	**op·er·a·tor**	opponant	**op·po·nent**
operatick	**op·er·at·ic**	opportuneism	**op·por·tun·ism**
operationel	**op·er·a·tion·al**	opposeable	**op·pos·a·ble**
operent	**op·er·ant**	opposeing	**op·pos·ing**
opereta	**op·er·et·ta**	opposission	**op·po·si·tion**
operible	**op·er·a·ble**	oppossite	**op·po·site**
opes	**opus**	oppossum	**opos·sum**
opeum	**opi·um**	oppresed	**op·pressed**
ophthamology	**oph·thal·mol·o·gy**	oppresion	**op·pres·sion**
opiam	**opi·um**	oppresser	**op·pres·sor**
opin	**open**	opprobrius	**op·pro·bri·ous**
opinian	**opin·ion**	oppulent	**op·u·lent**
opinionnated	**opin·ion·at·ed**	opra	**op·era**
oponent	**op·po·nent**	oprable	**op·er·a·ble**
oportune	**op·por·tune**	opratic	**op·er·at·ic**
		oprative	**op·er·a·tive**

147

WRONG	RIGHT	WRONG	RIGHT
opressed	**op·pressed**	orcesstra	**or·ches·tra**
opression	**op·pres·sion**	orched	**or·chid**
oprobrious	**op·pro·bri·ous**	orcherd	**or·chard**
opsional	**op·tion·al**	orchestrel	**or·ches·tral**
optacal	**op·ti·cal**	orchistra	**or·ches·tra**
optamal	**op·ti·mal**	orcid	**or·chid**
optamism	**op·ti·mism**	ordanal	**or·di·nal**
optamistic	**op·ti·mis·tic**	ordanance	**or·di·nance**
opthalmology			*(regulation)*
	oph·thal·mol·o·gy	ordanarily	**or·di·nar·i·ly**
optick	**op·tic**	ordanary	**or·di·nary**
opticle	**op·ti·cal**	ordanation	**or·di·na·tion**
optimel	**op·ti·mal**	ordane	**or·dain**
optimistick	**op·ti·mis·tic**	ordeel	**or·deal**
optimizm	**op·ti·mism**	orderley	**or·der·ly**
optionel	**op·tion·al**	ordinance	**ord·nance**
optitian	**op·ti·cian**		*(military weapons)*
optomatrist	**op·tom·e·trist**	ordinaraly	**or·di·nar·i·ly**
optomology		ordnance	**or·di·nance**
	oph·thal·mol·o·gy		*(regulation)*
opulant	**op·u·lent**	ordnarily	**or·di·nar·i·ly**
or	**oar** *(paddle)*	ordnary	**or·di·nary**
or	**ore** *(mineral)*	ordnation	**or·di·na·tion**
oracal	**or·a·cle** *(wise person)*	ordnence	**ord·nance**
orafice	**or·i·fice**		*(military weapons)*
oragin	**or·i·gin**	ore	**oar** *(paddle)*
oral	**au·ral** *(of the ear)*	ore	**or** *(conj.)*
orangatan	**orang·u·tan**	ore d'oeuvre	**hors d'oeu·vre**
orateing	**orat·ing**	oregeno	**oreg·a·no**
orater	**or·a·tor**	oreintal	**ori·en·tal**
oratoricle	**ora·tor·i·cal**	oreintate	**ori·en·tate**
orbet	**or·bit**	orel	**oral** *(of the mouth)*

WRONG	RIGHT	WRONG	RIGHT
orenge	**or·ange**	orregano	**oreg·a·no**
orfan	**or·phan**	orthadontist	**or·tho·don·tist**
organazation	**or·gan·i·za·tion**	orthadox	**or·tho·dox**
organick	**or·gan·ic**	orthapedics	**or·tho·pe·dics**
organizeing	**or·gan·iz·ing**	oscilate	**os·cil·late**
organizm	**or·gan·ism**	oscillater	**os·cil·la·tor**
orgazm	**or·gasm**	oseanic	**oce·an·ic**
orgeastic	**or·gi·as·tic**	oselot	**oce·lot**
orgen	**or·gan**	oshean	**ocean**
orgendy	**or·gan·dy**	osmossis	**os·mo·sis**
orgenism	**or·gan·ism**	ossafy	**os·si·fy**
orgenization	**or·gan·i·za·tion**	ossillate	**os·cil·late**
orgiastick	**or·gi·as·tic**	osstensible	**os·ten·si·ble**
oriantal	**ori·en·tal**	osstentatious	**os·ten·ta·tious**
oriantate	**ori·en·tate**	osteapath	**os·te·o·path**
oricle	**or·a·cle** *(wise person)*	ostensable	**os·ten·si·ble**
oriface	**or·i·fice**	ostentatius	**os·ten·ta·tious**
origanal	**orig·i·nal**	ostiopath	**os·te·o·path**
origen	**or·i·gin**	ostrasize	**os·tra·cize**
origenate	**orig·i·nate**	ostritch	**os·trich**
originallity	**orig·i·nal·i·ty**	otemeal	**oat·meal**
originaly	**orig·i·nal·ly**	oter	**ot·ter**
originel	**orig·i·nal**	othe	**oath**
Origon	**Or·e·gon**	Ottowa	**Ot·ta·wa**
orjiastic	**or·gi·as·tic**	ouht	**ought**
orjy	**or·gy**	oul	**owl**
ornamint	**or·na·ment**	ounse	**ounce**
ornry	**or·nery**	outragious	**out·ra·geous**
orphanege	**or·phan·age**	outriger	**out·rig·ger**
orphen	**or·phan**	outter	**out·er**
orrangutang	**orang·u·tan**	outting	**out·ing**
orratorical	**ora·tor·i·cal**	outword	**out·ward**

WRONG	*RIGHT*
ouze	**ooze**
ovature	**over·ture**
ovel	**oval**
overals	**over·alls**
overate	**over·rate**
	(rate too highly)
overawd	**over·awed**
overbering	**over·bear·ing**
overbord	**over·board**
overchure	**over·ture**
overlaping	**over·lap·ping**
overrought	**over·wrought**
overule	**over·rule**
overun	**over·run**
overwelm	**over·whelm**
overy	**ova·ry**
oveture	**over·ture**
ovewlation	**ovu·la·tion**
ovin	**ov·en**
ovry	**ova·ry**
ovuler	**ovu·lar**
ovullation	**ovu·la·tion**
ovurt	**overt**
oweing	**ow·ing**
owllish	**owl·ish**
ownce	**ounce**
ownly	**on·ly**
owst	**oust**
owter	**out·er**
oxedation	**ox·i·da·tion**
oxferd	**ox·ford**
oxidental	**oc·ci·den·tal**

WRONG	*RIGHT*
oxigen	**ox·y·gen**
oxydation	**ox·i·da·tion**
oze	**ooze**
ozmosis	**os·mo·sis**
ozzone	**ozone**

P

WRONG	*RIGHT*
pacefier	**pac·i·fi·er**
pacefist	**pac·i·fist**
pachiderm	**pach·y·derm**
pack	**pact** *(agreement)*
packedge	**pack·age**
packyderm	**pach·y·derm**
paddel	**pad·dle**
paddeling	**pad·dling**
paddy	**pat·ty** *(cake)*
padock	**pad·dock**
pageantrey	**pag·eant·ry**
pagen	**pa·gan**
pagenation	**pag·i·na·tion**
pagent	**pag·eant**
pail	**pale** *(white)*
pain	**pane** *(window)*
painfull	**pain·ful**
pair	**pare** *(trim)*
pair	**pear** *(fruit)*
pairody	**par·o·dy**
pajammas	**pa·ja·mas**
Pakestan	**Pa·ki·stan**
palacial	**pa·la·tial**
palate	**pal·let** *(bed; platform)*

WRONG	RIGHT	WRONG	RIGHT
palate	**pal·ette** *(paint board)*	papreka	**pa·pri·ka**
pale	**pail** *(bucket)*	paradice	**par·a·dise**
paletable	**pal·at·a·ble**	paradime	**par·a·digm**
palette	**pal·ate** *(roof of mouth)*	parady	**par·o·dy**
palette	**pal·let** *(bed; platform)*	parafin	**par·af·fin**
Palistine	**Pal·es·tine**	paralel	**par·al·lel**
pallace	**pal·ace**	paralize	**par·a·lyze**
paller	**pal·lor**	parallysis	**pa·ral·y·sis**
Pallestine	**Pal·es·tine**	parameter	**pe·rim·e·ter**
pallet	**pal·ate** *(roof of mouth)*		*(boundary)*
palletible	**pal·at·a·ble**	paraphenalia	
pallette	**pal·ette** *(paint board)*		**par·a·pher·na·lia**
pallsy	**pal·sy**	parden	**par·don**
palmestry	**palm·is·try**	pare	**pair** *(two)*
palpatate	**pal·pi·tate**	pare	**pear** *(fruit)*
palpible	**pal·pa·ble**	pareble	**par·a·ble**
palsey	**pal·sy**	paredigm	**par·a·digm**
paltrey	**pal·try** *(trifling)*	parefenalia	**par·a·pher·na·lia**
paltry	**poul·try** *(fowls)*	paregaric	**par·e·gor·ic**
pamflit	**pam·phlet**	paregraph	**par·a·graph**
panarama	**pan·o·ra·ma**	Pareguay	**Par·a·guay**
pancrias	**pan·cre·as**	parentheses	**pa·ren·the·sis**
pane	**pain** *(hurt)*		*(sing.)*
paned	**panned** *(pt. of pan)*	parenthesis	**pa·ren·the·ses**
panellist	**pan·el·ist**		*(pl.)*
paniking	**pan·ick·ing**	paresite	**par·a·site**
pannel	**pan·el**	parfay	**par·fait**
pansie	**pan·sy**	paridise	**par·a·dise**
pantamine	**pan·to·mime**	paridox	**par·a·dox**
paper–maché	**pa·pier–mâ·ché**	pariffin	**par·af·fin**
pappal	**pa·pal**	parigon	**par·a·gon**
pappaya	**pa·pa·ya**	parikeet	**par·a·keet**

WRONG	RIGHT	WRONG	RIGHT
parimount	**par·a·mount**	parrity	**par·i·ty**
parinoia	**par·a·noia**	parsel	**par·cel**
parish	**per·ish** (die)	parsen	**par·son**
parishute	**par·a·chute**	parsly	**pars·ley**
parisol	**par·a·sol**	partecle	**par·ti·cle**
paritrooper	**par·a·troop·er**	partesan	**par·ti·san**
parkay	**par·quet**	partiallity	**par·ti·al·i·ty**
parlay	**par·ley** (confer)	partialy	**par·tial·ly**
parler	**par·lor**	participial	**par·ti·ci·ple** (n.)
parley	**par·lay** (bet)	participle	**par·ti·cip·i·al** (adj.)
parliment	**par·lia·ment**	particuler	**par·tic·u·lar**
parocheal	**pa·ro·chi·al**	partime	**part–time**
parolled	**pa·roled**	partisipant	**par·tic·i·pant**
parot	**par·rot**	partisipeal	**par·ti·cip·i·al** (adj.)
parrable	**par·a·ble**	partisiple	**par·ti·ci·ple** (n.)
parrachute	**par·a·chute**	partrige	**par·tridge**
parrade	**pa·rade**	paruse	**pe·ruse**
parradox	**par·a·dox**	pasable	**pass·a·ble**
parragon	**par·a·gon**	pasage	**pas·sage**
parragraph	**par·a·graph**	pasay	**pas·sé**
parrakeet	**par·a·keet**	Pasedena	**Pas·a·de·na**
parralel	**par·al·lel**	pasemaker	**pace·mak·er**
parralysis	**pa·ral·y·sis**	pasenger	**pas·sen·ger**
parralyze	**par·a·lyze**	Pasific	**Pa·cif·ic**
parrameter	**pa·ram·e·ter**	pasionnate	**pas·sion·ate**
	(math constant)	pasive	**pas·sive**
parramount	**par·a·mount**	pasport	**pass·port**
parranoia	**par·a·noia**	passanger	**pas·sen·ger**
parraphrase	**par·a·phrase**	passed	**past** (over; beyond)
parrasol	**par·a·sol**	passege	**pas·sage**
parrental	**pa·ren·tal**	passeve	**pas·sive**
parret	**par·rot**	passible	**pass·a·ble**

WRONG	RIGHT	WRONG	RIGHT
passifier	**pac·i·fi·er**	patriat	**pa·tri·ot**
passifist	**pac·i·fist**	patrinagee	**pa·tron·age**
passionite	**pas·sion·ate**	patroleum	**pe·tro·le·um**
passtel	**pas·tel**	patroling	**pa·trol·ling**
passteurize	**pas·teur·ize**	patronnage	**pa·tron·age**
passtime	**pas·time**	patronnize	**pa·tron·ize**
passtrami	**pas·tra·mi**	pattent	**pat·ent**
past	**passed** (pt. of pass)	patternal	**pa·ter·nal**
paster	**pas·ture** (field)	pattriotic	**pa·tri·ot·ic**
paster	**pas·tor** (clergyman)	patturn	**pat·tern**
pasteral	**pas·to·ral**	patty	**pad·dy** (rice)
pastesh	**pas·tiche**	paun	**pawn**
pastor	**pas·ture** (field)	paverty	**pov·er·ty**
pastrey	**pas·try**	pavillion	**pa·vil·ion**
pastural	**pas·to·ral**	payible	**pay·a·ble**
pasture	**pas·tor** (clergyman)	peacan	**pe·can**
pastureize	**pas·teur·ize**	peace	**piece** (part)
patassium	**po·tas·si·um**	peacefull	**peace·ful**
pateo	**pa·tio**	peacemeal	**piece·meal**
patern	**pat·tern**	peak	**peek** (glance)
paternize	**pa·tron·ize**	peak	**pique** (offend)
pathas	**pa·thos**	peal	**peel** (skin)
pathelogical	**path·o·log·i·cal**	peany	**pe·o·ny**
patholegist	**pa·thol·o·gist**	pear	**pare** (trim)
pathollogical	**path·o·log·i·cal**	pear	**pair** (two)
patience	**pa·tients**	pearce	**pierce**
	(pl. of patient)	pearl	**purl** (stitch)
patients	**pa·tience**	peasantrey	**peas·ant·ry**
	(endurance)	peasent	**peas·ant**
patition	**pe·ti·tion**	peble	**peb·ble**
patrearch	**pa·tri·arch**	pecon	**pe·can**
patren	**pa·tron**	peculierity	**pecu·li·ar·i·ty**

WRONG	RIGHT
pedagree	**ped·i·gree**
pedal	**ped·dle** *(sell)*
peddeler	**ped·dler**
peddestal	**ped·es·tal**
peddestrian	**pe·des·tri·an**
peddle	**ped·al** *(foot lever)*
pedeatrician	**pe·di·a·tri·cian**
pedistal	**ped·es·tal**
peech	**peach**
peecock	**pea·cock**
peek	**peak** *(summit)*
peek	**pique** *(offend)*
peel	**peal** *(a ringing)*
peenut	**pea·nut**
peeple	**peo·ple**
peer	**pier** *(structure)*
peice	**piece** *(part)*
peir	**pier** *(structure)*
peirce	**pierce**
pejoritive	**pejo·ra·tive**
pelet	**pel·let**
pellican	**pel·i·can**
pellit	**pel·let**
pelvas	**pel·vis**
penacillin	**pen·i·cil·lin**
penall	**pe·nal**
penallize	**pe·nal·ize**
penant	**pen·nant**
penatentiary	**pen·i·ten·tia·ry**
pencel	**pen·cil** *(writing instrument)*
penchent	**pen·chant**

WRONG	RIGHT
pendullum	**pen·du·lum**
pengwin	**pen·guin**
penicilin	**pen·i·cil·lin**
penitentiery	**pen·i·ten·tia·ry**
penitration	**pen·e·tra·tion**
pennalize	**pe·nal·ize**
pennalty	**pen·al·ty**
pennance	**pen·ance**
pennent	**pen·nant**
pennetration	**pen·e·tra·tion**
pennicillin	**pen·i·cil·lin**
penninsula	**pen·in·su·la**
Pennsilvania	**Penn·syl·va·nia**
pensave	**pen·sive**
Pentacostal	**Pen·te·cos·tal**
pentamiter	**pen·tam·e·ter**
Pentatuch	**Pen·ta·teuch**
pentigon	**pen·ta·gon**
pention	**pen·sion**
peonie	**pe·o·ny**
pepermint	**pep·per·mint**
peragoric	**par·e·gor·ic**
perascope	**per·i·scope**
peratrooper	**par·a·troop·er**
percarious	**pre·car·i·ous**
percaution	**pre·cau·tion**
percedure	**pro·ce·dure**
perceed	**pro·ceed** *(go on)*
perceiveable	**per·ceiv·a·ble**
perceptably	**per·cep·ti·bly**
percession	**pre·ces·sion** *(precedence)*

WRONG	RIGHT
percession	**pro·ces·sion**
	(parade)
perchase	**pur·chase**
percieve	**per·ceive**
percipitation	**pre·cip·i·ta·tion**
percise	**pre·cise** *(definite)*
percision	**pre·ci·sion**
perclaim	**pro·claim**
perclude	**pre·clude**
percocious	**pre·co·cious**
percollator	**per·co·la·tor**
percure	**pro·cure**
percursor	**pre·cur·sor**
percushion	**per·cus·sion**
perdicament	**pre·dic·a·ment**
perdiction	**pre·dic·tion**
perdigious	**pro·di·gious**
perdominant	**pre·dom·i·nant**
perducer	**pro·duc·er**
perduction	**pro·duc·tion**
perelous	**per·il·ous**
perenial	**per·en·ni·al**
perenthesis	**pa·ren·the·sis**
	(sing.)
perfectable	**per·fect·i·ble**
perferate	**per·fo·rate**
perfess	**pro·fess**
perfessional	**pro·fes·sion·al**
perficient	**pro·fi·cient**
performence	**per·form·ance**
perfusion	**pro·fu·sion**
pergatory	**pur·ga·to·ry**

WRONG	RIGHT
pergressive	**pro·gres·sive**
perhibit	**pro·hib·it**
perifery	**pe·riph·ery**
perillous	**per·il·ous**
perimedic	**par·a·med·ic**
perimeter	**pa·ram·e·ter**
	(math constant)
perinoia	**par·a·noia**
perioddical	**pe·ri·od·i·cal**
peripharel	**pe·riph·er·al**
periphary	**pe·riph·ery**
perish	**par·ish** *(church district)*
perjection	**pro·jec·tion**
perjector	**pro·jec·tor**
perjery	**per·ju·ry**
perjorative	**pejo·ra·tive**
perkalator	**per·co·la·tor**
perl	**pearl** *(gem)*
perl	**purl** *(stitch)*
perliminary	**pre·lim·i·nary**
permenant	**per·ma·nent**
permiable	**per·me·a·ble**
permiate	**per·me·ate**
perminent	**per·ma·nent**
permisive	**per·mis·sive**
permissable	**per·mis·si·ble**
permited	**per·mit·ted**
permmutation	**per·mu·ta·tion**
pernounce	**pro·nounce**
pernunciation	
	pro·nun·ci·a·tion
perochial	**pa·ro·chi·al**

WRONG	RIGHT
perogative	**pre·rog·a·tive**
peroled	**pa·roled**
perpatrate	**per·pe·trate**
perpellant	**pro·pel·lant**
perpendiculer	
	per·pen·dic·u·lar
perpertrate	**per·pe·trate**
perpettuate	**per·pet·u·ate**
perpetualy	**per·pet·u·al·ly**
perpindicular	
	per·pen·dic·u·lar
perplexaty	**per·plex·i·ty**
perponderance	
	pre·pon·der·ance
perportionate	
	pro·por·tion·ate
perposely	**pur·pose·ly**
perposterous	**pre·pos·ter·ous**
perquisite	**pre·req·ui·site**
	(requirement)
perrenial	**per·en·ni·al**
perrimeter	**pe·rim·e·ter**
	(boundary)
perripheral	**pe·riph·er·al**
perriscope	**per·i·scope**
persacute	**per·se·cute**
	(harass)
persaverence	
	per·se·ver·ance
per–say	**per se**
perscribe	**pre·scribe** *(order)*
perscribe	**pro·scribe** *(forbid)*

WRONG	RIGHT
perscription	**pre·scrip·tion**
persecute	**pros·e·cute**
	(legal term)
persent	**per·cent**
persentable	**pre·sent·a·ble**
persentament	**pre·sen·ti·ment**
	(foreboding)
perseptibly	**per·cep·ti·bly**
perseption	**per·cep·tion**
perserve	**pre·serve**
perserverance	
	per·se·ver·ance
persistance	**per·sist·ence**
personafication	
	per·son·i·fi·ca·tion
personal	**per·son·nel**
	(employees)
personallity	**per·son·al·i·ty**
personel	**per·son·nel**
	(employees)
personel	**per·son·al** *(private)*
personible	**per·son·a·ble**
personnage	**per·son·age**
personnality	**per·son·al·i·ty**
personnel	**per·son·al** *(private)*
perspectave	**per·spec·tive**
	(view)
perspective	**pro·spec·tive**
	(expected)
persperation	**per·spi·ra·tion**
persuassive	**per·sua·sive**
persuation	**per·sua·sion**

WRONG	RIGHT	WRONG	RIGHT
persuede	**per·suade**	pettition	**pe·ti·tion**
persuit	**pur·suit**	peuter	**pew·ter**
persume	**pre·sume**	phantem	**phan·tom**
persumption	**pre·sump·tion**	pharmeceutical	
persumptuous			**phar·ma·ceu·ti·cal**
	pre·sump·tu·ous	pharmecy	**phar·ma·cy**
pertanent	**per·ti·nent**	Pharoh	**Phar·aoh**
pertector	**pro·tec·tor**		*(Egyptian ruler)*
pertend	**pre·tend** *(simulate)*	phase	**faze** *(disturb)*
pertend	**por·tend** *(foreshadow)*	phaze	**phase** *(stage)*
pertentious	**pre·ten·tious**	phenomenan	**phe·nom·e·non**
perterb	**per·turb**	phenominal	**phe·nom·e·nal**
perticipant	**par·tic·i·pant**	Pheonix	**Phoe·nix**
perticular	**par·tic·u·lar**	Pheraoh	**Phar·aoh**
pertition	**par·ti·tion**		*(Egyptian ruler)*
pervailing	**pre·vail·ing**	pheseant	**pheas·ant**
pervassive	**per·va·sive**	philbert	**fil·bert**
pervertion	**per·ver·sion**	Philedelphia	**Phil·a·del·phia**
pervurse	**per·verse**	philharmonnic	
pesant	**peas·ant**		**phil·har·mon·ic**
pessamism	**pes·si·mism**	Philipines	**Phil·ip·pines**
pestalence	**pes·ti·lence**	phillanthropist	
peta	**pi·ta**		**phi·lan·thro·pist**
pete moss	**peat moss**	philosipher	**phi·los·o·pher**
petigree	**ped·i·gree**	phisically	**phys·i·cal·ly**
petle	**pet·al**	phisiology	**phys·i·ol·o·gy**
petoonia	**pe·tu·nia**	phlem	**phlegm**
petrachemical		phobea	**pho·bia**
	pet·ro·chem·i·cal	phonegraph	**pho·no·graph**
petrefied	**pet·ri·fied**	phoney	**pho·ny**
petrollium	**pe·tro·le·um**	phonnetic	**pho·net·ic**
pettiecoat	**pet·ti·coat**	phosfate	**phos·phate**

WRONG	RIGHT	WRONG	RIGHT
phosforescence		pidgeon .... **pi·geon** *(bird)*	
.... **phos·pho·res·cence**		piece .... **peace** *(serenity)*	
phosforus .... **phos·pho·rus**		pier .... **peer** *(equal; look)*	
phosphoresence		piggon .... **pi·geon** *(bird)*	
.... **phos·pho·res·cence**		pigmie .... **pyg·my**	
photoes .... **pho·tos**		pijamas .... **pa·ja·mas**	
photogennic .... **pho·to·gen·ic**		pikaxe .... **pick·ax**	
photografer ... **pho·tog·ra·pher**		piknic .... **pic·nic**	
photosinthesis		pilage .... **pil·lage**	
.... **pho·to·syn·the·sis**		pilar .... **pil·lar**	
physicion .... **phy·si·cian**		pilet .... **pi·lot**	
physicly .... **phys·i·cal·ly**		pilgrem .... **pil·grim**	
physiollogy .... **phys·i·ol·o·gy**		pilgrimege .... **pil·grim·age**	
pianeer .... **pi·o·neer**		pillege .... **pil·lage**	
piannist .... **pi·an·ist**		piller .... **pil·lar**	
pianoes .... **pi·an·os**		pillgrim .... **pil·grim**	
piaty .... **pi·e·ty**		pilow .... **pil·low**	
pican .... **pe·can**		pimmento .... **pi·men·to**	
piceyune .... **pic·a·yune**		pimpel .... **pim·ple**	
picher .... **pitch·er**		pinacle .. **pi·noch·le** *(card game)*	
(hurler; container)		pinacle .... **pin·na·cle** *(acme)*	
pichfork .... **pitch·fork**		pinapple .... **pine·ap·ple**	
pickel .... **pick·le**		pinnacle .... **pi·noch·le**	
pickeling .... **pick·ling**		*(card game)*	
picknic .... **pic·nic**		pinnicle .... **pin·na·cle** *(acme)*	
pickyune .... **pic·a·yune**		pipeing .... **pip·ing**	
picnik .... **pic·nic**		pipline .... **pipe·line**	
picniking .... **pic·nick·ing**		piracey .... **pi·ra·cy**	
picollo .... **pic·co·lo**		piramid .... **pyr·a·mid**	
pictoral .... **pic·to·ri·al**		pire .... **pyre**	
picturresque ...... **pic·tur·esque**		piriodical .... **pe·ri·od·i·cal**	
picuniary .... **pe·cu·ni·ary**		piroette .... **pir·ou·ette**	

WRONG	RIGHT	WRONG	RIGHT
pirothechnics ..	**py·ro·tech·nics**	plantiff	**plain·tiff**
Pisees	**Pis·ces**	plasebo	**pla·ce·bo**
pistashio	**pis·ta·chio**	plasenta	**pla·cen·ta**
pistel	**pis·tol** *(firearm)*	plassid	**plac·id** *(calm)*
pistol	**pis·til** *(part of flower)*	plasster	**plas·ter**
pistun	**pis·ton**	plastec	**plas·tic**
pitcher	**pic·ture** *(likeness)*	plate	**plait** *(braid)*
pithetic	**pa·thet·ic**	plateu	**pla·teau**
pithey	**pithy**	platnum	**plat·i·num**
pithon	**py·thon**	platonnic	**pla·ton·ic**
pitta	**pi·ta**	platteau	**pla·teau**
pittence	**pit·tance**	plattypus	**plat·y·pus**
pituetary	**pi·tu·i·tary**	plausable	**plau·si·ble**
pitunia	**pe·tu·nia**	playright	**play·wright**
pityless	**pit·i·less**	plazma	**plas·ma**
pius	**pi·ous**	plazza	**pla·za**
pivetal	**piv·ot·al**	pleasantrey	**pleas·ant·ry**
pizzaria	**piz·ze·ria**	pleasent	**pleas·ant**
placcard	**plac·ard**	pleasurible	**pleas·ur·a·ble**
placed	**plac·id** *(calm)*	plee	**plea**
placibo	**pla·ce·bo**	pleed	**plead**
placque	**plaque**	pleet	**pleat**
plad	**plaid**	plege	**pledge**
plage	**plague**	plentaful	**plen·ti·ful**
plagerism	**pla·gia·rism**	plentious	**plen·te·ous**
plain	**plane** *(airplane; surface)*	pleseant	**pleas·ant**
plaintif	**plain·tiff**	plethera	**pleth·o·ra**
plait	**plate** *(dish)*	pleurasy	**pleu·ri·sy**
plancton	**plank·ton**	plexaglass	**Plex·i·glas**
plane	**plain** *(simple)*	plieing	**ply·ing**
planed	**planned** *(pt. of plan)*	plient	**pli·ant**
plannet	**plan·et**	plite	**plight**

WRONG	RIGHT	WRONG	RIGHT
ploted	**plot·ted**	poligamy	**po·lyg·a·my**
pluerisy	**pleu·ri·sy**	poligraph	**pol·y·graph**
plum	**plumb**	polimer	**pol·y·mer**
(to test; a lead weight)		polip	**pol·yp**
plumb	**plum** *(fruit)*	politacal	**po·lit·i·cal**
plummer	**plumb·er**	politically	**pol·i·tic·ly**
plumming	**plumb·ing**		*(prudently)*
plungeing	**plung·ing**	politicing	**pol·i·tick·ing**
plurallity	**plu·ral·i·ty**	politicion	**pol·i·ti·cian**
plurel	**plu·ral**	politicly	**po·lit·i·cal·ly**
plurisy	**pleu·ri·sy**		*(in a political manner)*
plyable	**pli·a·ble**	poll	**pole** *(rod)*
plyers	**pli·ers**	pollice	**po·lice**
Plymuth	**Ply·mouth**	pollicy	**pol·i·cy**
pnuematic	**pneu·mat·ic**	pollin	**pol·len**
pnuemonia	**pneu·mo·nia**	pollish	**pol·ish**
poched	**poached**	pollite	**po·lite**
pockit	**pock·et**	pollitical	**po·lit·i·cal**
podeum	**po·di·um**	pollup	**pol·yp**
poetecal	**po·et·i·cal**	pollutent	**pol·lu·tant**
pogoda	**pa·go·da**	pollyester	**pol·y·es·ter**
poinant	**poign·ant**	Pollynesian	**Pol·y·ne·sian**
poinsetta	**poin·set·tia**	poltry	**poul·try** *(fowls)*
poisenous	**poi·son·ous**	polutant	**pol·lu·tant**
Polanesian	**Pol·y·ne·sian**	polyesther	**pol·y·es·ter**
polarazation	**polar·i·za·tion**	polyethelene	**pol·y·eth·yl·ene**
polatician	**pol·i·ti·cian**	polygemy	**po·lyg·a·my**
pole	**poll** *(vote)*	polyunsaterated	
polecy	**pol·i·cy**		**pol·y·un·sat·u·rat·ed**
polen	**pol·len**	pome	**po·em** *(verse)*
poler	**po·lar** *(of the poles)*	pomegranite	**pome·gran·ate**
polerization	**polar·i·za·tion**	pomel	**pom·mel**

160

WRONG	RIGHT	WRONG	RIGHT
pompus	**pom·pous** *(pretentious)*	portfollio	**port·fo·lio**
ponch	**paunch**	portible	**port·a·ble**
pontifacate	**pon·tif·i·cate**	portrade	**por·trayed**
pooberty	**pu·ber·ty**	portraid	**por·trayed**
poodel	**poo·dle**	portret	**por·trait**
poper	**pau·per**	posative	**pos·i·tive**
poplar	**pop·u·lar** *(common)*	poschulate	**pos·tu·late**
popler	**pop·lar** *(tree)*	poschumous	**post·hu·mous**
popourri	**pot·pour·ri**	posession	**pos·ses·sion**
populace	**pop·u·lous** *(crowded)*	posessive	**pos·ses·sive**
popular	**pop·lar** *(tree)*	posibility	**pos·si·bil·i·ty**
popularety	**pop·u·lar·i·ty**	posible	**pos·si·ble**
populer	**pop·u·lar** *(common)*	pospone	**post·pone**
populous	**pop·u·lace** *(the people)*	possably	**pos·si·bly**
		posscript	**post·script**
porcelin	**por·ce·lain**	possebility	**pos·si·bil·i·ty**
porcipine	**por·cu·pine**	possesive	**pos·ses·sive**
pore	**pour** *(flow)*	possition	**po·si·tion**
porfolio	**port·fo·lio**	postege	**post·age**
poridge	**por·ridge**	posteraty	**pos·ter·i·ty**
porkupine	**por·cu·pine**	posthumus	**post·hu·mous**
pornogerphy	**por·nog·ra·phy**	post–mortum	**post–mor·tem**
porpous	**por·poise**	postoolate	**pos·tu·late**
porrage	**por·ridge**	postumous	**post·hu·mous**
porselain	**por·ce·lain**	potant	**po·tent**
portant	**por·tent** *(omen)*	potatos	**po·ta·toes**
Porta Rico	**Puer·to Ri·co**	potensial	**po·ten·tial**
portel	**por·tal**	potery	**pot·tery**
portend	**por·tent** *(omen)*	poting	**pot·ting**
portent	**por·tend** *(foreshadow)*	potpoorri	**pot·pour·ri**
		pottary	**pot·tery**
		pottasium	**po·tas·si·um**

WRONG	*RIGHT*
pouder	**pow·der**
poultrey	**poul·try** *(fowls)*
poultry	**pal·try** *(trifling)*
pour	**pore** *(opening; ponder)*
povarty	**pov·er·ty**
powncing	**pounc·ing**
powt	**pout**
pracee	**pré·cis** *(summary)*
practecal	**prac·ti·cal**
practiceing	**prac·tic·ing**
practicianer	**prac·ti·tion·er**
practicly	**prac·ti·cal·ly**
pragmattic	**prag·mat·ic**
praisworthy	**praise·wor·thy**
prarie	**prai·rie**
praun	**prawn**
pray	**prey** *(victim)*
prean	**preen**
precapice	**prec·i·pice**
precarius	**pre·car·i·ous**
precedance	**prec·e·dence** *(priority)*
precedence	**pre·ced·ent** *(example)*
preceed	**pre·cede** *(come before)*
preceedence	**prec·e·dence** *(priority)*
precense	**pres·ence**
precession	**pro·ces·sion** *(parade)*
precice	**pre·cise** *(definite)*

WRONG	*RIGHT*
precipatation	**pre·cip·i·ta·tion**
precipiece	**prec·i·pice**
precise	**pré·cis** *(summary)*
precission	**pre·ci·sion**
precius	**pre·cious**
preconseption	**pre·con·cep·tion**
precosious	**pre·co·cious**
precurser	**pre·cur·sor**
predacate	**pred·i·cate**
predater	**pred·a·tor**
predesessor	**pred·e·ces·sor**
predesposed	**pre·dis·posed**
predicsion	**pre·dic·tion**
predicument	**pre·dic·a·ment**
predillection	**pre·di·lec·tion**
preditor	**pred·a·tor**
predjudice	**prej·u·dice**
predomanent	**pre·dom·i·nant**
preech	**preach**
preemanant	**pre·em·i·nent**
prefabercate	**pre·fab·ri·cate**
preferance	**pref·er·ence**
prefered	**pre·ferred**
preferible	**pref·er·a·ble**
preferrential	**pref·er·en·tial**
prefertory	**pref·a·to·ry**
prefface	**pref·ace**
preffered	**pre·ferred**
prefferential	**pref·er·en·tial**
pregnent	**preg·nant**
preisthood	**priest·hood**

WRONG	RIGHT
prejidace	**prej·u·dice**
prelimanary	**pre·lim·i·nary**
prellude	**prel·ude**
premanition	**pre·mo·ni·tion**
premedetated	**pre·med·i·tat·ed**
premeir	**pre·mier**
	(first; prime minister)
premeire	**pre·mière**
	(first performance)
premerital	**pre·mar·i·tal**
premeum	**pre·mi·um**
premiere	**pre·mier**
	(first; prime minister)
preminent	**pre·em·i·nent**
premmise	**prem·ise**
prempt	**pre·empt**
preocuppied	**pre·oc·cu·pied**
prepair	**pre·pare**
prepatory	**pre·par·a·to·ry**
preperation	**prep·a·ra·tion**
prepisition	**prep·o·si·tion**
preponderence	**pre·pon·der·ance**
prepostorous	**pre·pos·ter·ous**
prepposition	**prep·o·si·tion**
prerequesite	**pre·req·ui·site**
	(requirement)
prerequisite	**per·qui·site**
	(privilege)
prerie	**prai·rie**
prerogitive	**pre·rog·a·tive**

WRONG	RIGHT
presadency	**pres·i·den·cy**
presance	**pres·ence**
Presbiterian	**Pres·by·te·ri·an**
prescribe	**pro·scribe** *(forbid)*
prescriptian	**pre·scrip·tion**
presede	**pre·cede**
	(come before)
presedence	**prec·e·dence**
	(priority)
presedent	**prec·ed·ent**
	(example)
presentible	**pre·sent·a·ble**
presentment	**pre·sen·ti·ment**
	(foreboding)
presept	**pre·cept**
presidancy	**pres·i·den·cy**
presinct	**pre·cinct**
presious	**pre·cious**
presipitation	**pre·cip·i·ta·tion**
presise	**pre·cise** *(definite)*
presision	**pre·ci·sion**
prespective	**pro·spec·tive**
	(expected)
prespiration	**per·spi·ra·tion**
pressage	**pres·age**
pressence	**pres·ence**
presservative	**pre·ser·va·tive**
pressidency	**pres·i·den·cy**
pressipice	**prec·i·pice**
prestegious	**pres·ti·gious**
prestiege	**pres·tige**
presumtion	**pre·sump·tion**

presumtuous	....	probabillity	.... **prob·a·bil·i·ty**
	.... **pre·sump·tu·ous**	probbably	.... **prob·a·bly**
presure	.... **pres·sure**	probbation	.... **pro·ba·tion**
pretensious	.... **pre·ten·tious**	probibility	.... **prob·a·bil·i·ty**
pretention	.... **pre·ten·sion**	probibly	.... **prob·a·bly**
pretex	.... **pre·text**	problimatic	...... **prob·lem·at·ic**
pretsel	.... **pret·zel**	procede	.... **pro·ceed** (go on)
prevaling	.... **pre·vail·ing**	proceed	.... **pre·cede**
prevelant	.... **prev·a·lent**		(come before)
preveous	.... **pre·vi·ous**	proceedure	.... **pro·ce·dure**
preversion	.... **per·ver·sion**	procession	.... **pre·ces·sion**
prey	.... **pray** (implore)		(precedence)
prickley	.... **prick·ly**	proclame	.... **pro·claim**
prier	.... **pri·or** (earlier)	proclimation	... **proc·la·ma·tion**
primative	.... **prim·i·tive**	procrasstinate	....
primerily	.... **pri·ma·ri·ly**		.... **pro·cras·ti·nate**
primery	.... **pri·ma·ry**	procriation	.... **pro·cre·a·tion**
primevil	.... **pri·me·val**	procter	.... **proc·tor**
primmitive	.... **prim·i·tive**	prodduct	.... **prod·uct**
principal	.... **prin·ci·ple**	prodegal	.... **prod·i·gal**
	(basic rule)	prodege	.... **pro·té·gé**
principle	.... **prin·ci·pal** (chief)		(one helped by another)
princley	.... **prince·ly**	prodigee	.... **prod·i·gy** (genius)
prior	.... **pri·er** (one who pries)	prodigias	.... **pro·di·gious**
priorrity	.... **pri·or·i·ty**	producktion	.... **pro·duc·tion**
prisem	.... **prism**	produser	.... **pro·duc·er**
prisen	.... **pris·on**	profain	.... **pro·fane**
prisonner	.... **pris·on·er**	profannity	.... **pro·fan·i·ty**
privecy	.... **pri·va·cy**	profecy	.... **proph·e·cy** (n.)
privelage	.... **priv·i·lege**	profesional	...... **pro·fes·sion·al**
privite	.... **pri·vate**	professer	.... **pro·fes·sor**
prizm	.... **prism**	profesy	.... **proph·e·sy** (v.)

proffess	**pro·fess**	promiscuety	**prom·is·cu·i·ty**
proffessor	**pro·fes·sor**	promiscuos	**pro·mis·cu·ous**
proffet	**proph·et**	promissing	**prom·is·ing**
	(one who predicts)	promp	**prompt**
profficient	**pro·fi·cient**	pronounciation	....
proffile	**pro·file**		**pro·nun·ci·a·tion**
proffit	**prof·it** *(gain)*	pronounse	**pro·nounce**
proffusion	**pro·fu·sion**	proove	**prove**
proficiant	**pro·fi·cient**	propasition	**prop·o·si·tion**
profillactic	**pro·phy·lac·tic**	propelent	**pro·pel·lant**
profit	**proph·et**	propellor	**pro·pel·ler**
	(one who predicts)	propencity	**pro·pen·si·ty**
profitible	**prof·it·a·ble**	prophallactic	**pro·phy·lac·tic**
profuzion	**pro·fu·sion**	prophecy	**proph·e·sy** *(v.)*
prognoses	**prog·no·sis** *(sing.)*	prophesy	**proph·e·cy** *(n.)*
prognosis	**prog·no·ses** *(pl.)*	prophet	**prof·it** *(gain)*
prognostecation	....	propicious	**pro·pi·tious**
	prog·nos·ti·ca·tion	propigate	**prop·a·gate**
programor	**pro·gram·mer**	propoganda	**prop·a·gan·da**
progresive	**pro·gres·sive**	proponant	**pro·po·nent**
progriss	**prog·ress**	proportionnate	....
prohabition	**pro·hi·bi·tion**		**pro·por·tion·ate**
proibition	**pro·hi·bi·tion**	proposel	**pro·pos·al**
projeck	**proj·ect**	proppeller	**pro·pel·ler**
projecter	**pro·jec·tor**	propper	**prop·er**
prolifferate	**pro·lif·er·ate**	propperty	**prop·er·ty**
proliffic	**pro·lif·ic**	propponent	**pro·po·nent**
prolitariate	**pro·le·tar·iat**	propposition	**prop·o·si·tion**
prolliferate	**pro·lif·er·ate**	propriatery	**pro·pri·e·tary**
prologe	**pro·logue**	proprieter	**pro·pri·e·tor**
prominade	**prom·e·nade**	propullsion	**pro·pul·sion**
prominance	**prom·i·nence**	prosayic	**pro·sa·ic**

WRONG	RIGHT	WRONG	RIGHT
proscribe	**pre·scribe** *(order)*	protien	**pro·tein** *(substance)*
prosecute	**per·se·cute**	Protistant	**Prot·es·tant**
	(harass)	protocall	**pro·to·col**
prosecuter	**pros·e·cu·tor**	protracter	**pro·trac·tor**
proselitize	**pros·e·lyt·ize**	protrussion	**pro·tru·sion**
prosessed	**proc·essed**	protuberence	
prosession	**pro·ces·sion**		**pro·tu·ber·ance**
	(parade)	provance	**prov·ince**
prosicute	**pros·e·cute**	provedence	**prov·i·dence**
	(legal term)	proverbeal	**pro·ver·bi·al**
prosicution	**pros·e·cu·tion**	provication	**prov·o·ca·tion**
prosletyze	**pros·e·lyt·ize**	providance	**prov·i·dence**
prosparity	**pros·per·i·ty**	provintial	**pro·vin·cial**
prosparous	**pros·per·ous**	provocitive	**pro·voc·a·tive**
prospecter	**pros·pec·tor**	prowel	**prowl**
prospective	**per·spec·tive**	proximaty	**prox·im·i·ty**
	(view)	prudance	**pru·dence**
prosperrity	**pros·per·i·ty**	pruriant	**pru·ri·ent**
prossecution	**pros·e·cu·tion**	pseudanim	**pseu·do·nym**
prossetics	**pros·thet·ics**	psiche	**psy·che** *(mind; soul)*
prosspect	**pros·pect**	psichedelic	**psy·che·del·ic**
prostate	**pros·trate** *(prone)*	psichiatrist	**psy·chi·a·trist**
prostatute	**pros·ti·tute**	psichic	**psy·chic**
prostheesis	**pros·the·sis**	psichological	
prostrate	**pros·tate** *(gland)*		**psy·cho·log·i·cal**
protaganist	**pro·tag·o·nist**	psichosis	**psy·cho·sis** *(sing.)*
protan	**pro·ton**	psolm	**psalm**
protaplasm	**pro·to·plasm**	psorriasis	**pso·ri·a·sis**
protatype	**pro·to·type**	psuedonym	**pseu·do·nym**
protecol	**pro·to·col**	psycapath	**psy·cho·path**
protecter	**pro·tec·tor**	psych	**psy·che** *(mind; soul)*
protein	**pro·te·an** *(changeable)*	psychadelic	**psy·che·del·ic**

WRONG	*RIGHT*	*WRONG*	*RIGHT*
psyche	**psych** *(excite; outwit)*	pulmenary	**pul·mo·nary**
psychec	**psy·chic**	pulpet	**pul·pit**
psychoanallysis		pulvarize	**pul·ver·ize**
	psy·cho·a·nal·y·sis	pumise	**pum·ice**
psychollogy	**psy·chol·o·gy**	pumkin	**pump·kin**
psychologecal		punative	**pu·ni·tive**
	psy·cho·log·i·cal	punctuetion	**punc·tu·a·tion**
psychosamatic		punctule	**punc·tu·al**
	psy·cho·so·mat·ic	puneshment	**pun·ish·ment**
psychoses ...	**psy·cho·sis** *(sing.)*	puney	**pu·ny**
psychotheripy		pungant	**pun·gent**
	psy·cho·ther·apy	punkin	**pump·kin**
psyciatrist	**psy·chi·a·trist**	punktual	**punc·tu·al**
psycoanalysis		punktuation	**punc·tu·a·tion**
	psy·cho·a·nal·y·sis	punkture	**punc·ture**
psycological ..	**psy·cho·log·i·cal**	punnishment	**pun·ish·ment**
psycotic	**psy·chot·ic**	punnitive	**pu·ni·tive**
psyschosis	**psy·cho·ses** *(pl.)*	pupel	**pu·pil**
pubarty	**pu·ber·ty**	puppit	**pup·pet**
pubec	**pu·bic**	puray	**pu·rée**
publec	**pub·lic**	purcent	**per·cent**
publecation	**pub·li·ca·tion**	purception	**per·cep·tion**
publesher	**pub·lish·er**	purchace	**pur·chase**
publisity	**pub·lic·i·ty**	purcolator	**per·co·la·tor**
puding	**pud·ding**	purcussion	**per·cus·sion**
pudle	**pud·dle**	puré	**pu·rée**
puker	**puck·er**	purefication	**puri·fi·ca·tion**
pullmonary	**pul·mo·nary**	pureley	**pure·ly**
pullpit	**pul·pit**	Puretan	**Pu·ri·tan**
pullsate	**pul·sate**	purety	**pu·ri·ty**
pullverize	**pul·ver·ize**	purfectible	**per·fect·i·ble**
pully	**pul·ley**	purforate	**per·fo·rate**

WRONG	*RIGHT*
purformance	.... **per·form·ance**
purgery	.... **per·ju·ry**
purgetory	.... **pur·ga·to·ry**
purient	.... **pru·ri·ent**
purifecation	.... **puri·fi·ca·tion**
puritannical	.... **puri·tan·i·cal**
purl	.... **pearl** *(gem)*
purmeate	.... **per·me·ate**
purmutation	.... **per·mu·ta·tion**
purpel	.... **pur·ple**
purpendicular	....
	.... **per·pen·dic·u·lar**
purplexity	.... **per·plex·i·ty**
purposly	.... **pur·pose·ly**
pursute	.... **pur·suit**
purterb	.... **per·turb**
puss	.... **pus** *(matter)*
pusstule	.... **pus·tule**
put	.... **putt** *(golf stroke)*
putred	.... **pu·trid**
puttie	.... **put·ty**
puzzeling	.... **puz·zling**
pweblo	.... **pueb·lo**
pyremid	.... **pyr·a·mid**
pyrotecnics	..... **py·ro·tech·nics**
pythan	.... **py·thon**

Q

WRONG	*RIGHT*
qeue	.... **queue** *(line)*
Quaalood	.... **Quaa·lude**
quackary	.... **quack·ery**

WRONG	*RIGHT*
quadralateral	....
	.... **quad·ri·lat·er·al**
quadraplegic	.... **quad·ri·ple·gic**
quadratick	.... **quad·rat·ic**
quadrent	.... **quad·rant**
quadrilion	.... **quad·ril·lion**
quadrillateral	....
	.... **quad·ri·lat·er·al**
quadriplejic	..... **quad·ri·ple·gic**
quadrupel	.... **quad·ru·ple**
quadruplette	...... **quad·ru·plet**
quafe	.... **quaff**
quagmier	.... **quag·mire**
qualafication	... **qual·i·fi·ca·tion**
quale	.... **quail** *(bird; cower)*
qualety	.... **qual·i·ty**
quallified	.... **qual·i·fied**
quallitative	.... **qual·i·ta·tive**
quallity	.... **qual·i·ty**
Qualude	.... **Quaa·lude**
quam	.... **qualm**
quandry	.... **quan·da·ry**
quanitative	..... **quan·ti·ta·tive**
quanity	.... **quan·ti·ty**
quantafy	.... **quan·ti·fy**
quante	.... **quaint**
quantety	.... **quan·ti·ty**
quantom	.... **quan·tum**
quarel	.... **quar·rel**
quarrantine	.... **quar·an·tine**
quarterley	.... **quar·ter·ly**
quartor	.... **quar·ter**

WRONG	RIGHT	WRONG	RIGHT
quarts	**quartz** *(mineral)*	quintilion	**quin·til·lion**
quarulous	**quer·u·lous**	quintissential	
quarum	**quo·rum**		**quin·tes·sen·tial**
quary	**quar·ry**	quints	**quince**
quazar	**qua·sar**	quintupplet	**quin·tu·plet**
quazi	**qua·si**	quiry	**que·ry**
que	**queue** *(line)*	quisine	**cui·sine**
quear	**queer**	quite	**qui·et** *(silence)*
queazy	**quea·sy**	quiting	**quit·ting**
Quebeck	**Que·bec**	quivver	**quiv·er**
queche	**quiche**	quixatic	**quix·ot·ic**
queery	**que·ry**	quizical	**quiz·zi·cal**
queesy	**quea·sy**	quorentine	**quar·an·tine**
queiscent	**qui·es·cent**	quorril	**quar·rel**
quel	**quell**	quorry	**quar·ry**
quentessential		quort	**quart**
	quin·tes·sen·tial	quorter	**quar·ter**
queralous	**quer·u·lous**	quortet	**quar·tet**
querk	**quirk**	quoteable	**quot·a·ble**
quesstion	**ques·tion**	quotiant	**quo·tient**
questionaire	**ques·tion·naire**		
questionible	**ques·tion·a·ble**		**R**
quesy	**quea·sy**		
quey	**quay** *(wharf)*	rabbel	**rab·ble**
quible	**quib·ble**	rabbenical	**rab·bin·i·cal**
quicksotic	**quix·ot·ic**	rabbet	**rab·bit** *(animal)*
quiessent	**qui·es·cent**	rabbid	**rab·id**
quiet	**quite** *(entirely)*	rabbie	**rab·bi**
quiettude	**qui·e·tude**	rabbies	**ra·bies** *(disease)*
quillt	**quilt**	rabed	**rab·id**
quinesential	**quin·tes·sen·tial**	rabellion	**re·bel·lion**
quinnine	**qui·nine**	rabi	**rab·bi**

WRONG	*RIGHT*	*WRONG*	*RIGHT*
rabinical	**rab·bin·i·cal**	raggoo	**ra·gout**
rabit	**rab·bit** *(animal)*	raglen	**rag·lan**
rable	**rab·ble**	ragou	**ra·gout**
racey	**racy**	railling	**rail·ing**
rachet	**ratch·et**	railrode	**rail·road**
racizm	**rac·ism**	rain	**reign** *(rule)*
rackit	**rack·et**	rain	**rein** *(a leather strap)*
racous	**rau·cous**	raindeer	**rein·deer**
radacal	**rad·i·cal** *(extreme)*	raise	**raze** *(demolish)*
raddar	**ra·dar**	raisen	**rai·sin**
raddial	**ra·di·al**	rak	**rack** *(framework)*
raddically	**rad·i·cal·ly**	rak	**wrack** *(torment)*
raddio	**ra·dio**	rakeing	**rak·ing**
raddish	**rad·ish**	rakket	**rack·et**
rade	**raid**	rale	**rail**
radeal	**ra·di·al**	ralley	**ral·ly**
radeating	**ra·di·at·ing**	ramafication	**ram·i·fi·ca·tion**
radeo	**ra·dio**	rambeling	**ram·bling**
radeoactive	**ra·di·o·ac·tive**	ramblor	**ram·bler**
radeology	**ra·di·ol·o·gy**	rambunktious	
radeus	**ra·di·us**		**ram·bunc·tious**
radiactive	**ra·di·o·ac·tive**	ramedial	**re·me·di·al**
radialogy	**ra·di·ol·o·gy**	rammification	
radiateing	**ra·di·at·ing**		**ram·i·fi·ca·tion**
radiater	**ra·di·a·tor**	rammpage	**ram·page**
radicaly	**rad·i·cal·ly**	rampent	**ramp·ant**
radicle	**rad·i·cal** *(extreme)*	ramshakle	**ram·shack·le**
radience	**ra·di·ance**	rancer	**ran·cor**
raffel	**raf·fle**	randezvous	**ren·dez·vous**
raffter	**raft·er**	rane	**reign** *(rule)*
raged	**rag·ged** *(tattered)*	rane	**rein** *(a leather strap)*
rageing	**rag·ing**	ranewal	**re·new·al**

WRONG	RIGHT	WRONG	RIGHT
rangeing	**rang·ing**	raskal	**ras·cal**
rangey	**rangy**	rassberry	**rasp·ber·ry**
rangle	**wran·gle**	rassion	**ra·tion**
rankor	**ran·cor**	ratan	**rat·tan**
ransak	**ran·sack**	ratchit	**ratch·et**
ransid	**ran·cid**	ratefy	**rat·i·fy**
ransome	**ran·som**	rateing	**rat·ing**
rap	**wrap** (cover)	rateo	**ra·tio**
rapchure	**rap·ture**	rath	**wrath** (rage)
rapiar	**ra·pi·er**	ratial	**ra·cial**
raping	**rap·ping** (tapping)	rational	**ra·tion·a·le**
raport	**rap·port** (harmony)		(explanation)
raport	**re·port** (an account)	rationallize	**ration·al·ize**
rappid	**rap·id**	rationel	**ra·tion·al** (reasoning)
rappidity	**ra·pid·i·ty**	ratle	**rat·tle**
rappier	**ra·pi·er**	ratlesnake	**rat·tle·snake**
rappist	**rap·ist**	ratten	**rat·tan**
rappor	**rap·port** (harmony)	rattify	**rat·i·fy**
rapprochment		rattion	**ra·tion**
	rap·proche·ment	rattional	**ra·tion·al** (reasoning)
rapsody	**rhap·so·dy**	rattleling	**rat·tling**
raquetball	**rac·quet·ball**	rattlsnake	**rat·tle·snake**
rarety	**rar·i·ty**	raucus	**rau·cous**
rarify	**rar·e·fy**	raunchey	**raun·chy**
rarly	**rare·ly**	ravageing	**rav·ag·ing**
rascel	**ras·cal**	ravanous	**rav·e·nous**
rase	**raise** (lift)	ravege	**rav·age**
rase	**raze** (demolish)	raveing	**rav·ing**
rase	**race** (contest)	ravene	**ra·vine**
rashal	**ra·cial**	ravenus	**rav·e·nous**
rasin	**rai·sin**	raveoli	**ra·vi·o·li**
rasism	**rac·ism**	ravle	**rav·el**

WRONG	RIGHT	WRONG	RIGHT
ravvish	**rav·ish**	rearange	**re·ar·range**
rawide	**raw·hide**	rearrangment	
rayan	**ray·on**		**re·ar·range·ment**
raze	**raise** *(lift)*	reasen	**rea·son**
razer	**ra·zor**	reasonible	**rea·son·a·ble**
razzberry	**rasp·ber·ry**	reath	**wreath** *(a band)*
reacktionary	**re·ac·tion·ary**	reathe	**wreathe** *(to encircle)*
reactavate	**re·ac·ti·vate**	reazon	**rea·son**
reacter	**re·ac·tor**	rebait	**re·bate**
reactionery	**re·ac·tion·ary**	rebbel	**reb·el**
read	**reed** *(plant)*	rebbellious	**re·bel·lious**
readilly	**read·i·ly**	rebbuttal	**re·but·tal**
readjusment	**re·ad·just·ment**	rebeling	**reb·el·ling**
readyness	**read·i·ness**	rebelion	**re·bel·lion**
reaf	**reef**	rebelious	**re·bel·lious**
reajustment	**re·ad·just·ment**	reble	**reb·el**
reak	**reek** *(smell)*	rebownd	**re·bound**
real	**reel** *(whirl; spool)*	rebutal	**re·but·tal**
realaty	**re·al·i·ty** *(fact)*	recalsitrant	**re·cal·ci·trant**
realine	**re·a·lign**	recampense	**rec·om·pense**
realistick	**re·al·is·tic**	recanize	**rec·og·nize**
reality	**re·al·ty** *(real estate)*	recannoiter	**rec·on·noi·ter**
reallign	**re·a·lign**	recapitchulation	
reallism	**re·al·ism**		**re·ca·pit·u·la·tion**
reallistic	**re·al·is·tic**	reccognise	**rec·og·nize**
reallity	**re·al·i·ty** *(fact)*	reccognition	**rec·og·ni·tion**
reallization	**real·i·za·tion**	reccolect	**rec·ol·lect**
realstate	**real es·tate**	reccommend	**rec·om·mend**
realty	**re·al·i·ty** *(fact)*	recconciliation	
realy	**re·al·ly**		**rec·on·cil·i·a·tion**
reancarnation		recconning	**reck·on·ing**
	re·in·car·na·tion	receed	**re·cede**

receiveable	**re·ceiv·a·ble**	recompence	**rec·om·pense**
recent	**re·sent** *(feel a hurt)*	reconaissance	
recepe	**rec·i·pe**		**re·con·nais·sance**
recepter	**re·cep·tor**	reconcileable	**rec·on·cil·a·ble**
recepticle	**re·cep·ta·cle**	reconcilliation	
recerd	**re·cord**		**rec·on·cil·i·a·tion**
recesion	**re·ces·sion**	reconnaisance	
receve	**re·ceive**		**re·con·nais·sance**
rech	**retch** *(vomit)*	reconoiter	**rec·on·noi·ter**
reciept	**re·ceipt**	reconsiliation	
recieve	**re·ceive**		**rec·on·cil·i·a·tion**
recint	**re·cent** *(new)*	reconstatute	**re·con·sti·tute**
recipiant	**re·cip·i·ent**	reconstrucktion	
recipracal	**re·cip·ro·cal**		**re·con·struc·tion**
recipracate	**re·cip·ro·cate**	recoop	**re·coup**
recitel	**re·cit·al**	recooperate	**re·cu·per·ate**
reck	**wreck**	recorse	**re·course**
reckening	**reck·on·ing**	recoverey	**re·cov·er·y**
reckoncilible	**rec·on·cil·a·ble**	requirement	**re·quire·ment**
reckord	**re·cord**	recquisite	**req·ui·site**
reckreational	**rec·re·a·tion·al**	recquisition	**req·ui·si·tion**
recktify	**rec·ti·fy**	recreationel	**rec·re·a·tion·al**
recktitude	**rec·ti·tude**	recrute	**re·cruit**
reclaimation	**rec·la·ma·tion**	rectafy	**rec·ti·fy**
reclame	**re·claim**	rectanguler	**rec·tan·gu·lar**
reclineing	**re·clin·ing**	rectatude	**rec·ti·tude**
recloose	**rec·luse**	rectel	**rec·tal**
recoarse	**re·course**	recter	**rec·tor**
recognizence	**re·cog·ni·zance**	rectery	**rec·to·ry**
recognizible	**rec·og·niz·a·ble**	recuparate	**re·cu·per·ate**
recolleck	**rec·ol·lect**	recurence	**re·cur·rence**
recomend	**rec·om·mend**	recuring	**re·cur·ring**

WRONG	RIGHT	WRONG	RIGHT
recurrance	**re·cur·rence**	refering	**re·fer·ring**
recykle	**re·cy·cle**	referrel	**re·fer·ral**
red	**read** (pt. of read)	refferee	**ref·er·ee**
reddolent	**red·o·lent**	refference	**ref·er·ence**
reddy	**ready**	refferendum	**ref·er·en·dum**
redeam	**re·deem**	refferring	**re·fer·ring**
redemtion	**re·demp·tion**	reffuge	**ref·uge**
rediculous	**ridic·u·lous**	reffugee	**ref·u·gee**
redolant	**red·o·lent**	reffuse	**ref·use** (trash)
redondancy	**re·dun·dan·cy**	refinary	**re·fin·ery**
reduceing	**re·duc·ing**	refinment	**re·fine·ment**
reducktion	**re·duc·tion**	refleck	**re·flect**
redundency	**re·dun·dan·cy**	reflecks	**re·flex** (response)
redundent	**re·dun·dant**	reflecktion	**re·flec·tion**
redusing	**re·duc·ing**	refoose	**re·fuse** (decline)
reed	**read** (understand)	reformitory	**re·form·a·to·ry**
reek	**wreak** (inflict)	refracktion	**re·frac·tion**
reel	**real** (actual)	refrane	**re·frain**
reelly	**re·al·ly**	refrence	**ref·er·ence**
reem	**ream**	refreshmint	**re·fresh·ment**
reemburse	**re·im·burse**	refridgerator	**re·frig·er·a·tor**
reencarnation		refun	**re·fund**
	re·in·car·na·tion	refusel	**re·fus·al**
reenforcement		refuze	**re·fuse** (decline)
	re·in·force·ment	regae	**reg·gae**
reep	**reap**	regail	**re·gale** (entertain)
reeson	**rea·son**	regale	**re·gal** (royal)
refecktory	**re·fec·to·ry**	regallia	**re·ga·lia**
referal	**re·fer·ral**	regamen	**reg·i·men**
referance	**ref·er·ence**	regament	**reg·i·ment**
refered	**re·ferred**	regel	**re·gal** (royal)
referindum	**ref·er·en·dum**	regeme	**re·gime**

WRONG	RIGHT	WRONG	RIGHT
regenarate	**re·gen·er·ate**	rejime	**re·gime**
regergitation		rejimen	**reg·i·men**
	re·gur·gi·ta·tion	rejiment	**reg·i·ment**
regester	**reg·is·ter**	rejister	**reg·is·ter**
reggay	**reg·gae**	rejoiceing	**re·joic·ing**
regimint	**reg·i·ment**	rejoiner	**re·join·der**
regin	**re·gion**	rejoyce	**re·joice**
reginal	**re·gion·al**	rejuvanate	**re·ju·ve·nate**
regincy	**re·gen·cy**	reke	**reek** *(smell)*
regint	**re·gent**	rekless	**reck·less**
regionel	**re·gion·al**	rekluse	**rec·luse**
regon	**re·gion**	reknowned	**re·nowned**
regresion	**re·gres·sion**	relacks	**re·lax**
regretable	**re·gret·ta·ble**	relagate	**rel·e·gate**
regualation	**reg·u·la·tion**	relaid	**re·layed** *(conveyed)*
reguard	**re·gard**	relateing	**re·lat·ing**
regulater	**reg·u·la·tor**	relativaty	**rel·a·tiv·i·ty**
reguler	**reg·u·lar**	relavant	**rel·e·vant**
regurjitation	**re·gur·gi·ta·tion**	releese	**re·lease**
reguvenate	**re·ju·ve·nate**	releif	**re·lief** *(n.)*
rehabillitate	**re·ha·bil·i·tate**	releive	**re·lieve** *(v.)*
rehearsel	**re·hears·al**	relevent	**rel·e·vant**
reign	**rein** *(a leather strap)*	relick	**rel·ic**
reimberse	**re·im·burse**	relie	**re·ly**
rein	**reign** *(rule)*	relieable	**re·li·a·ble**
reinforcemint		relient	**re·li·ant**
	re·in·force·ment	religin	**re·li·gion**
reitarate	**re·it·er·ate**	religous	**re·li·gious**
rejeck	**re·ject**	relization	**real·i·za·tion**
rejency	**re·gen·cy**	rellative	**rel·a·tive**
rejenerate	**re·gen·er·ate**	rellativity	**rel·a·tiv·i·ty**
rejent	**re·gent**	rellegate	**rel·e·gate**

WRONG	RIGHT	WRONG	RIGHT
rellentless	**re·lent·less**	ren	**wren**
rellevant	**rel·e·vant**	renagade	**ren·e·gade**
rellic	**rel·ic**	renaissence	**ren·ais·sance**
relligion	**re·li·gion**	renavate	**ren·o·vate**
relligious	**re·li·gious**	rench	**wrench**
rellinquish	**re·lin·quish**	rendavous	**ren·dez·vous**
rellish	**rel·ish**	rendring	**ren·der·ing**
relluctance	**re·luc·tance**	renewel	**re·new·al**
relm	**realm**	renig	**re·nege**
reluctently	**re·luc·tant·ly**	rennaissance	**ren·ais·sance**
relyable	**re·li·a·ble**	rennegade	**ren·e·gade**
remady	**rem·e·dy**	rennovate	**ren·o·vate**
remander	**re·main·der**	renouned	**re·nowned**
remane	**re·main**	renownce	**re·nounce**
remann	**re·mand**	rentel	**rent·al**
remarkible	**re·mark·a·ble**	renumeration	
remedeal	**re·me·di·al**		**re·mu·ner·a·tion**
remembrence		renunsiation	**re·nun·ci·a·tion**
	re·mem·brance	repare	**re·pair**
remenisce	**rem·i·nisce**	repayed	**re·paid**
remine	**re·mind**	repeel	**re·peal**
reminisence	**rem·i·nis·cence**	repeet	**re·peat**
reminiss	**rem·i·nisce**	repeling	**re·pel·ling**
remision	**re·mis·sion**	repell	**re·pel** *(drive back)*
remitance	**re·mit·tance**	repellant	**re·pel·lent**
remminisce	**rem·i·nisce**	repentent	**re·pent·ant**
remminiscence		reperations	**rep·a·ra·tions**
	rem·i·nis·cence	repercusion	**re·per·cus·sion**
remnent	**rem·nant**	repersent	**rep·re·sent**
remourse	**re·morse**	repertoiar	**rep·er·toire**
removeable	**re·mov·a·ble**	repete	**re·peat**
removel	**re·mov·al**	repetitius	**rep·e·ti·tious**

WRONG	RIGHT	WRONG	RIGHT
repetoire	**rep·er·toire**	repreive	**re·prieve**
repetory	**rep·er·to·ry**	represe	**re·prise**
repettitive	**re·pet·i·tive**	represion	**re·pres·sion**
repitition	**rep·e·ti·tion**	repriman	**rep·ri·mand**
repititious	**rep·e·ti·tious**	reprizal	**re·pris·al**
replaca	**rep·li·ca**	reprize	**re·prise**
replacment	**re·place·ment**	reproche	**re·proach**
repleat	**re·plete**	reproduse	**re·pro·duce**
replennish	**re·plen·ish**	reptle	**rep·tile**
replie	**re·ply**	republick	**re·pub·lic**
reposatory	**re·pos·i·to·ry**	repudeate	**re·pu·di·ate**
reposession	**re·pos·ses·sion**	repugnent	**re·pug·nant**
repparations	**rep·a·ra·tions**	repullsive	**re·pul·sive**
reppartee	**rep·ar·tee**	requasition	**req·ui·si·tion**
reppel	**re·pel** *(drive back)*	requess	**re·quest**
reppercussion		requierment	**re·quire·ment**
	re·per·cus·sion	requiset	**req·ui·site**
reppertory	**rep·er·to·ry**	resadue	**res·i·due**
reppetition	**rep·e·ti·tion**	resaleable	**re·sal·a·ble**
repport	**re·port** *(an account)*	resalution	**res·o·lu·tion**
reppresent	**rep·re·sent**	résamé	**ré·su·mé**
reppudiate	**re·pu·di·ate**	rescend	**re·scind**
repputation	**rep·u·ta·tion**	rescusitator	**re·sus·ci·ta·tor**
reprabate	**rep·ro·bate**	resede	**re·cede**
repraduce	**re·pro·duce**	resedential	**res·i·den·tial**
reprahensible		resegnation	**res·ig·na·tion**
	rep·re·hen·si·ble	reseipt	**re·ceipt**
repramand	**rep·ri·mand**	reseive	**re·ceive**
reprasentative		resemblence	**re·sem·blance**
	rep·re·sent·a·tive	resent	**re·cent** *(new)*
reprehensable		reseptacle	**re·cep·ta·cle**
	rep·re·hen·si·ble	reseption	**re·cep·tion**

WRONG	RIGHT	WRONG	RIGHT
reseptor	**re·cep·tor**	respirater	**res·pi·ra·tor**
reserch	**re·search**	respit	**res·pite**
resergent	**re·sur·gent**	resplendant	**re·splend·ent**
reserrection	**res·ur·rec·tion**	responsability	
resess	**re·cess**		**re·spon·si·bil·i·ty**
resession	**re·ces·sion**	responsable	**re·spon·si·ble**
resevoir	**res·er·voir**	respratory	**res·pi·ra·to·ry**
residancy	**res·i·den·cy**	resservation	**res·er·va·tion**
residencial	**res·i·den·tial**	restaration	**res·to·ra·tion**
residew	**res·i·due**	restatution	**res·ti·tu·tion**
resiliance	**re·sil·ience**	resterant	**res·tau·rant**
resind	**re·scind**	restle	**wres·tle**
resine	**re·sign**	restrant	**re·straint**
resipe	**rec·i·pe**	restrant	**res·tau·rant**
resipient	**re·cip·i·ent**	restrick	**re·strict**
resiprocal	**re·cip·ro·cal**	resultent	**re·sult·ant**
resiprocate	**re·cip·ro·cate**	résumae	**ré·su·mé**
resistence	**re·sist·ance**	resumtion	**re·sump·tion**
resister	**re·sis·tor**	resurection	**res·ur·rec·tion**
	(electrical device)	resurgant	**re·sur·gent**
resistor	**re·sist·er**	resussitator	**re·sus·ci·ta·tor**
	(one who resists)	resycle	**re·cy·cle**
resital	**re·cit·al**	retale	**re·tail**
resitation	**rec·i·ta·tion**	retalliate	**re·tal·i·ate**
resonater	**res·o·na·tor**	retane	**re·tain**
resonence	**res·o·nance**	retanue	**ret·i·nue**
resorceful	**re·source·ful**	retch	**wretch**
resownding	**re·sound·ing**		*(miserable person)*
respand	**re·spond**	retecence	**ret·i·cence**
respeck	**re·spect**	retension	**re·ten·tion**
respectible	**re·spect·a·ble**	retern	**re·turn**
resperation	**res·pi·ra·tion**	retisence	**ret·i·cence**

WRONG	RIGHT
retna	**ret·i·na**
retorical	**rhe·tor·i·cal**
retrabution	**ret·ri·bu·tion**
retrack	**re·tract**
retraspect	**ret·ro·spect**
retreet	**re·treat**
retreival	**re·triev·al**
retrospeck	**ret·ro·spect**
retticence	**ret·i·cence**
rettina	**ret·i·na**
rettinue	**ret·i·nue**
rettribution	**ret·ri·bu·tion**
reumatic	**rheu·mat·ic**
revalation	**rev·e·la·tion**
revalutionary	
	rev·o·lu·tion·ary
revanue	**rev·e·nue**
reveer	**re·vere**
reveiw	**re·view** (survey)
reveiw	**re·vue** (musical show)
revellation	**rev·e·la·tion**
revelle	**re·veil·le** (bugle call)
revellry	**rev·el·ry** (festivity)
revelry	**rev·er·ie** (daydream)
revelry	**re·veil·le** (bugle call)
reverance	**rev·er·ence**
reverbarate	**re·ver·ber·ate**
reversable	**re·vers·i·ble**
revery	**rev·er·ie** (daydream)
revery	**rev·el·ry** (festivity)
revinge	**re·venge**
revission	**re·vi·sion**

WRONG	RIGHT
revivel	**re·viv·al**
revize	**re·vise**
revolutionery	
	rev·o·lu·tion·ary
revolveing	**re·volv·ing**
revrence	**rev·er·ence**
revullsion	**re·vul·sion**
rezentment	**re·sent·ment**
rezervation	**res·er·va·tion**
rezervoir	**res·er·voir**
rezide	**re·side**
rezidency	**res·i·den·cy**
rezidential	**res·i·den·tial**
rezidual	**re·sid·u·al**
rezidue	**res·i·due**
rezign	**re·sign**
rezignation	**res·ig·na·tion**
rezin	**res·in**
rezistance	**re·sist·ance**
rezolution	**res·o·lu·tion**
rezolved	**re·solved**
rezonance	**res·o·nance**
rezonator	**res·o·na·tor**
rezort	**re·sort**
rezounding	**re·sound·ing**
rezultant	**re·sult·ant**
rezumption	**re·sump·tion**
rhapsady	**rhap·so·dy**
rhetoricle	**rhe·tor·i·cal**
rheumatick	**rheu·mat·ic**
rhime	**rhyme** (verse)
rhinoseros	**rhi·noc·er·os**

WRONG	RIGHT	WRONG	RIGHT
rhithm	**rhythm**	rifle	**rif·fle** *(shuffle)*
rhodadendron	**rho·do·den·dron**	riformatory	**re·form·a·to·ry**
		rifrigerator	**re·frig·er·a·tor**
rhyme	**rime** *(frost)*	rifute	**re·fute**
rhythem	**rhythm**	rigalia	**re·ga·lia**
rhythymical	**rhyth·mi·cal**	rigamaroll	**rig·ma·role**
ribben	**rib·bon**	rige	**ridge**
ricachet	**ric·o·chet**	rigerous	**rig·or·ous**
riceptacle	**re·cep·ta·cle**	riggatoni	**ri·ga·to·ni**
riciprocate	**re·cip·ro·cate**	rigger	**rig·or** *(hardship)*
ricital	**re·cit·al**	riggle	**wrig·gle**
ricketts	**rick·ets**	right	**rite** *(ritual)*
ricognizance	**re·cog·ni·zance**	right	**write** *(inscribe)*
ricoshet	**ric·o·chet**	rightous	**right·eous**
ricruit	**re·cruit**	riging	**rig·ging**
ridacule	**rid·i·cule**	rigor	**rig·ger** *(one who rigs)*
riddel	**rid·dle**	rigorus	**rig·or·ous**
riddence	**rid·dance**	rigression	**re·gres·sion**
riddicule	**rid·i·cule**	rigurgitation	**re·gur·gi·ta·tion**
rideem	**re·deem**		
rideing	**rid·ing**	rilationship	**re·la·tion·ship**
ridemption	**re·demp·tion**	rilease	**re·lease**
ridgid	**rig·id**	rilentless	**re·lent·less**
ridickulous	**ridic·u·lous**	rilief	**re·lief** *(n.)*
ridle	**rid·dle**	rilieve	**re·lieve** *(v.)*
ridress	**re·dress**	rimand	**re·mand**
riducing	**re·duc·ing**	rimember	**re·mem·ber**
riduction	**re·duc·tion**	rimiss	**re·miss**
riduplication	**re·du·pli·ca·tion**	rimission	**re·mis·sion**
		rimuneration	**re·mu·ner·a·tion**
rie	**rye** *(grain)*		
riffle	**ri·fle** *(gun)*	rine	**rind**

rinege	**re·nege**	rivue	**re·vue** (*musical show*)
rinestone	**rhine·stone**	rivulsion	**re·vul·sion**
ring	**wring** (*twist*)	robbin	**rob·in**
rinoceros	**rhi·noc·er·os**	robbot	**ro·bot**
riotus	**ri·ot·ous**	roben	**rob·in**
riplenish	**re·plen·ish**	robery	**rob·bery**
ripository	**re·pos·i·to·ry**	roche	**roach**
riprisal	**re·pris·al**	rockit	**rock·et**
ripugnant	**re·pug·nant**	rodant	**ro·dent**
ripulsive	**re·pul·sive**	rodao	**ro·deo**
riscind	**re·scind**	rododendron	
risentment	**re·sent·ment**		**rho·do·den·dron**
risidual	**re·sid·u·al**	roge	**rogue**
riskey	**risky** (*dangerous*)	roil	**roy·al** (*regal*)
risky	**ris·qué** (*indecent*)	role	**roll** (*turn*)
risourceful	**re·source·ful**	roler	**roll·er**
rispond	**re·spond**	roll	**role** (*an actor's part*)
risponsible	**re·spon·si·ble**	romane	**ro·maine**
ritchual	**rit·u·al**	romanse	**ro·mance**
rite	**right** (*correct*)	rome	**roam**
rite	**write** (*inscribe*)	rommantic	**ro·man·tic**
rithe	**writhe**	ronchy	**raun·chy**
rithm	**rhythm**	rondezvous	**ren·dez·vous**
ritort	**re·tort**	rone	**roan**
ritten	**writ·ten**	roomate	**room·mate**
rivallry	**ri·val·ry**	roomor	**room·er** (*lodger*)
rivelry	**ri·val·ry**	root	**route** (*way*)
riverberate	**re·ver·ber·ate**	rootabaga	**ru·ta·ba·ga**
rivision	**re·vi·sion**	rosery	**ro·sa·ry**
rivit	**riv·et**	rosey	**rosy**
rivoke	**re·voke**	rost	**roast**
rivolt	**re·volt**	roten	**rot·ten**

WRONG	RIGHT	WRONG	RIGHT
rotery	**ro·ta·ry**	ruge	**rouge**
rotiserie	**rotis·serie**	rulette	**rou·lette**
rotonda	**ro·tun·da**	rumage	**rum·mage**
roudy	**row·dy**	rumanant	**ru·mi·nant**
rouff	**rough** *(not smooth)*	rumatic	**rheu·mat·ic**
roughege	**rough·age**	rumenate	**ru·mi·nate**
rouje	**rouge**	rumer	**ru·mor** *(gossip)*
roulet	**rou·lette**	ruminent	**ru·mi·nant**
rout	**route** *(way)*	rummege	**rum·mage**
route	**rout** *(defeat)*	rung	**wrung** *(pt. of wring)*
route	**root** *(source)*	runing	**run·ning**
routene	**rou·tine**	rupchure	**rup·ture**
row	**roe** *(fish eggs)*	rurel	**ru·ral**
rowse	**rouse**	ruset	**rus·set**
rowst	**roust**	russle	**rus·tle**
rowt	**rout** *(defeat)*	rutine	**rou·tine**
royal	**roil** *(stir up)*	ruttabaga	**ru·ta·ba·ga**
royel	**roy·al** *(regal)*	rutter	**rud·der**
royelty	**roy·al·ty**	ruze	**ruse**
rozin	**ros·in**	rye	**wry** *(twisted; ironic)*
rubarb	**rhu·barb**	ryme	**rime** *(frost)*
rubbry	**rub·bery**	ryme	**rhyme** *(verse)*
rubela	**ru·bel·la**	rythm	**rhythm**
ruber	**rub·ber**	rythmical	**rhyth·mi·cal**
rubey	**ru·by**		
rubish	**rub·bish**		
rudamentary	**rudi·men·ta·ry**	**S**	
rudy	**rud·dy**		
ruff	**rough** *(not smooth)*	sabattical	**sab·bat·i·cal**
ruffage	**rough·age**	Sabbeth	**Sab·bath**
rufian	**ruf·fi·an**	sabbotage	**sab·o·tage**
rufle	**ruf·fle**	sabboteur	**sab·o·teur**
		sabor	**sa·ber**

WRONG	RIGHT
saboter	**sab·o·teur**
saccarine	**sac·cha·rine**
	(too sweet)
sacerfice	**sac·ri·fice**
sacerficial	**sac·ri·fi·cial**
sacerligous	**sac·ri·le·gious**
sacharine	**sac·cha·rin**
	(sugar substitute)
sachel	**satch·el**
sacheration	**sat·u·ra·tion**
sack	**sac** *(organic pouch)*
sackroiliac	**sa·cro·il·i·ac**
sacraficial	**sac·ri·fi·cial**
sacrefice	**sac·ri·fice**
sacrelige	**sac·ri·lege**
sacreligious	**sac·ri·le·gious**
sacrement	**sac·ra·ment**
sacrid	**sa·cred**
sacrine	**sac·cha·rine**
	(too sweet)
sacroilliac	**sa·cro·il·i·ac**
saddeling	**sad·dling**
saddistic	**sa·dis·tic**
sadesm	**sad·ism**
saduce	**se·duce**
saence	**sé·ance**
safegaurd	**safe·guard**
saffari	**sa·fa·ri**
safire	**sap·phire**
saflower	**saf·flow·er**
safron	**saf·fron**
safty	**safe·ty**

WRONG	RIGHT
sagga	**sa·ga**
Saggitarius	**Sag·it·ta·rius**
Sahera	**Sa·ha·ra**
saidism	**sad·ism**
saige	**sage**
sail	**sale** *(business exchange)*
sailer	**sail·or** *(person)*
sailor	**sail·er** *(boat)*
sakred	**sa·cred**
salary	**cel·e·ry** *(vegetable)*
salavate	**sal·i·vate**
sale	**sail** *(boat's canvas)*
salemn	**sol·emn**
saliant	**sa·lient**
sallad	**sal·ad**
sallamander	**sal·a·man·der**
sallami	**sa·la·mi**
sallary	**sal·a·ry** *(pay)*
sallient	**sa·lient**
salline	**sa·line**
salliva	**sa·li·va**
sallivate	**sal·i·vate**
sallon	**sa·lon**
salloon	**sa·loon**
sallutation	**sal·u·ta·tion**
sallute	**sa·lute**
salm	**psalm**
salman	**salm·on**
salow	**sal·low**
salstice	**sol·stice**
saltsellar	**salt·cel·lar**
salution	**so·lu·tion**

WRONG	RIGHT	WRONG	RIGHT
salvege	**sal·vage**	sarkophagus	**sar·coph·a·gus**
samantics	**se·man·tics**	Sarracen	**Sar·a·cen**
sammon	**salm·on**	sarri	**sa·ri** *(Hindu garment)*
samorai	**sam·u·rai**	sarsparilla	**sar·sa·pa·ril·la**
sampeling	**sam·pling**	sasafras	**sas·sa·fras**
sanatarium	**san·i·tar·i·um**	sashay	**sa·chet**
sanatation	**san·i·ta·tion**		*(perfumed powder)*
sanctefied	**sanc·ti·fied**	sashiate	**sa·ti·ate**
sanctuery	**sanc·tu·ary**	sasparilla	**sar·sa·pa·ril·la**
San Deigo	**San Di·e·go**	satannic	**sa·tan·ic**
sandle	**san·dal**	satchle	**satch·el**
Sandskrit	**San·skrit**	satelite	**sat·el·lite**
sandwitch	**sand·wich**	saten	**sat·in** *(fabric)*
sanetary	**san·i·tary**	sater	**sat·yr** *(deity)*
sanety	**san·i·ty**	Saterday	**Sat·ur·day**
sangwin	**san·guine**	saterize	**sat·i·rize**
saniterium	**san·i·tar·i·um**	Satern	**Sat·urn**
sanktion	**sanc·tion**	satesfaction	**sat·is·fac·tion**
sannitation	**san·i·ta·tion**	Satin	**Sa·tan** *(devil)*
Sanscrit	**San·skrit**	satisfactery	**sat·is·fac·to·ry**
sanwich	**sand·wich**	sattanic	**sa·tan·ic**
saphire	**sap·phire**	sattelite	**sat·el·lite**
saprano	**so·pra·no**	sattin	**sat·in** *(fabric)*
Sarasen	**Sar·a·cen**	sattire	**sat·ire** *(ridicule)*
sarcasem	**sar·casm**	sattyr	**sat·yr** *(deity)*
sarcasticly	**sar·cas·ti·cal·ly**	saturration	**sat·u·ra·tion**
sarcofagus	**sar·coph·a·gus**	saucey	**sau·cy**
sardene	**sar·dine**	sauercraut	**sau·er·kraut**
sardonnic	**sar·don·ic**	saught	**sought**
sargeant	**ser·geant**	saunna	**sau·na**
saringe	**sy·ringe**	saurkraut	**sau·er·kraut**
sarkastically	**sar·cas·ti·cal·ly**	sause	**sauce**

WRONG	RIGHT	WRONG	RIGHT
sausege	**sau·sage**	scandilous	**scan·dal·ous**
sauser	**sau·cer**	scaner	**scan·ner**
sautté	**sau·té**	scaning	**scan·ning**
savagrey	**sav·age·ry**	scapgoat	**scape·goat**
save	**salve** (ointment)	scarceley	**scarce·ly**
savege	**sav·age**	scarcety	**scar·ci·ty**
saveing	**sav·ing**	scared	**scarred** (marred)
saver	**sa·vor** (taste or smell)	scarey	**scary**
saver	**sav·ior** (rescuer)	scarlit	**scar·let**
savery	**sa·vory**	scarred	**scared** (frightened)
savier	**sav·ior** (rescuer)	scarsely	**scarce·ly**
savier	**sav·er**	scarsity	**scar·ci·ty**
	(keeper; one who saves)	scatering	**scat·ter·ing**
savoir-fair	**sa·voir–faire**	scatheing	**scath·ing**
savor	**sav·ior** (rescuer)	scavinger	**scav·eng·er**
savor	**sav·er**	sceen	**scene** (location)
	(keeper; one who saves)	scematic	**sche·mat·ic**
savuar-faire	**sa·voir–faire**	scemed	**schemed**
savy	**sav·vy**	scenary	**sce·nery**
saxaphone	**sax·o·phone**	scennario	**sce·nar·io**
Saxen	**Sax·on**	scent	**cent** (money)
sayed	**said**	scent	**sent** (pt. of send)
scafold	**scaf·fold**	scepticle	**skep·ti·cal**
scaleing	**scal·ing**	sceptor	**scep·ter**
scaley	**scaly**	scewer	**skew·er**
scalion	**scal·lion**	schedual	**sched·ule**
scallap	**scal·lop**	schedulling	**sched·ul·ing**
scalled	**scald** (burn)	scheemed	**schemed**
scalpul	**scal·pel**	scheenario	
scandallize	**scan·dal·ize**		**schiz·o·phre·nia**
Scandanavia	**Scan·di·na·via**	schnopps	**schnapps**
scandel	**scan·dal**	schnouzer	**schnau·zer**

scholer	**schol·ar**	scraped ... **scrapped** *(discarded)*	
schollastic	**scho·las·tic**	scrapped ...... **scraped** *(rubbed)*	
schoolling	**school·ing**	scraul	**scrawl**
sciense	**sci·ence**	scrauny	**scraw·ny**
scientiffic	**sci·en·tif·ic**	screach	**screech**
scimmed	**skimmed**	screeming	**scream·ing**
scimpy	**skimpy**	scribling	**scrib·bling**
scintilate	**scin·til·late**	scrimage	**scrim·mage**
scirmish	**skir·mish**	scrip	**script** *(manuscript)*
scism	**schism**	scripcher	**scrip·ture**
scismatic	**schis·mat·ic**	script	**scrip** *(certificate)*
scisors	**scis·sors**	scrole	**scroll**
scithe	**scythe**	scroopulous	**scru·pu·lous**
scizophrenia	**schiz·o·phre·nia**	scrootinize	**scru·ti·nize**
sclirosis	**scle·ro·sis**	scrownge	**scrounge**
scoch	**scotch**	scrubed	**scrubbed**
scolar	**schol·ar**	scrupullous	**scru·pu·lous**
scolastic	**scho·las·tic**	scrutenize	**scru·ti·nize**
scooling	**school·ing**	scruteny	**scru·ti·ny**
scooner	**schoon·er**	scuad	**squad**
scoreing	**scor·ing**	scufle	**scuf·fle**
scornfull	**scorn·ful**	scull	**skull** *(head)*
Scorpeo	**Scor·pio**	sculpcher	**sculp·ture**
scorpeon	**scor·pi·on**	sculpter	**sculp·tor**
Scotish	**Scot·tish**	scunk	**skunk**
scoul	**scowl**	scurge	**scourge**
scower	**scour**	scurilous	**scur·ril·ous**
scowndrel	**scoun·drel**	scurvey	**scur·vy**
scowt	**scout**	scury	**scur·ry**
scrachy	**scratchy**	scutle	**scut·tle**
scragly	**scrag·gly**	scyth	**scythe**
scrambeling	**scram·bling**	sea	**see** *(perceive)*

seady	**seedy**	sed	**said**
sealent	**seal·ant**	sedament	**sed·i·ment**
sealing	**ceil·ing**	sedantary	**sed·en·tary**
	(overhead covering)	sedar	**ce·dar**
seam	**seem** *(appear)*	seddan	**se·dan**
seamly	**seem·ly**	seddation	**se·da·tion**
seamstriss	**seam·stress**	seddative	**sed·a·tive**
seapage	**seep·age**	sedductive	**se·duc·tive**
sear	**seer** *(prophet)*	sede	**cede** *(give up)*
seasaw	**see·saw**	sedentery	**sed·en·tary**
seasen	**sea·son**	sedimant	**sed·i·ment**
seasening	**sea·son·ing**	seditive	**sed·a·tive**
Sebtember	**Sep·tem·ber**	seductave	**se·duc·tive**
seccede	**se·cede** *(withdraw)*	see	**sea** *(body of water)*
seccessive	**suc·ces·sive**	seed	**cede** *(give up)*
seccular	**sec·u·lar**	seege	**siege**
seceed	**se·cede** *(withdraw)*	seem	**seam** *(line)*
secertary	**sec·re·tary**	seemstress	**seam·stress**
seclussion	**se·clu·sion**	seemy	**seamy**
secondery	**sec·ond·ary**	seen	**scene** *(location)*
secracy	**se·cre·cy**	seenile	**se·nile**
secratary	**sec·re·tary**	seepege	**seep·age**
secrative	**se·cre·tive**	seequel	**se·quel**
secreet	**se·crete**	seequin	**se·quin**
secreetion	**se·cre·tion**	seer	**sear** *(burn)*
secresy	**se·cre·cy**	seeth	**seethe**
secs	**sects** *(factions)*	seeting	**seat·ing**
secter	**sec·tor**	segmint	**seg·ment**
seculer	**sec·u·lar**	segragation	**seg·re·ga·tion**
secullarize	**sec·u·lar·ize**	seige	**siege**
secundary	**sec·ond·ary**	seirra	**si·er·ra**
securety	**se·cu·ri·ty**	seismagraph	**seis·mo·graph**

WRONG	RIGHT	WRONG	RIGHT
seive	**sieve**	sennile	**se·nile**
seizeing	**seiz·ing**	senority	**sen·ior·i·ty**
sekts	**sects** *(factions)*	sensability	**sen·si·bil·i·ty**
seldum	**sel·dom**	sensable	**sen·si·ble**
selectave	**se·lec·tive**	sensasional	**sen·sa·tion·al**
self–concious		sensative	**sen·si·tive**
	self–con·scious	sensativity	**sen·si·tiv·i·ty**
self–rightious	**self–right·eous**	sensatize	**sen·si·tize**
sell	**cell** *(room)*	sensery	**sen·so·ry**
sellar	**sell·er** *(vendor)*	sensitivaty	**sen·si·tiv·i·ty**
sellection	**se·lec·tion**	sensor	**cen·sor** *(prohibiter)*
sellective	**se·lec·tive**	sensuallity	**sen·su·al·i·ty**
seller	**cel·lar** *(basement)*	sensuas	**sen·su·ous**
seltser	**selt·zer**	sensule	**sen·su·al**
semafore	**sem·a·phore**	sensus	**cen·sus**
semalina	**sem·o·li·na**	sent	**cent** *(money)*
semanary	**sem·i·nary**	sent	**scent** *(smell)*
sembelance	**sem·blance**	sentamental	**sen·ti·men·tal**
semenal	**sem·i·nal**	sentement	**sen·ti·ment**
Semetic	**Se·mit·ic**	sentense	**sen·tence**
seminery	**sem·i·nary**	sentinnel	**sen·ti·nel**
semmantics	**se·man·tics**	sentrey	**sen·try**
semmester	**se·mes·ter**	sentury	**cen·tu·ry**
semmicolon	**sem·i·co·lon**	separration	**sep·a·ra·tion**
semminary	**sem·i·nary**	seperable	**sep·a·ra·ble**
Semmitic	**Se·mit·ic**	seperate	**sep·a·rate**
senario	**sce·nar·io**	seperation	**sep·a·ra·tion**
senater	**sen·a·tor**	Septembar	**Sep·tem·ber**
senatoreal	**sen·a·to·ri·al**	septer	**scep·ter**
sence	**sense**	sequal	**se·quel**
senier	**sen·ior**	sequance	**se·quence**
sennator	**sen·a·tor**	sequen	**se·quin**

WRONG	RIGHT	WRONG	RIGHT
seranade	**ser·e·nade**	servent	**serv·ant**
serch	**search**	servial	**ser·vile**
sercharge	**sur·charge**	servicable	**serv·ice·a·ble**
serenety	**se·ren·i·ty**	servise	**serv·ice**
serf	**surf** *(waves)*	servival	**sur·viv·al**
serface	**sur·face**	sesami	**ses·a·me**
serfboard	**surf·board**	sesede	**se·cede** *(withdraw)*
serge	**surge**	sessame	**ses·a·me**
	(sudden increase; wave)	sessian	**ses·sion** *(meeting)*
sergent	**ser·geant**	session	**ces·sion** *(a giving up)*
sergeon	**sur·geon**	sesspool	**cess·pool**
sergery	**sur·gery**	setteler	**set·tler**
sergical	**sur·gi·cal**	settlement	**set·tle·ment**
serial	**ce·re·al** *(grain)*	seudonym	**pseu·do·nym**
seriusness	**seri·ous·ness**	sevanth	**sev·enth**
serloin	**sir·loin**	sevarel	**sev·er·al**
serly	**sur·ly** *(rude)*	sevarance	**sev·er·ance**
serman	**ser·mon**	sevarity	**se·ver·i·ty**
sermise	**sur·mise**	seveer	**se·vere**
serpant	**ser·pent**	seventeith	**sev·en·ti·eth**
serpassed	**sur·passed**	severrity	**se·ver·i·ty**
serplus	**sur·plus** *(excess)*	sevinteen	**sev·en·teen**
serreal	**sur·real** *(fantastic)*	sevral	**sev·er·al**
serrenade	**ser·e·nade**	sevrance	**sev·er·ance**
serrene	**se·rene** *(calm)*	sevver	**sev·er**
serrenity	**se·ren·i·ty**	sew	**sow** *(plant)*
serrogate	**sur·ro·gate**	sew	**sue** *(prosecute)*
serrum	**se·rum**	sewege	**sew·age**
sertax	**sur·tax**	sexey	**sexy**
servace	**serv·ice**	sextent	**sex·tant**
servatude	**ser·vi·tude**	sexuallity	**sex·u·al·i·ty**
serveillance	**sur·veil·lance**	sfere	**sphere**

WRONG	RIGHT	WRONG	RIGHT
shabbie	**shab·by**	sheer	**shear** *(clip)*
Shablis	**Cha·blis**	sheeth	**sheath** *(n.)*
shackeled	**shack·led**	sheeth	**sheathe** *(v.)*
shaddow	**shad·ow**	shef	**chef** *(cook)*
shadey	**shady**	sheik	**chic** *(fashionable)*
shaggie	**shag·gy**	sheild	**shield**
shakey	**shaky**	sheperd	**shep·herd**
shakled	**shack·led**	sherbert	**sher·bet**
Shakspeare	**Shake·speare**	sherif	**sher·iff** *(law officer)*
shalet	**cha·let**	sherrie	**sher·ry**
shalot	**shal·lot** *(onion)*	shicanery	**chi·can·ery**
shalow	**shal·low** *(not deep)*	shiek	**sheik** *(Arab chief)*
shambels	**sham·bles**	shiling	**shil·ling**
shamful	**shame·ful**	shillac	**shel·lac**
shamois	**cham·ois**	shimer	**shim·mer**
shampane	**cham·pagne** *(wine)*	shiney	**shiny**
		shingel	**shin·gle**
shampo	**sham·poo**	shining	**shin·ning** *(climbing)*
shandelier	**chan·de·lier**	shinning	**shin·ing** *(radiant)*
Shanghi	**Shang·hai**	shiped	**shipped**
shantey	**shan·ty** *(shack)*	shirtail	**shirt·tail**
shantie	**chan·tey** *(song)*	shivver	**shiv·er**
shapliness	**shape·li·ness**	shlock	**schlock**
sharade	**cha·rade**	shmorgasbord	
shassis	**chas·sis**		**smor·gas·bord**
shateau	**châ·teau**	shnapps	**schnapps**
shater	**shat·ter**	shnauzer	**schnau·zer**
shaul	**shawl**	shnitzel	**schnit·zel**
shear	**sheer** *(thin; steep)*	shody	**shod·dy**
sheathe	**sheath** *(n.)*	sholder	**shoul·der**
sheef	**sheaf**	shoot	**chute** *(trough)*
sheek	**sheik** *(Arab chief)*	shortning	**short·en·ing**

WRONG	RIGHT	WRONG	RIGHT
shovinism	**chau·vin·ism**	siesmograph	**seis·mo·graph**
showey	**showy**	siethe	**seethe**
shrapnle	**shrap·nel**	siezing	**seiz·ing**
shreek	**shriek**	siezure	**sei·zure**
shreud	**shrewd**	siffilis	**syph·i·lis**
shrinkege	**shrink·age**	sifon	**si·phon**
shrivvel	**shriv·el**	sight	**cite** *(quote)*
shrowd	**shroud**	sight	**site** *(location)*
shrubery	**shrub·bery**	sightseing	**sight·see·ing**
shufled	**shuf·fled**	sign	**sine** *(ratio)*
shulder	**shoul·der**	signat	**sig·net**
shurbit	**sher·bet**	signefy	**sig·ni·fy**
shurely	**sure·ly** *(certainly)*	signel	**sig·nal**
shurk	**shirk**	signeture	**sig·na·ture**
shuter	**shut·ter**	significanse	**sig·nif·i·cance**
shutteling	**shut·tling**	silacone	**sil·i·cone** *(compound)*
shuvel	**shov·el**	silecon	**sil·i·con** *(element)*
shyed	**shied**	silense	**si·lence**
Siammese	**Si·a·mese**	silhuette	**sil·hou·ette**
siatica	**sci·at·i·ca**	silia	**cil·ia**
sibbeling	**sib·ling**	silkan	**silk·en**
Sibiria	**Si·ber·ia**	sillabic	**syl·lab·ic**
sicada	**ci·ca·da**	sillable	**syl·la·ble**
sicamore	**syc·a·more**	sillabus	**syl·la·bus**
sick	**sic** *(set upon; incite)*	sillica	**sil·i·ca**
sickel	**sick·le**	sillicon	**sil·i·con** *(element)*
siclusion	**se·clu·sion**	sillicone	**sil·i·cone**
sidition	**se·di·tion**		*(compound)*
siduce	**se·duce**	sillogism	**syl·lo·gism**
sience	**sci·ence**	sillos	**si·los**
sientific	**sci·en·tif·ic**	sillouette	**sil·hou·ette**
siera	**si·er·ra**	siloes	**si·los**

WRONG	RIGHT	WRONG	RIGHT
silverey	**sil·very**	sinder	**cin·der**
simbiotic	**sym·bi·ot·ic**	sindicate	**syn·di·cate**
simbol	**sym·bol** (mark)	sindrome	**syn·drome**
simbolism	**sym·bol·ism**	sine	**sign** (signal)
simbollize	**sym·bol·ize**	sinester	**sin·is·ter**
simean	**sim·i·an**	sinfuel	**syn·fu·el**
simeltaneous	**simul·ta·ne·ous**	sinfull	**sin·ful**
simer	**sim·mer**	singeling	**sin·gling**
simfony	**sym·pho·ny**	singing	**singe·ing** (burning)
similation	**sim·u·la·tion**	singuler	**sin·gu·lar**
similer	**sim·i·lar**	sink	**sync** (synchronize)
simmetrical	**sym·met·ri·cal**	sinkronize	**syn·chro·nize**
simmetry	**sym·me·try**	sinnew	**sin·ew**
simmian	**sim·i·an**	sinnister	**sin·is·ter**
simmulation	**sim·u·la·tion**	sinnopses	**syn·op·ses** (pl.)
simpathetic	**sym·pa·thet·ic**	sinnuous	**sin·u·ous**
simpathy	**sym·pa·thy**	sinonym	**syn·o·nym**
simpelton	**sim·ple·ton**	sinopsis	**syn·op·sis** (sing.)
simphonic	**sym·phon·ic**	sinous	**si·nus**
simplefy	**sim·pli·fy**	sinserely	**sin·cere·ly**
simplicety	**sim·plic·i·ty**	sinserity	**sin·cer·i·ty**
simposium	**sym·po·si·um**	sintax	**syn·tax**
simptom	**symp·tom**	sinthesis	**syn·the·sis** (sing.)
simular	**sim·i·lar**	sinthetic	**syn·thet·ic**
simulater	**sim·u·la·tor**	sintillate	**scin·til·late**
simultanious	**simul·ta·ne·ous**	sinue	**sin·ew**
sinagogue	**syn·a·gogue**	sion	**sci·on**
sincerly	**sin·cere·ly**	siphen	**si·phon**
sincerrity	**sin·cer·i·ty**	siphilis	**syph·i·lis**
sinchronize	**syn·chro·nize**	sircharge	**sur·charge**
sinchronous	**syn·chro·nous**	sirene	**se·rene** (calm)
sincopation	**syn·co·pa·tion**	Siria	**Syr·ia**

WRONG	RIGHT	WRONG	RIGHT
sirial	**se·ri·al** *(in a series)*	skamper	**scam·per**
sirin	**si·ren**	Skandinavia	**Scan·di·na·via**
siringe	**sy·ringe**	skanty	**scanty**
sirly	**sur·ly** *(rude)*	skathing	**scath·ing**
sirmon	**ser·mon**	skavenger	**scav·eng·er**
sirname	**sur·name**	skech	**sketch**
sirpent	**ser·pent**	skedule	**sched·ule**
sirrup	**syr·up**	skee	**ski**
sirtax	**sur·tax**	skeing	**ski·ing**
sirum	**se·rum**	skeleten	**skel·e·ton**
sism	**schism**	skeptacism	**skep·ti·cism**
sissors	**scis·sors**	skeptecal	**skep·ti·cal**
sistem	**sys·tem**	skewar	**skew·er**
sistematic	**sys·tem·at·ic**	skien	**skein**
sistern	**cis·tern**	skilfull	**skill·ful**
sitation	**ci·ta·tion**	skimpie	**skimpy**
site	**cite** *(quote)*	sking	**ski·ing**
site	**sight** *(vision)*	skiped	**skipped**
sither	**zith·er**	skoff	**scoff**
siting	**sit·ting** *(prp. of sit)*	skooner	**schoon·er**
sittuation	**sit·u·a·tion**	skooter	**scoot·er**
siutcase	**suit·case**	skope	**scope**
sixteith	**six·ti·eth**	skorch	**scorch**
sizeing	**siz·ing**	skorpion	**scor·pi·on**
sizemograph	**seis·mo·graph**	skotch	**scotch**
sizmatic	**schis·mat·ic**	skowl	**scowl**
sizzeling	**siz·zling**	skrawny	**scraw·ny**
skab	**scab**	skreen	**screen**
skain	**skein**	skrimp	**scrimp**
skald	**scald** *(burn)*	skroll	**scroll**
skallion	**scal·lion**	skuba	**scu·ba**
skalp	**scalp**	skuff	**scuff**

WRONG	RIGHT	WRONG	RIGHT
skull	**scull** *(oar; boat)*	slite	**sleight** *(dexterity)*
skulptor	**sculp·tor**	slithary	**slith·ery**
skum	**scum**	slo	**sloe** *(fruit)*
skurmish	**skir·mish**	slober	**slob·ber**
skwid	**squid**	slogen	**slo·gan**
skwint	**squint**	slolom	**sla·lom**
skyskraper	**sky·scrap·er**	slooth	**sleuth**
slalem	**sla·lom**	slopy	**slop·py**
slandorous	**slan·der·ous**	sloted	**slot·ted**
slaternly	**slat·tern·ly**	slothe	**sloth**
slath	**sloth**	slou	**slough**
slaugter	**slaugh·ter**	sloughter	**slaugh·ter**
slavvery	**slav·ery**	slovvenly	**slov·en·ly**
Slavvic	**Slav·ic**	slow	**sloe** *(fruit)*
slay	**sleigh** *(vehicle)*	sluce	**sluice**
sleak	**sleek**	sludje	**sludge**
sleat	**sleet**	slueth	**sleuth**
sleave	**sleeve** *(arm covering)*	sluf	**slough**
sleazie	**slea·zy**	slugard	**slug·gard**
sleepally	**sleep·i·ly**	slugish	**slug·gish**
sleevless	**sleeve·less**	slurr	**slur**
sleezy	**slea·zy**	smaterring	**smat·ter·ing**
slege	**sledge**	smeer	**smear**
sleight	**slight** *(thin)*	smely	**smelly**
sley	**slay** *(kill)*	smerch	**smirch**
sliceing	**slic·ing**	smerk	**smirk**
sliegh	**sleigh** *(vehicle)*	smokey	**smoky** *(of smoke)*
slight	**sleight** *(dexterity)*	smollder	**smol·der**
slimey	**slimy**	smootch	**smooch**
sliped	**slipped**	smorgasboard	
slipry	**slip·pery**		**smor·gas·bord**
slising	**slic·ing**	smuggeling	**smug·gling**

194

smurch	**smirch**	sodder	**sol·der** *(metal alloy)*
smurk	**smirk**	sodeum	**so·di·um**
smuther	**smoth·er**	soffa	**so·fa**
snach	**snatch**	soffener	**sof·ten·er**
snair	**snare**	sofistication	**sophis·ti·ca·tion**
snakey	**snaky**	sofistry	**soph·is·try**
snappie	**snap·py**	sofomore	**soph·o·more**
sneeky	**sneaky**	softner	**sof·ten·er**
snich	**snitch**	sojurn	**so·journ**
sniffeling	**snif·fling**	solase	**sol·ace**
sniped	**snipped** *(cut)*	solatude	**sol·i·tude**
snivling	**sniv·el·ing**	solder	**sol·dier**
snoball	**snow·ball**		*(person in army)*
snobery	**snob·bery**	sole	**soul** *(spirit)*
snorkle	**snor·kel**	soled	**sol·id** *(substantial)*
snowey	**snowy**	soledarity	**sol·i·dar·i·ty**
snuggeling	**snug·gling**	soler	**so·lar**
so	**sew** *(stitch)*	soletaire	**sol·i·taire**
so	**sow** *(plant)*	soletary	**sol·i·tary**
soar	**sore** *(painful)*	soley	**sole·ly**
soberiety	**so·bri·e·ty**	solice	**sol·ace**
socable	**so·cia·ble**	soliciter	**so·lic·i·tor**
sociallism	**so·cial·ism**	solidefy	**so·lid·i·fy**
sociallize	**so·cial·ize**	soliderity	**sol·i·dar·i·ty**
socialogical	**so·ci·o·log·i·cal**	solilequy	**so·lil·o·quy**
socialy	**so·cial·ly**	solisitor	**so·lic·i·tor**
sociaty	**so·ci·e·ty**	sollace	**sol·ace**
sociologecal	**so·ci·o·log·i·cal**	sollar	**so·lar**
socker	**soc·cer**	sollemn	**sol·emn**
sockit	**sock·et**	sollicitor	**so·lic·i·tor**
Socrites	**Soc·ra·tes**	sollid	**sol·id** *(substantial)*
sodda	**so·da**	solliloquy	**so·lil·o·quy**

WRONG	RIGHT	WRONG	RIGHT
sollitaire	**sol·i·taire**	sorow	**sor·row**
sollitary	**sol·i·tary**	sorrority	**so·ror·i·ty**
sollitude	**sol·i·tude**	sorry	**sa·ri** (Hindu garment)
Sollomon	**Sol·o·mon**	sorserer	**sor·cer·er**
sollution	**so·lu·tion**	sorsery	**sor·cery**
solstise	**sol·stice**	sosiable	**so·cia·ble**
solumn	**sol·emn**	sosialism	**so·cial·ism**
solvant	**sol·vent**	sosially	**so·cial·ly**
sombody	**some·body**	sosiety	**so·ci·e·ty**
sombraro	**som·bre·ro**	soterne	**sau·terne**
somersalt	**som·er·sault**	souflé	**souf·flé**
sonec	**son·ic**	soul	**sole** (single; bottom)
sonnar	**so·nar**	sourkraut	**sau·er·kraut**
sonnata	**so·na·ta**	sourse	**source**
sonnic	**son·ic**	southren	**south·ern**
sonnit	**son·net**	southword	**south·ward**
sooflé	**souf·flé**	souvanir	**sou·ve·nir**
sooth	**soothe** (make calm)	Soux	**Sioux**
soovenir	**sou·ve·nir**	soviat	**so·vi·et**
sophestry	**soph·is·try**	sovreign	**sov·er·eign**
sophistecation		sow	**sew** (stitch)
	sophis·ti·ca·tion	sowse	**souse**
sophmore	**soph·o·more**	spachula	**spat·u·la**
sopranno	**so·pra·no**	spacial	**spa·tial**
sorcary	**sor·cery**	spacific	**spe·cif·ic**
sorce	**source**	spacifically	**spe·cif·i·cal·ly**
sorceror	**sor·cer·er**	spacous	**spa·cious**
sord	**sword** (weapon)	spade	**spayed** (pt. of spay)
sorded	**sor·did**	spagetti	**spa·ghet·ti**
sore	**soar** (fly)	spangeled	**span·gled**
soriasis	**pso·ri·a·sis**	spanniel	**span·iel**
sorley	**sore·ly**	Spannish	**Span·ish**

WRONG	RIGHT	WRONG	RIGHT
sparce	**sparse**	spector	**spec·ter**
sparibs	**spare·ribs**	spectrem	**spec·trum**
sparing	**spar·ring** (boxing)	speculitive	**spec·u·la·tive**
sparkeler	**spar·kler**	specullation	**spec·u·la·tion**
sparow	**spar·row**	spedometer	**speed·om·e·ter**
sparr	**spar**	speek	**speak**
sparring	**spar·ing** (saving)	speer	**spear**
spasem	**spasm**	speermint	**spear·mint**
spasious	**spa·cious**	spekled	**speck·led**
spasmoddic	**spas·mod·ic**	spektrum	**spec·trum**
spaun	**spawn**	spelbound	**spell·bound**
spazm	**spasm**	speradic	**spo·rad·ic**
speach	**speech**	spern	**spurn**
speccify	**spec·i·fy**	sperrow	**spar·row**
specculation	**spec·u·la·tion**	spert	**spurt**
specefication	**spec·i·fi·ca·tion**	spesial	**spe·cial**
specemin	**spec·i·men**	spesialize	**spe·cial·ize**
speciallist	**spe·cial·ist**	spesify	**spec·i·fy**
speciallize	**spe·cial·ize**	spesimen	**spec·i·men**
specie	**spe·cies** (variety)	sphear	**sphere**
speciel	**spe·cial**	spheracle	**spher·i·cal**
specielty	**spe·cial·ty**	sphynx	**sphinx**
species	**spe·cie** (coin)	spicey	**spicy**
specifecation	**spec·i·fi·ca·tion**	spicket	**spig·ot**
speciffic	**spe·cif·ic**	spidary	**spi·dery**
specificly	**spe·cif·i·cal·ly**	spiggot	**spig·ot**
speckeled	**speck·led**	spimoni	**spu·mo·ni**
speckter	**spec·ter**	spindel	**spin·dle**
spectacel	**spec·ta·cle**	spindely	**spin·dly**
spectater	**spec·ta·tor**	spinel	**spi·nal** (of the spine)
specteral	**spec·tral**	spiney	**spiny**
specticle	**spec·ta·cle**	spinich	**spin·ach**

WRONG	RIGHT	WRONG	RIGHT
spinnoff	**spin·off**	spummoni	**spu·mo·ni**
spiratual	**spir·it·u·al**	spunge	**sponge**
spirel	**spi·ral**	spured	**spurred**
spiret	**spir·it**	spurm	**sperm**
spiritted	**spir·it·ed**	spurrious	**spu·ri·ous**
spirituallity	**spir·it·u·al·i·ty**	sputer	**sput·ter**
spiritule	**spir·it·u·al**	spyre	**spire**
spirral	**spi·ral**	squable	**squab·ble**
spirrit	**spir·it**	squadren	**squad·ron**
spitefull	**spite·ful**	squallid	**squal·id**
splean	**spleen**	squallor	**squal·or**
splended	**splen·did**	squauk	**squawk**
splender	**splen·dor**	squeek	**squeak**
sploch	**splotch**	squeel	**squeal**
spoillage	**spoil·age**	squeemish	**squeam·ish**
spoilling	**spoil·ing**	squeltch	**squelch**
spongey	**spon·gy**	squerm	**squirm**
sponser	**spon·sor**	squerrel	**squir·rel**
spontanious	**spon·ta·ne·ous**	squert	**squirt**
sponteneity	**spon·ta·ne·i·ty**	squigly	**squig·gly**
sporradic	**spo·rad·ic**	squirel	**squir·rel**
spoted	**spot·ted**	squonder	**squan·der**
spoutted	**spout·ed**	squosh	**squash**
spowse	**spouse**	squot	**squat**
spralled	**sprawled**	stabed	**stabbed**
spraned	**sprained**	stabel	**sta·ble**
sprauled	**sprawled**	stabillity	**sta·bil·i·ty**
spred	**spread**	stabillize	**sta·bi·lize**
sprinkeling	**sprin·kling**	stableize	**sta·bi·lize**
spritely	**spright·ly**	stacatto	**stac·ca·to**
sprowt	**sprout**	stachure	**stat·ure**
spue	**spew**	stackade	**stock·ade**

WRONG	RIGHT	WRONG	RIGHT
stacking	**stock·ing** *(sock)*	standerdize	**stand·ard·ize**
stadeum	**sta·di·um**	stansa	**stan·za**
staff	**staph** *(bacterium)*	stanse	**stance**
stagerring	**stag·ger·ing**	stanstill	**stand·still**
stagey	**stagy**	stapel	**sta·ple**
stagnent	**stag·nant**	stapeling	**sta·pling**
staid	**stayed** *(pt. of stay)*	stappler	**sta·pler**
staidium	**sta·di·um**	stare	**stair** *(step)*
stail	**stale**	stared	**starred**
stailmate	**stale·mate**		*(marked with a star)*
stair	**stare** *(gaze)*	stareo	**ster·eo**
staive	**stave**	starred	**stared** *(pt. of stare)*
stake	**steak** *(meat slice)*	startch	**starch**
stalacmite	**sta·lag·mite**	starteling	**star·tling**
	(lime deposit on floor)	stary	**star·ry**
stalagtite	**sta·lac·tite**	statastition	**stat·is·ti·cian**
	(lime deposit from roof)	statchute	**stat·ute**
stalid	**stol·id** *(impassive)*	statick	**stat·ic**
stalion	**stal·lion**	stationary	**sta·tion·ery**
stallactite	**sta·lac·tite**		*(writing materials)*
	(lime deposit from roof)	stationery	**sta·tion·ary** *(still)*
stallagmite	**sta·lag·mite**	statis	**sta·tus**
	(lime deposit on floor)	statly	**state·ly**
stallwart	**stal·wart**	stattic	**stat·ic**
stalmate	**stale·mate**	stattistics	**sta·tis·tics**
stamena	**stam·i·na**	stattue	**stat·ue**
stamerer	**stam·mer·er**	statture	**stat·ure**
stamin	**sta·men**	stattutory	**stat·u·to·ry**
stammina	**stam·i·na**	statuery	**stat·u·ary**
stampeed	**stam·pede**	statueske	**stat·u·esque**
stanby	**stand·by**	statuet	**stat·u·ette**
standerd	**stand·ard**	stauk	**stalk** *(stem)*

WRONG	RIGHT	WRONG	RIGHT
staul	**stall**	sterness	**stern·ness**
staut	**stout**	sterreo	**ster·eo**
stawnch	**staunch**	sterreophonic	
stayed	**staid** (sober)		**ster·e·o·phon·ic**
stead	**steed** (horse)	sterreotype	**ster·e·o·type**
steak	**stake** (post; share)	sterrile	**ster·ile**
steal	**steel** (metal)	stethiscope	**steth·o·scope**
steap	**steep**	stewerd	**stew·ard**
steaple	**stee·ple**	stewerdess	**stew·ard·ess**
stear	**steer**	stiched	**stitched**
stearage	**steer·age**	stie	**sty**
sted	**stead** (place)	stien	**stein**
stedy	**steady**	stifen	**stiff·en**
steed	**stead** (place)	stifness	**stiff·ness**
steel	**steal** (rob)	stigmatism	**astig·ma·tism**
steem	**steam**		(lens distortion)
steepel	**stee·ple**	stigme	**stig·ma**
steller	**stel·lar**	stigmitism	**stig·ma·tism**
stelthy	**stealthy**		(condition of normal lens)
stennographer		stikler	**stick·ler**
	ste·nog·ra·pher	stile	**style** (manner)
stensil	**sten·cil**	stilletto	**sti·let·to**
stentch	**stench**	stilus	**sty·lus**
step	**steppe** (plain)	stimie	**sty·mie**
steral	**ster·ile**	stimmulate	**stim·u·late**
steralize	**ster·i·lize**	stimulas	**stim·u·lus**
sterdy	**stur·dy**	stimulent	**stim·u·lant**
stereofonic	**ster·e·o·phon·ic**	stine	**stein**
stereotipe	**ster·e·o·type**	stingey	**stin·gy**
sterillization	**ster·i·li·za·tion**	stipand	**sti·pend**
sterio	**ster·eo**	stipled	**stip·pled**
steriotype	**ster·e·o·type**	stippend	**sti·pend**

stippulation	**stip·u·la·tion**	straned	**strained**
stired	**stirred**	strangel	**stran·gle**
stirene	**sty·rene**	strangellation	
stirling	**ster·ling**		**stran·gu·la·tion**
stirup	**stir·rup**	strangness	**strange·ness**
stlactite	**sta·lac·tite**	stratagy	**strat·e·gy**
(lime deposit from roof)		stratajem	**strat·a·gem**
stlagmite	**sta·lag·mite**	strateegic	**stra·te·gic**
(lime deposit on floor)		stratefy	**strat·i·fy**
stock	**stalk** *(stem)*	stratigem	**strat·a·gem**
stodgey	**stodgy**	stratisphere	**strat·o·sphere**
(dull; unfashionable)		strattegy	**strat·e·gy**
stogey	**sto·gie** *(cigar)*	strattify	**strat·i·fy**
stokyard	**stock·yard**	strecher	**stretch·er**
stollen	**stol·en** *(pp. of steal)*	streek	**streak**
stollid	**stol·id** *(impassive)*	streem	**stream**
stomich	**stom·ach**	streemlined	**stream·lined**
stonch	**staunch**	strennuous	**stren·u·ous**
stoney	**stony**	strenthen	**strength·en**
stoped	**stopped**	strepp	**strep** *(bacterium)*
storie	**sto·ry**	streusal	**streu·sel**
storrage	**stor·age**	strick	**strict** *(rigid)*
stowe	**stow**	stricly	**strict·ly**
stowic	**sto·ic**	stringant	**strin·gent**
stowt	**stout**	strip	**strep** *(bacterium)*
stradling	**strad·dling**	striped	**stripped** *(pp. of strip)*
straggeling	**strag·gling**	stripped ..	**striped** *(pp. of stripe)*
stragle	**strag·gle**	stroabe	**strobe**
straight	**strait**	stroginoff	**stro·ga·noff**
(narrow passage)		stroler	**stroll·er**
straigten	**straight·en**	structurel	**struc·tur·al**
strait	**straight** *(even)*	struesel	**streu·sel**

WRONG	RIGHT	WRONG	RIGHT
struggeling	**strug·gling**	subdude	**sub·dued**
stuard	**stew·ard**	suberban	**sub·ur·ban**
stubborness	**stub·born·ness**	subgigate	**sub·ju·gate**
stuble	**stub·ble**	subjeck	**sub·ject**
stucko	**stuc·co**	subjegate	**sub·ju·gate**
studant	**stu·dent**	subjektive	**sub·jec·tive**
studdied	**stud·ied**	sublemate	**sub·li·mate**
studdious	**stu·di·ous**	sublimmation	**sub·li·ma·tion**
studeing	**stud·y·ing**	sublimminal	**sub·lim·i·nal**
studeous	**stu·di·ous**	submerine	**sub·ma·rine**
studing	**stud·y·ing**	submersable	**sub·mers·i·ble**
stufy	**stuffy**	submision	**sub·mis·sion**
stumbeling	**stum·bling**	submisive	**sub·mis·sive**
stuped	**stu·pid**	submited	**sub·mit·ted**
stuper	**stu·por**	submurge	**sub·merge**
stupidety	**stu·pid·i·ty**	submursion	**sub·mer·sion**
stupify	**stu·pe·fy**	suborddinate	**sub·or·di·nate**
stuppendous	**stu·pen·dous**	subordenation	
stuppor	**stu·por**		**sub·or·di·na·tion**
sturling	**ster·ling**	subpeena	**sub·poe·na**
sturred	**stirred**	subplant	**sup·plant**
sturrup	**stir·rup**	subpoenied	**sub·poe·naed**
stuterring	**stut·ter·ing**	subsadize	**sub·si·dize**
stylesh	**styl·ish**	subsaquent	**sub·se·quent**
styllus	**sty·lus**	subscribsion	**sub·scrip·tion**
styreen	**sty·rene**	subsedy	**sub·si·dy**
subblimate	**sub·li·mate**	subserviant	**sub·ser·vi·ent**
subblime	**sub·lime**	subsidiery	**sub·sid·i·ary**
subbordinate	**sub·or·di·nate**	subsiquant	**sub·se·quent**
subburban	**sub·ur·ban**	subsistance	**sub·sist·ence**
subconsious	**sub·con·scious**	subsitute	**sub·sti·tute**
subdew	**sub·due**	subsitution	**sub·sti·tu·tion**

WRONG	RIGHT	WRONG	RIGHT
substancial	**sub·stan·tial**	sucker	**suc·cor** *(help)*
substanciate	**sub·stan·ti·ate**	suckotash	**suc·co·tash**
substatute	**sub·sti·tute**	sucksion	**suc·tion**
substence	**sub·stance**	suckumb	**suc·cumb**
substetution	**sub·sti·tu·tion**	sucor	**suc·cor** *(help)*
subsurvient	**sub·ser·vi·ent**	sucroce	**su·crose**
subtel	**sub·tle**	sucsess	**suc·cess**
subteler	**sub·tler**	sucsinct	**suc·cinct**
subtelty	**sub·tle·ty**	suculent	**suc·cu·lent**
subterranian		sucumb	**suc·cumb**
....	**sub·ter·ra·ne·an**	suecidal	**su·i·ci·dal**
subturanéan ..	**sub·ter·ra·ne·an**	suer	**sew·er**
subturfuge	**sub·ter·fuge**	sufering	**suf·fer·ing**
subversave	**sub·ver·sive**	sufferage	**suf·frage**
succatash	**suc·co·tash**	suffex	**suf·fix**
succede	**suc·ceed**	sufficate	**suf·fo·cate**
	(follow; achieve)	suffisiency	**suf·fi·cien·cy**
succeed	**se·cede** *(withdraw)*	suffring	**suf·fer·ing**
succesion	**suc·ces·sion**	sufice	**suf·fice**
successer	**suc·ces·sor**	suficiency	**suf·fi·cien·cy**
succion	**suc·tion**	sufix	**suf·fix**
succulant	**suc·cu·lent**	sufocate	**suf·fo·cate**
suceed	**suc·ceed**	sufrage	**suf·frage**
	(follow; achieve)	sufuse	**suf·fuse**
suceptibility		suger	**sug·ar**
....	**sus·cep·ti·bil·i·ty**	sugest	**sug·gest**
sucess	**suc·cess**	sugestion	**sug·ges·tion**
sucession	**suc·ces·sion**	sugestive	**sug·ges·tive**
sucessive	**suc·ces·sive**	suggary	**sug·ary**
sucessor	**suc·ces·sor**	suisidal	**su·i·ci·dal**
suchure	**su·ture**	suit	**su·et** *(fat)*
suckeled	**suck·led**	suit	**suite** *(apartment)*

WRONG	RIGHT	WRONG	RIGHT
suite .. **suit** (clothes; legal action)		super .... **sup·per** (dinner)	
suiter .... **suit·or**		superceed .... **su·per·sede**	
suitible .... **suit·a·ble**		supercillious .... **su·per·cil·i·ous**	
sulfer .... **sul·fur**		superempose ... **su·per·im·pose**	
sullin .... **sul·len**		supereority .... **su·pe·ri·or·i·ty**	
sullky .... **sulky**		superfishal .... **su·per·fi·cial**	
sulpher .... **sul·fur**		superflewas ..... **su·per·flu·ous**	
sulten .... **sul·tan**		superintendant	
sultrey .... **sul·try**		.... **su·per·in·tend·ent**	
sumarrize .... **sum·ma·rize**		superletive .... **su·per·la·tive**	
sumary .... **sum·ma·ry**		supernateral ... **su·per·nat·u·ral**	
(brief account)		superseed .... **su·per·sede**	
sumbrero .... **som·bre·ro**		supersilious ..... **su·per·cil·i·ous**	
sumed .... **summed**		supersonnic .... **su·per·son·ic**	
sumer .... **sum·mer**		supersticious .. **su·per·sti·tious**	
sumit .... **sum·mit**		superstission .. **su·per·sti·tion**	
summen .... **sum·mon**		supervizer .... **su·per·vi·sor**	
summerize .... **sum·ma·rize**		supirior .... **su·pe·ri·or**	
summersalt .... **som·er·sault**		suplamentary	
summery .... **sum·ma·ry**		.... **sup·ple·men·ta·ry**	
(brief account)		suplant .... **sup·plant**	
summet .... **sum·mit**		suple .... **sup·ple**	
sumon .... **sum·mon**		suplement .... **sup·ple·ment**	
sumptious .... **sump·tu·ous**		suplication ..... **sup·pli·ca·tion**	
sunbath .... **sun·bathe** (v.)		suply .... **sup·ply**	
sunbathe .... **sun·bath** (n.)		supoena .... **sub·poe·na**	
sunbern .... **sun·burn**		suport .... **sup·port**	
sunday .... **sun·dae** (dessert)		supose .... **sup·pose**	
sundile .... **sun·di·al**		suposedly .... **sup·pos·ed·ly**	
sundrey .... **sun·dry**		suposition .... **sup·po·si·tion**	
sunkin .... **sunk·en**		supossitory ...... **sup·pos·i·to·ry**	
suovenir .... **sou·ve·nir**		suppel .... **sup·ple**	

WRONG	RIGHT	WRONG	RIGHT
supper	**su·per** *(great)*	surge	**serge** *(fabric)*
supperb	**su·perb**	surgecal	**sur·gi·cal**
supperficial	**su·per·fi·cial**	surgen	**sur·geon**
supperior	**su·pe·ri·or**	surgury	**sur·gery**
suppperlative	**su·per·la·tive**	surloin	**sir·loin**
supplecation	**sup·pli·ca·tion**	surly	**sure·ly** *(certainly)*
supplementery		surmize	**sur·mise**
	sup·ple·men·ta·ry	suroggate	**sur·ro·gate**
suppliment	**sup·ple·ment**	suround	**sur·round**
supposetory	**sup·pos·i·to·ry**	suroundings	**sur·round·ings**
suppossedly	**sup·pos·ed·ly**	surpased	**sur·passed**
suppremacy	**su·prem·a·cy**	surplice	**sur·plus** *(excess)*
suppreme	**su·preme**	surprize	**sur·prise**
suppresion	**sup·pres·sion**	surreel	**sur·real** *(fantastic)*
suppressent	**sup·pres·sant**	surrendar	**sur·ren·der**
supreem	**su·preme**	surrepetitious	**sur·rep·ti·tious**
supremmacy	**su·prem·a·cy**	surry	**sur·rey**
supress	**sup·press**	surtain	**cer·tain**
supressant	**sup·pres·sant**	survay	**sur·vey**
suprise	**sur·prise**	surveilance	**sur·veil·lance**
supscription	**sub·scrip·tion**	surveyer	**sur·vey·or**
supterfuge	**sub·ter·fuge**	survile	**ser·vile**
supurb	**su·perb**	survivel	**sur·viv·al**
supurfluous	**su·per·flu·ous**	survix	**cer·vix**
sureal	**sur·real** *(fantastic)*	susceptable	**sus·cep·ti·ble**
surely	**sur·ly** *(rude)*	suseptability	
surender	**sur·ren·der**		**sus·cep·ti·bil·i·ty**
sureptitious	**sur·rep·ti·tious**	suspeck	**sus·pect**
surf	**serf** *(slave)*	suspence	**sus·pense**
surfbord	**surf·board**	suspendors	**sus·pend·ers**
surfice	**sur·face**	suspention	**sus·pen·sion**
surfiet	**sur·feit**	suspision	**sus·pi·cion**

WRONG	RIGHT	WRONG	RIGHT
suspisious	**sus·pi·cious**	swindel	**swin·dle**
susseptibility		swindeler	**swin·dler**
	sus·cep·ti·bil·i·ty	Switserland	**Switz·er·land**
susseptible	**sus·cep·ti·ble**	swivvle	**swiv·el**
sustane	**sus·tain**	swizel	**swiz·zle**
sustinence	**sus·te·nance**	swolen	**swol·len**
sutcase	**suit·case**	swollow	**swal·low**
sutherly	**south·er·ly**	sword	**sward** *(turf)*
suthern	**south·ern**	sworm	**swarm**
sutle	**sub·tle**	sworthy	**swarthy**
sutor	**suit·or**	swoted	**swat·ted**
swade	**suede**	swoth	**swath** *(strip)*
swadling	**swad·dling**	swurl	**swirl**
swager	**swag·ger**	swurve	**swerve**
swalow	**swal·low**	syanide	**cy·a·nide**
swaped	**swapped**	sycemore	**syc·a·more**
sward	**sword** *(weapon)*	syche	**psy·che** *(mind; soul)*
swated	**swat·ted**	sychedelic	**psy·che·del·ic**
swath	**swathe** *(to wrap)*	sychoanalysis	
swave	**suave**		**psy·cho·a·nal·y·sis**
sweator	**sweat·er**	sychological	**psy·cho·log·i·cal**
sweepsteaks	**sweep·stakes**	sychoses	**psy·cho·ses** *(pl.)*
sweet	**suite** *(apartment)*	syclone	**cy·clone**
sweethart	**sweet·heart**	syfilis	**syph·i·lis**
sweetner	**sweet·en·er**	sylabbic	**syl·lab·ic**
sweltring	**swel·ter·ing**	sylabbus	**syl·la·bus**
swepped	**swept**	sylable	**syl·la·ble**
swet	**sweat**	sylinder	**cyl·in·der**
swetter	**sweat·er**	sylogism	**syl·lo·gism**
swich	**switch**	symbalism	**sym·bol·ism**
swieback	**zwie·back**	symbelize	**sym·bol·ize**
swiming	**swim·ming**	symbeotic	**sym·bi·ot·ic**

WRONG	RIGHT	WRONG	RIGHT
symble	**sym·bol** *(mark)*	systemmatic	**sys·tem·at·ic**
symbol	**cym·bal** *(brass plate)*	sythe	**scythe**
symbollic	**sym·bol·ic**		
symetrical	**sym·met·ri·cal**		
symfonic	**sym·phon·ic**		**T**
symmatry	**sym·me·try**		
symmetrecal	**sym·met·ri·cal**	tabacco	**to·bac·co**
sympethetic	**sym·pa·thet·ic**	tabbernacle	**tab·er·nac·le**
sympethize	**sym·pa·thize**	tabboo	**ta·boo**
sympethy	**sym·pa·thy**	tabercular	**tuber·cu·lar**
symphany	**sym·pho·ny**	taberculosis	**tuber·cu·lo·sis**
symposeum	**sym·po·si·um**	tabernackle	**tab·er·nac·le**
symptem	**symp·tom**	tableu	**tab·leau**
symptommatic		tablit	**tab·let**
	symp·to·mat·ic	taboggan	**to·bog·gan**
synanym	**syn·o·nym**	tabuler	**tab·u·lar**
synchopation	**syn·co·pa·tion**	taburnacle	**tab·er·nac·le**
syncronize	**syn·chro·nize**	tacet	**tac·it** *(implied)*
syncronous	**syn·chro·nous**	tachameter	**tachom·e·ter**
syndecate	**syn·di·cate**	tacitern	**tac·i·turn**
synical	**cyn·i·cal**	tack	**tact** *(sensitivity)*
synogog	**syn·a·gogue**	tackel	**tack·le**
synonimous	**syn·on·y·mous**	tackometer	**tachom·e·ter**
synopses	**syn·op·sis** *(sing.)*	tacks	**tax** *(payment)*
synopsis	**syn·op·ses** *(pl.)*	tacticks	**tac·tics**
synthasis	**syn·the·sis** *(sing.)*	tactitian	**tac·ti·cian**
synthettic	**syn·thet·ic**	tactle	**tac·tile**
synthises	**syn·the·ses** *(pl.)*	tafeta	**taf·fe·ta**
syphalis	**syph·i·lis**	taffey	**taf·fy**
syrringe	**sy·ringe**	tagether	**to·geth·er**
syrrup	**syr·up**	tail	**tale** *(story)*
systam	**sys·tem**	tailer	**tai·lor** *(clothes maker)*
		tailight	**tail·light**

WRONG	RIGHT	WRONG	RIGHT
tailling	**tail·ing**	tanjelo	**tan·ge·lo**
takeing	**tak·ing**	tanjent	**tan·gent**
tako	**ta·co**	tanjerine	**tan·ge·rine**
Talahassee	**Tal·la·has·see**	tant	**taint**
talant	**tal·ent**	tantallize	**tan·ta·lize**
talasman	**tal·is·man**	tantemount	**tan·ta·mount**
	(good luck charm)	tantrem	**tan·trum**
talcam	**tal·cum**	tapastry	**tap·es·try**
tale	**tail** *(rear end)*	tapeing	**tap·ing** *(using tape)*
talen	**tal·on**	tapeoca	**tap·i·o·ca**
talesman	**tal·is·man**	taper	**ta·pir** *(animal)*
	(good luck charm)	taping	**tap·ping** *(rapping)*
talk	**talc** *(powder)*	tapir	**ta·per** *(candle)*
Tallahasee	**Tal·la·has·see**	tapography	**topog·ra·phy**
tallent	**tal·ent**	tappestry	**tap·es·try**
tallisman	**tal·is·man**	taranchula	**ta·ran·tu·la**
	(good luck charm)	tardyness	**tar·di·ness**
tallon	**tal·on**	tarif	**tar·iff**
talow	**tal·low**	tarnesh	**tar·nish**
taly	**tal·ly**	taro	**tar·ot** *(cards)*
tamahawk	**tom·a·hawk**	tarot	**ta·ro** *(plant)*
tamalle	**ta·ma·le**	tarpaulen	**tar·pau·lin**
tamato	**to·ma·to**	tarrantula	**ta·ran·tu·la**
tamborine	**tam·bou·rine**	tarro	**ta·ro** *(plant)*
tammale	**ta·ma·le**	tarrot	**tar·ot** *(cards)*
tamultuous	**tumul·tu·ous**	tarten	**tar·tan**
tanalize	**tan·ta·lize**	tarter	**tar·tar**
tanamount	**tan·ta·mount**	tasit	**tac·it** *(implied)*
tandum	**tan·dem**	tasiturn	**tac·i·turn**
tangable	**tan·gi·ble**	tassle	**tas·sel**
tangalo	**tan·ge·lo**	tasteing	**tast·ing**
tangarine	**tan·ge·rine**	tastey	**tasty**

WRONG	RIGHT	WRONG	RIGHT
taters	**tat·ters** *(rags)*	tedeous	**te·di·ous**
tatler	**tat·tler**	tee	**tea** *(beverage)*
tatoo	**tat·too**	teek	**teak**
tattletail	**tat·tle·tale**	teem	**team** *(group)*
taudry	**taw·dry**	teeth	**teethe** *(grow teeth)*
taught	**taut** *(tight)*	teethe	**teeth** *(pl. of tooth)*
tauny	**taw·ny**	telacast	**tel·e·cast**
Taurrus	**Tau·rus**	telagram	**tel·e·gram**
taut	**taught** *(pt. of teach)*	telagraph	**tel·e·graph**
tavurn	**tav·ern**	telaphone	**tel·e·phone**
tawney	**taw·ny**	telascope	**tel·e·scope**
tawt	**taut** *(tight)*	telathon	**tel·e·thon**
taxadermy	**tax·i·der·my**	telavision	**tel·e·vi·sion**
taxible	**tax·a·ble**	telefone	**tel·e·phone**
taxie	**taxi**	telegraf	**tel·e·graph**
tea	**tee** *(ball–holder)*	tellecast	**tel·e·cast**
team	**teem** *(be full of)*	tellegram	**tel·e·gram**
teamate	**team·mate**	tellegraphy	**te·leg·ra·phy**
tear	**tier** *(row)*	tellepathy	**te·lep·a·thy**
technicallity	**tech·ni·cal·i·ty**	tellescope	**tel·e·scope**
technicke	**tech·nique**	tellevision	**tel·e·vi·sion**
technicle	**tech·ni·cal**	teltale	**tell·tale**
technitian	**tech·ni·cian**	temarity	**te·mer·i·ty**
technolagical		tempel	**tem·ple**
	tech·no·log·i·cal	temperal	**tem·po·ral**
tecknical	**tech·ni·cal**	temperary	**tem·po·rary**
tecknique	**tech·nique**	temperchure	**tem·per·a·ture**
tecknological		temperence	**tem·per·ance**
	tech·no·log·i·cal	tempermental	
tecnicality	**tech·ni·cal·i·ty**		**tem·per·a·men·tal**
tecnician	**tech·ni·cian**	tempestous	**tem·pes·tu·ous**
tecnique	**tech·nique**	tempist	**tem·pest**

WRONG	RIGHT	WRONG	RIGHT
temporery	**tem·po·rary**	tention	**ten·sion**
tempra	**tem·pera**	tentitive	**ten·ta·tive**
templral	**tem·po·ral**	tenuos	**ten·u·ous** *(slight)*
tempramental		tenur ... **ten·or** *(singer; meaning)*	
	tem·per·a·men·tal	teppid	**tep·id**
temprance	**tem·per·ance**	tequela	**te·qui·la**
temprate	**tem·per·ate**	terace	**ter·race**
temprature	**tem·per·a·ture**	terain	**ter·rain**
temtation	**temp·ta·tion**	terarium	**ter·rar·i·um**
tenacius	**te·na·cious**	terbine	**tur·bine** *(engine)*
tenacle	**ten·ta·cle**	terbulence	**tur·bu·lence**
tenament	**ten·e·ment**	terce	**terse** *(concise)*
tenasity	**te·nac·i·ty**	terestrial	**ter·res·tri·al**
tenatious	**te·na·cious**	terf	**turf**
tenative	**ten·ta·tive**	terible	**ter·ri·ble**
tence	**tense**	terier	**ter·ri·er**
tendancy	**tend·en·cy**	teriff	**tar·iff**
tenden	**ten·don**	terific	**ter·rif·ic**
tendonitis	**ten·di·ni·tis**	teritorial	**ter·ri·to·ri·al**
tenent	**ten·ant**	terkey	**tur·key**
tener ... **ten·or** *(singer; meaning)*		termanation	**ter·mi·na·tion**
Tenessee	**Ten·nes·see**	termanology	**ter·mi·nol·o·gy**
tenible	**ten·a·ble**	terminel	**ter·mi·nal**
tenis	**ten·nis**	termoil	**tur·moil**
tenit	**ten·et**	ternip	**tur·nip**
tennable	**ten·a·ble**	teror	**ter·ror**
tenner .. **ten·or** *(singer; meaning)*		terot	**tar·ot** *(cards)*
tenner	**ten·ure** *(time held)*	terpentine	**tur·pen·tine**
Tennesee	**Ten·nes·see**	terquoise	**tur·quoise**
tenor	**ten·ure** *(time held)*	terrable	**ter·ri·ble**
tensle	**ten·sile** *(flexible)*	terrareum	**ter·rar·i·um**
tenticle	**ten·ta·cle**	terratorial	**ter·ri·to·ri·al**

WRONG	RIGHT	WRONG	RIGHT
terrer	**ter·ror**	theif	**thief** (n.)
terrice	**ter·race**	their	**they're** (they are)
terriffic	**ter·rif·ic**	their	**there** (adv.)
terriyaki	**ter·i·ya·ki**	theirs	**there's** (there is)
terry	**tar·ry** (linger)	theive	**thieve** (v.)
tershiary	**ter·ti·ary**	theivery	**thiev·ery**
tertle	**tur·tle**	themomater	**ther·mom·e·ter**
teryaki	**ter·i·ya·ki**	then	**than** (conj.; prep.)
tess	**test**	theologen	**the·o·lo·gi·an**
testacle	**tes·ti·cle**	theraputic	**ther·a·peu·tic**
testafy	**tes·ti·fy**	there	**their** (poss.)
testamonial	**tes·ti·mo·ni·al**	there	**they're** (they are)
testamony	**tes·ti·mo·ny**	therem	**the·o·rem**
testement	**tes·ta·ment**	theres	**there's** (there is)
testical	**tes·ti·cle**	there's	**theirs** (poss.)
tetnus	**tet·a·nus**	theretical	**the·o·ret·i·cal**
Teusday	**Tues·day**	therfore	**there·fore** (hence)
texbook	**text·book**	thermameter	**ther·mom·e·ter**
texchual	**tex·tu·al**	thermastat	**ther·mo·stat**
texchure	**tex·ture**	thermel	**ther·mal** (of heat)
textle	**tex·tile**	thermus	**ther·mos**
thach	**thatch**	Thersday	**Thurs·day**
than	**then** (at that time)	therteen	**thir·teen**
thankfull	**thank·ful**	therty	**thir·ty**
thealogian	**the·o·lo·gi·an**	thesarus	**the·sau·rus**
thealogy	**the·ol·o·gy**	theses	**the·sis** (sing.)
thearem	**the·o·rem**	thesis	**the·ses** (pl.)
thearetical	**the·o·ret·i·cal**	thesorus	**the·sau·rus**
theary	**the·o·ry**	theyre	**they're** (they are)
theatricle	**the·at·ri·cal**	they're	**there** (adv.)
theem	**theme**	they're	**their** (poss.)
theeter	**the·a·ter**	thickning	**thick·en·ing**

WRONG	RIGHT	WRONG	RIGHT
thief	**thieve** (v.)	throws	**throes**
thieve	**thief** (n.)		(spasm; struggle)
thievry	**thiev·ery**	thru	**threw** (pt. of throw)
thimbel	**thim·ble**	thum	**thumb**
thime	**thyme** (herb)	thumtack	**thumb·tack**
thiner	**thin·ner**	thundring	**thun·der·ing**
thiroid	**thy·roid**	thursty	**thirsty**
thirstey	**thirsty**	thwort	**thwart**
thirteith	**thir·ti·eth**	tic	**tick** (mite)
thissel	**this·tle**	tick	**tic** (spasm)
thorney	**thorny**	tickeling	**tick·ling**
thorobred	**thor·ough·bred**	tickit	**tick·et**
thorou	**thor·ough** (absolute)	ticklesh	**tick·lish**
thorough	**through**	tidel	**tid·al** (of tides)
	(from end to end)	tidey	**ti·dy**
thousanth	**thou·sandth**	tiecoon	**ty·coon**
thousend	**thou·sand**	tieing	**ty·ing**
thout	**thought**	tiephoon	**ty·phoon**
thowsand	**thou·sand**	tigger	**ti·ger**
threatning	**threat·en·ing**	timber	**tim·bre**
thred	**thread**		(quality of sound)
threshhold	**thresh·old**	timbre	**tim·ber** (wood)
thret	**threat**	time	**thyme** (herb)
thretening	**threat·en·ing**	timed	**tim·id** (shy)
threw	**through**	timeing	**tim·ing**
	(from end to end)	timerity	**te·mer·i·ty**
thriler	**thrill·er**	timerous	**tim·or·ous**
throes	**throws** (pitches)	timley	**time·ly**
throte	**throat**	timmid	**tim·id** (shy)
throtle	**throt·tle**	tinacity	**te·nac·i·ty**
through	**threw** (pt. of throw)	tingley	**tin·gly**
through	**thor·ough** (absolute)	tinje	**tinge**

WRONG	RIGHT	WRONG	RIGHT
tinkture	**tinc·ture**	tommato	**to·ma·to**
tinsel	**ten·sile** *(flexible)*	tomorow	**to·mor·row**
tinsle	**tin·sel**	tomstone	**tomb·stone**
tipe	**type**	tong	**tongue** *(taste organ)*
tiphoid	**ty·phoid**	tonick	**ton·ic**
tiphus	**ty·phus**	tonsilectomy	**ton·sil·lec·to·my**
tipical	**typ·i·cal**	tonsles	**ton·sils**
tiquila	**te·qui·la**	too	**to** *(prep.)*
tirannical	**tyran·ni·cal**	too	**two** *(number)*
tiranny	**tyr·an·ny**	toomb	**tomb**
tirant	**ty·rant**	toomult	**tu·mult**
tiresum	**tire·some**	tootelage	**tu·te·lage**
tirrade	**ti·rade**	toothake	**tooth·ache**
tisshue	**tis·sue**	topagraphy	**topog·ra·phy**
titaler	**tit·u·lar**	tope	**taupe** *(brownish gray)*
titchular	**tit·u·lar**	topick	**top·ic**
titen	**ti·tan**	tople	**top·ple**
tittillate	**tit·il·late**	torchure	**tor·ture**
to	**too** *(also; overly)*	torent	**tor·rent**
to	**two** *(number)*	torential	**tor·ren·tial**
tobbacco	**to·bac·co**	torid	**tor·rid**
tobogan	**to·bog·gan**	torist	**tour·ist**
todler	**tod·dler**	tork	**torque**
toe	**tow** *(pull)*	tormenter	**tor·men·tor**
tofee	**tof·fee**	tornament	**tour·na·ment**
toillet	**toi·let**	torped	**tor·pid**
tokan	**to·ken**	torper	**tor·por**
tole	**toll** *(a tax)*	torreador	**tor·e·a·dor**
tole	**told** *(pt. of tell)*	torrencial	**tor·ren·tial**
tollerable	**tol·er·a·ble**	torrint	**tor·rent**
tollerance	**tol·er·ance**	torrpid	**tor·pid**
tommahawk	**tom·a·hawk**	Torrus	**Tau·rus**

213

WRONG	RIGHT	WRONG	RIGHT
tortila	**tor·til·la**	tragec	**trag·ic**
tortion	**tor·sion**	tragidy	**trag·e·dy**
tortuous	**tor·tur·ous**	trailler	**trail·er**
	(causing pain)	traiter	**trai·tor**
torturous	**tor·tu·ous** *(twisting)*	trajedy	**trag·e·dy**
tortus	**tor·toise**	traktor	**trac·tor**
totallitarian	**total·i·tar·i·an**	trale	**trail**
totaly	**to·tal·ly**	traler	**trail·er**
totel	**to·tal**	trama	**trau·ma**
tottler	**tod·dler**	trambone	**trom·bone**
totum	**to·tem**	tramendous	**tre·men·dous**
toupay	**tou·pee**	trampolene	**tram·po·line**
tournaquet	**tour·ni·quet**	tranqualizer	**tran·quil·iz·er**
tourniment	**tour·na·ment**	tranquel	**tran·quil**
toussel	**tou·sle**	transaktion	**trans·ac·tion**
tow	**toe** *(digit of a foot)*	transative	**tran·si·tive**
towle	**tow·el**	transcrip	**tran·script**
toword	**to·ward**	transe	**trance**
towring	**tow·er·ing**	transeint	**tran·sient**
towsle	**tou·sle**	transendental	
towt	**tout**		**tran·scen·den·tal**
toxec	**tox·ic**	transet	**trans·it**
toylet	**toi·let**	transferance	**trans·fer·ence**
traceing	**trac·ing**	transfered	**trans·ferred**
track	**tract** *(area)*	transfuzion	**trans·fu·sion**
tracktable	**trac·ta·ble**	transiant	**tran·sient**
tracktion	**trac·tion**	transision	**tran·si·tion**
tracter	**trac·tor**	transister	**tran·sis·tor**
tractible	**trac·ta·ble**	translater	**trans·la·tor**
traddition	**tra·di·tion**	translusent	**trans·lu·cent**
tradeing	**trad·ing**	transmision	**trans·mis·sion**
trafic	**traf·fic**	transmiting	**trans·mit·ting**

WRONG	RIGHT	WRONG	RIGHT
transparancy	**trans·par·en·cy**	tremer	**trem·or**
transperent	**trans·par·ent**	tremulus	**trem·u·lous**
transpertation		trenchent	**trench·ant**
	trans·por·ta·tion	treo	**trio**
transsend	**tran·scend**	trepadation	**trep·i·da·tion**
transum	**tran·som**	tressel	**tres·tle**
transvurse	**trans·verse**	tresspass	**tres·pass**
tranzaction	**trans·ac·tion**	tresure	**treas·ure** *(wealth)*
trappeze	**tra·peze**	tresurer	**treas·ur·er**
trase	**trace**	tretise	**trea·tise**
trate	**trait**	trey	**tray** *(flat receptacle)*
trator	**trai·tor**	triangel	**tri·an·gle**
traval	**trav·el** *(journey)*	trianguler	**tri·an·gu·lar**
travel	**trav·ail** *(toil; agony)*	tribbulation	**trib·u·la·tion**
travisty	**trav·es·ty**	tribel	**trib·al**
travurse	**trav·erse**	tributery	**trib·u·tary**
treacherus	**treach·er·ous**	trickey	**tricky**
treasen	**trea·son**	trico	**tri·cot**
treaserer	**treas·ur·er**	triel	**tri·al**
treasurey	**treas·ury**	trifel	**tri·fle**
treatey	**trea·ty**	triganometry	
treatiss	**trea·tise**		**trig·o·nom·e·try**
treazure	**treas·ure** *(wealth)*	triger	**trig·ger**
trecherous	**treach·er·ous**	trikle	**trick·le**
treck	**trek**	trilion	**tril·lion**
trecot	**tri·cot**	trillogy	**tril·o·gy**
tred	**tread**	triming	**trim·ming**
treeson	**trea·son**	trinkit	**trin·ket**
trelis	**trel·lis**	trinnity	**trin·i·ty**
tremalous	**trem·u·lous**	triping	**trip·ping**
trembel	**trem·ble**	triplacate	**trip·li·cate**
tremendus	**tre·men·dous**	triplit	**tri·plet**

WRONG	RIGHT	WRONG	RIGHT
tripple	**tri·ple**	truent	**tru·ant**
trist	**tryst**	truging	**trudg·ing**
trisycle	**tri·cy·cle**	trumpit	**trum·pet**
tritly	**trite·ly**	trunkate	**trun·cate**
triumf	**tri·umph**	truse	**truce**
triumphent	**tri·um·phant**	trusseau	**trous·seau**
triveal	**triv·i·al**	trustee	**trusty** (dependable)
troff	**trough**	trusty	**trus·tee** (manager)
trofy	**tro·phy**	trusworthy	**trust·wor·thy**
trogh	**trough**	truthfull	**truth·ful**
trole	**troll**	trycicle	**tri·cy·cle**
troley	**trol·ley**	tryed	**tried**
troop	**troupe** (group of actors)	trypod	**tri·pod**
trophey	**tro·phy**	trys	**tries**
tropicks	**trop·ics**	tuberculer	**tuber·cu·lar**
tropicle	**trop·i·cal**	tubercullosis	**tuber·cu·lo·sis**
troting	**trot·ting**	tubuler	**tu·bu·lar**
troubador	**trou·ba·dour**	tucksedo	**tux·e·do**
troubble	**trou·ble**	tuetion	**tu·i·tion**
troublesum	**trou·ble·some**	tuff	**tough** (strong)
troule	**trow·el**	tuff	**tuft** (clump)
trounse	**trounce**	tuision	**tu·i·tion**
trouseau	**trous·seau**	tullip	**tu·lip**
trouzers	**trou·sers**	tumbeling	**tum·bling**
trowl	**trow·el**	tumer	**tu·mor**
trownce	**trounce**	tumulltuous	**tumul·tu·ous**
trowsers	**trou·sers**	tun	**ton** (2000 lbs.)
trowt	**trout**	tunec	**tu·nic**
trubadour	**trou·ba·dour**	tunel	**tun·nel**
truculant	**truc·u·lent**	tungue	**tongue** (taste organ)
trueism	**tru·ism**	tupee	**tou·pee**
truely	**tru·ly**	turban	**tur·bine** (engine)

WRONG	RIGHT
turbine	**tur·ban**
	(head covering)
turbulance	**tur·bu·lence**
turcoise	**tur·quoise**
turet	**tur·ret**
turine	**tu·reen**
turist	**tour·ist**
turky	**tur·key**
turm	**term**
turminal	**ter·mi·nal**
turmination	**ter·mi·na·tion**
turminology	**ter·mi·nol·o·gy**
turn	**tern** *(bird)*
turnament	**tour·na·ment**
turniquet	**tour·ni·quet**
turnup	**tur·nip**
turpintine	**tur·pen·tine**
turquoize	**tur·quoise**
turrit	**tur·ret**
turse	**terse** *(concise)*
turtel	**tur·tle**
Tusday	**Tues·day**
Tuson	**Tuc·son**
tussel	**tus·sle**
tuter	**tu·tor**
tutilage	**tu·te·lage**
tutoreal	**tu·to·ri·al**
tuxido	**tux·e·do**
twead	**tweed**
tweater	**tweet·er**
tweek	**tweak**
twelf	**twelfth**

WRONG	RIGHT
twerl	**twirl**
twich	**twitch**
twinje	**twinge**
twurl	**twirl**
tye	**tie**
tyfoid	**ty·phoid**
tyfoon	**ty·phoon**
tyfus	**ty·phus**
tykoon	**ty·coon**
tyme	**thyme** *(herb)*
typacal	**typ·i·cal**
typeriter	**type·writ·er**
typewritting	**type·writ·ing**
tyrade	**ti·rade**
tyrany	**tyr·an·ny**
tyrent	**ty·rant**
tyrrannical	**tyran·ni·cal**

U

WRONG	RIGHT
ubickuitous	**ubiq·ui·tous**
udder	**ut·ter** *(speak)*
uder	**ud·der** *(milk gland)*
ukalele	**uku·le·le**
ulcerus	**ul·cer·ous**
ulltra	**ul·tra**
ulser	**ul·cer**
ulserous	**ul·cer·ous**
ultamate	**ul·ti·mate**
ultamatum	**ul·ti·ma·tum**
ulterier	**ul·te·ri·or**
ultrasanic	**ul·tra·son·ic**

WRONG	RIGHT	WRONG	RIGHT
ultravilet	**ul·tra·vi·o·let**	uneque	**unique**
umbillical	**um·bil·i·cal**	unerth	**un·earth**
umbrege	**um·brage**	unifacation	**uni·fi·ca·tion**
umbrela	**um·brel·la**	uniformaty	**uni·form·i·ty**
umpier	**um·pire**	unike	**unique**
unabriged	**un·a·bridged**	unisun	**uni·son**
unacorn	**uni·corn**	unisycle	**uni·cy·cle**
unacycle	**uni·cy·cle**	uniteing	**unit·ing**
unafication	**uni·fi·ca·tion**	univursal	**uni·ver·sal**
unalienable	**in·al·ien·a·ble**	univursity	**uni·ver·si·ty**
unanamous	**unan·i·mous**	unkemt	**un·kempt**
unason	**uni·son**	unkle	**un·cle**
unatural	**un·nat·u·ral**	unkouth	**un·couth**
unaty	**uni·ty**	unmaned	**un·manned**
unaversal	**uni·ver·sal**	unmentionibles	
unaversity	**uni·ver·si·ty**		**un·men·tion·a·bles**
uncany	**un·can·ny**	unmistakeable	
unconshunable			**un·mis·tak·a·ble**
	un·con·scion·a·ble	unmitagated	**un·mit·i·gat·ed**
uncuth	**un·couth**	unnecessaryly	
undenyable	**un·de·ni·a·ble**		**un·nec·es·sar·i·ly**
underite	**un·der·write**	unruley	**un·ruly**
underneth	**un·der·neath**	unscrupulus	**un·scru·pu·lous**
undiniable	**un·de·ni·a·ble**	untenible	**un·ten·a·ble**
undoutedly	**un·doubt·ed·ly**	untill	**un·til**
undullate	**un·du·late**	untye	**un·tie**
undur	**un·der**	unwanted	**un·wont·ed**
unecessarily			*(not usual)*
	un·nec·es·sar·i·ly	unwonted	**un·want·ed**
unecessary	**un·nec·es·sary**		*(not wanted)*
uneform	**uni·form**	unyon	**un·ion**
unefy	**uni·fy**	upan	**up·on**

WRONG	RIGHT
upbrade	**up·braid**
uper	**up·per**
upheval	**up·heav·al**
upolstery	**up·hol·stery**
upriseing	**up·ris·ing**
uprite	**up·right**
uprorious	**up·roar·i·ous**
upword	**up·ward**
uranal	**uri·nal**
uraneum	**ura·ni·um**
Urannus	**Ura·nus**
urathane	**ure·thane**
urban	**ur·bane** (refined)
urbane	**ur·ban** (of a city)
urchen	**ur·chin**
uren	**urine**
urgincy	**ur·gen·cy**
urgint	**ur·gent**
urinel	**uri·nal**
urjency	**ur·gen·cy**
urmine	**er·mine**
urr	**err** (be wrong)
usefull	**use·ful**
usege	**us·age**
useing	**us·ing**
userp	**usurp**
ushur	**ush·er**
ussage	**us·age**
usualy	**usu·al·ly**
utensle	**uten·sil**
uteran	**uter·ine**
uterance	**ut·ter·ance**

WRONG	RIGHT
utillitarian	**util·i·tar·i·an**
utillity	**util·i·ty**
utillize	**uti·lize**
utopea	**uto·pia**
utter	**ud·der** (milk gland)
utterence	**ut·ter·ance**
uturus	**uter·us**
uzually	**usu·al·ly**

V

WRONG	RIGHT
vacansy	**va·can·cy**
vacashun	**va·ca·tion**
vaccanate	**vac·ci·nate**
vaccene	**vac·cine**
vaccum	**vac·u·um**
vacency	**va·can·cy**
vacent	**va·cant**
vacilate	**vac·il·late**
vacine	**vac·cine**
vacksinate	**vac·ci·nate**
vadeville	**vaude·ville**
vage	**vague**
vagery	**va·gary**
vagibond	**vag·a·bond**
vagrent	**va·grant**
vain	**vein** (blood vessel)
vain	**vane** (blade)
vajina	**va·gi·na**
valadate	**val·i·date**
valadictorian	**val·e·dic·to·ri·an**

219

WRONG	RIGHT	WRONG	RIGHT
valance	**va·lence**	valu	**val·ue**
	(chemistry term)	valueable	**val·u·a·ble**
valantine	**val·en·tine**	valume	**vol·ume**
valay	**val·et**	valuminous	**volu·mi·nous**
vale	**veil** *(screen)*	valuntary	**vol·un·tary**
valed	**val·id**	valunteer	**vol·un·teer**
valedictorion		vanaty	**van·i·ty**
	val·e·dic·to·ri·an	vandelism	**van·dal·ism**
valence	**val·ance** *(curtain)*	vane	**vain** *(conceited)*
valer	**val·or**	vane	**vein** *(blood vessel)*
valese	**va·lise**	vaneer	**ve·neer**
valey	**val·ley**	vangard	**van·guard**
validaty	**va·lid·i·ty**	vanila	**va·nil·la**
valient	**val·iant**	vankuish	**van·quish**
valit	**val·et**	vannish	**van·ish**
valition	**vo·li·tion**	vantege	**van·tage**
vallance	**val·ance** *(curtain)*	vaped	**vap·id**
valledictorian		vaper	**va·por**
	val·e·dic·to·ri·an	vaperizer	**va·por·iz·er**
vallentine	**val·en·tine**	varanda	**ve·ran·da**
vallet	**val·et**	vareable	**var·i·a·ble**
valley	**vol·ley**	vareagated	**var·i·e·gat·ed**
	(discharge; ball return)	vareation	**var·i·a·tion**
valliant	**val·iant**	varecose	**var·i·cose**
vallid	**val·id**	vareous	**var·i·ous**
vallidate	**val·i·date**	variaty	**va·ri·e·ty**
vallidity	**va·lid·i·ty**	varient	**var·i·ant**
vallise	**va·lise**	varius	**var·i·ous**
valluable	**val·u·a·ble**	varnnish	**var·nish**
vallue	**val·ue**	varsaty	**var·si·ty**
vally	**val·ley**	vary	**very** *(exceedingly)*
valt	**vault**	varyed	**var·ied**

WRONG	RIGHT	WRONG	RIGHT
vasal	**vas·sal** *(subordinate)*	vejetate	**veg·e·tate**
vasaline	**vas·e·line**	velacity	**ve·loc·i·ty**
vasculer	**vas·cu·lar**	vellour	**ve·lour**
vasecktomy	**vas·ec·to·my**	velosity	**ve·loc·i·ty**
vaselene	**vas·e·line**	velum	**vel·lum** *(paper)*
vasillate	**vac·il·late**	velvit	**vel·vet**
vass	**vast** *(great)*	venal	**ve·ni·al** *(excusable)*
vassal	**ves·sel** *(container)*	venarate	**ven·er·ate**
vassel	**vas·sal** *(subordinate)*	venchure	**ven·ture**
Vattican	**Vat·i·can**	vendeta	**ven·det·ta**
vaudville	**vaude·ville**	venel	**ve·nal** *(corrupt)*
vaxine	**vac·cine**	venemous	**ven·om·ous**
vaze	**vase**	venerial	**ve·ne·re·al**
veamently	**vehe·ment·ly**	venerible	**ven·er·a·ble**
vear	**veer**	Venetion	**Ve·ne·tian**
vecter	**vec·tor**	venew	**ven·ue**
veel	**veal**	vengefull	**venge·ful**
vegatarian	**veg·e·tar·i·an**	vengence	**venge·ance**
vegatate	**veg·e·tate**	venial	**ve·nal** *(corrupt)*
vegtable	**veg·e·ta·ble**	venilate	**ven·ti·late**
vehementley	**vehe·ment·ly**	venire	**ve·neer**
vehical	**ve·hi·cle**	venireal	**ve·ne·re·al**
vehiculer	**ve·hic·u·lar**	vennison	**ven·i·son**
vehimently	**vehe·ment·ly**	ventalate	**ven·ti·late**
veicle	**ve·hi·cle**	ventillator	**ven·ti·la·tor**
veil	**vale** *(valley)*	ventrical	**ven·tri·cle**
vein	**vane** *(blade)*	ventrilloquist	**ven·tril·o·quist**
vein	**vain** *(conceited)*	veola	**vi·o·la**
veinglorious	**vain·glo·ri·ous**	veracious	**vo·ra·cious** *(greedy)*
veiw	**view**	veracius	**ve·ra·cious** *(truthful)*
vejetable	**veg·e·ta·ble**	verafiable	**ver·i·fi·a·ble**
vejetarian	**veg·e·tar·i·an**	verafy	**ver·i·fy**

verasimilitude		verses .... **ver·sus** _(against)_	
.... **ver·i·si·mil·i·tude**		versitile .... **ver·sa·tile**	
verasity .... **ve·rac·i·ty**		vertabra .... **ver·te·bra**	
veratable .... **ver·i·ta·ble**		vertago .... **ver·ti·go**	
verbatem .... **ver·ba·tim**		verticle .... **ver·ti·cal**	
verbeage .... **ver·bi·age**		vertually .... **vir·tu·al·ly**	
verbel .... **ver·bal**		very .... **vary** _(alter)_	
verdent .... **ver·dant**		verzion .... **ver·sion**	
verdick .... **ver·dict**		vesa .... **vi·sa**	
verginal .... **vir·gin·al**		vessal .... **ves·sel** _(container)_	
verginity .... **vir·gin·i·ty**		vessel .... **vas·sal** _(subordinate)_	
Vergo .... **Vir·go**		vestabule .... **ves·ti·bule**	
veriable .... **var·i·a·ble**		vestage .... **ves·tige**	
veriant .... **var·i·ant**		veteren .... **vet·er·an**	
veriation .... **var·i·a·tion**		veternarian .... **vet·er·i·nar·i·an**	
vericose .... **var·i·cose**		vetos .... **ve·toes**	
veriegated .... **var·i·e·gat·ed**		vetran .... **vet·er·an**	
veriety .... **va·ri·e·ty**		vetrinarian ..... **vet·er·i·nar·i·an**	
verifyable .... **ver·i·fi·a·ble**		vial .... **vile** _(evil)_	
verile .... **vir·ile**		vialate .... **vi·o·late**	
verious .... **var·i·ous**		vialence .... **vi·o·lence**	
verismillitude		vialet .... **vi·o·let**	
.... **ver·i·si·mil·i·tude**		vialin .... **vi·o·lin**	
veritible .... **ver·i·ta·ble**		vibrateing .... **vi·brat·ing**	
vermacelli .... **ver·mi·celli**		vibrater .... **vi·bra·tor**	
vermen .... **ver·min**		vibrent .... **vi·brant**	
vermillion .... **ver·mil·ion**		vicarius .... **vi·car·i·ous**	
vermuth .... **ver·mouth**		vice .... **vise** _(clamp)_	
vernaculer .... **ver·nac·u·lar**		vicissatude .... **vicis·si·tude**	
verneer .... **ve·neer**		vicius .... **vi·cious**	
verrisimilitude		vicker .... **vic·ar**	
.... **ver·i·si·mil·i·tude**		victem .... **vic·tim**	

WRONG	RIGHT	WRONG	RIGHT
victer	**vic·tor**	virgenal	**vir·gin·al**
victorius	**vic·to·ri·ous**	virgenity	**vir·gin·i·ty**
victry	**vic·to·ry**	virtous	**vir·tu·ous**
vidio	**vid·eo**	virtully	**vir·tu·al·ly**
vieing	**vy·ing**	virtuossity	**vir·tu·os·i·ty**
viel	**veil** *(screen)*	virulant	**vir·u·lent**
vigel	**vig·il**	visable	**vis·i·ble**
vigerous	**vig·or·ous**	visator	**vis·i·tor**
vigilence	**vig·i·lance**	viscus	**vis·cous** *(adj.)*
vijil	**vig·il**	vise	**vice** *(wickedness)*
vijilance	**vig·i·lance**	visege	**vis·age**
vilage	**vil·lage**	viser	**vi·sor**
vilain	**vil·lain** *(scoundrel)*	viseral	**vis·cer·al**
vile	**vi·al** *(bottle)*	vise versa	**vi·ce ver·sa**
vilet	**vi·o·let**	vishiate	**vi·ti·ate**
villege	**vil·lage**	vishus	**vi·cious**
villein	**vil·lain** *(scoundrel)*	visibillity	**vis·i·bil·i·ty**
vindacate	**vin·di·cate**	visinity	**vi·cin·i·ty**
vindictave	**vin·dic·tive**	visissitude	**vicis·si·tude**
vinereal	**ve·ne·re·al**	vitallity	**vi·tal·i·ty**
Vinetian	**Ve·ne·tian**	vitamen	**vi·ta·min**
vineyerd	**vine·yard**	vitel	**vi·tal**
vinigar	**vin·e·gar**	vivacius	**vi·va·cious**
vinil	**vi·nyl**	vivasection	**viv·i·sec·tion**
vinilla	**va·nil·la**	vived	**viv·id**
vinnegar	**vin·e·gar**	viza	**vi·sa**
vintege	**vin·tage**	vizage	**vis·age**
vinyard	**vine·yard**	viz–a–ve	**vis·à·vis**
violance	**vi·o·lence**	vizibility	**vis·i·bil·i·ty**
virchually	**vir·tu·al·ly**	vizible	**vis·i·ble**
virel	**vir·ile**	vizion	**vi·sion**
vires	**vi·rus**	vizit	**vis·it**

WRONG	RIGHT	WRONG	RIGHT
vizitor	**vis·i·tor**	voteing	**vot·ing**
vizual	**vis·u·al**	votery	**vo·ta·ry**
vocabulery	**vo·cab·u·lary**	vowl	**vow·el**
vocallize	**vo·cal·ize**	voyce	**voice**
vocul	**vo·cal**	voyd	**void**
vodeville	**vaude·ville**	voyege	**voy·age**
voge	**vogue**	voyure	**vo·yeur**
voise	**voice**	vue	**view**
vokabulary	**vo·cab·u·lary**	vulcanic	**vol·can·ic**
volatle	**vol·a·tile**	vulcano	**vol·ca·no**
volcanick	**vol·can·ic**	vulchure	**vul·ture**
voley	**vol·ley**	vulgarety	**vul·gar·i·ty**
	(discharge; ball return)	vulger	**vul·gar**
volision	**vo·li·tion**	vulnerible	**vul·ner·a·ble**
vollatile	**vol·a·tile**	vurbal	**ver·bal**
vollcano	**vol·ca·no**	vurbatim	**ver·ba·tim**
volluble	**vol·u·ble**	vurdict	**ver·dict**
vollume	**vol·ume**	vurge	**verge**
volluminous	**volu·mi·nous**	vurginal	**vir·gin·al**
volluntary	**vol·un·tary**	vurmin	**ver·min**
volluptuous	**volup·tu·ous**	vurse	**verse**
volly	**vol·ley**	vursus	**ver·sus** *(against)*
	(discharge; ball return)	vurtebra	**ver·te·bra**
voltege	**volt·age**	vurtical	**ver·ti·cal**
volumenous	**volu·mi·nous**	vurtigo	**ver·ti·go**
volunter	**vol·un·teer**	vurtue	**vir·tue**
voluntery	**vol·un·tary**	vurtuous	**vir·tu·ous**
volupchuous	**volup·tu·ous**	vurve	**verve**
vommit	**vom·it**	vyable	**vi·a·ble**
voracious	**ve·ra·cious**	vye	**vie**
	(truthful)		
voratious	**vo·ra·cious** *(greedy)*		

W

WRONG	RIGHT
wabble	**wob·ble**
wach	**watch**
wack	**whack**
wackey	**wacky**
wacks	**wax**
waddle	**wat·tle** (fold of skin)
wadeing	**wad·ing**
wading	**wad·ding** (stuffing)
wadle	**wad·dle** (toddle)
wafe	**waif**
waff	**waft** (float)
waffer	**wa·fer**
wafle	**waf·fle**
wagen	**wag·on**
wagish	**wag·gish**
wagle	**wag·gle**
waigh	**weigh** (measure weight of)
wail	**wale** (ridge)
wail	**whale** (animal)
waist	**waste** (squander)
wait	**weight** (heaviness)
waive	**wave** (curving motion)
waje	**wage**
wajer	**wa·ger**
wakeing	**wak·ing**
wale	**whale** (animal)
wale	**wail** (cry)
walet	**wal·let**
wallbord	**wall·board**
wallnut	**wal·nut**
wallrus	**wal·rus**
walop	**wal·lop**
walow	**wal·low**
walris	**wal·rus**
walz	**waltz**
wan	**won** (pt. of win)
wander	**won·der** (marvel)
wandrings	**wan·der·ings**
waneing	**wan·ing**
wann	**wan** (pale; feeble)
want	**wont** (accustomed)
wan ton	**won ton** (food)
warant	**war·rant**
wardon	**war·den**
ware	**wear** (to dress in)
ware	**where** (adv.)
warewolf	**were·wolf**
warey	**wary**
warf	**wharf**
warhouse	**ware·house**
warior	**war·ri·or**
warmunger	**war·mon·ger**
warn	**worn** (pp. of wear)
warrent	**war·rant**
warrenty	**war·ran·ty**
warrier	**war·ri·or**
warsh	**wash**
waryness	**war·i·ness**
wasail	**was·sail**
wasent	**wasn't**
washible	**wash·a·ble**

wassel	**was·sail**	weal	**wheel** (disc)
wastbasket	**waste·bas·ket**	weapen	**weap·on**
waste	**waist** (middle section)	wear	**ware** (merchandise)
wastege	**wast·age**	wearyness	**wea·ri·ness**
wasteing	**wast·ing**	weasle	**wea·sel**
wat	**watt**	weather	**wheth·er** (if)
watage	**watt·age**	weaveing	**weav·ing**
wate	**wait** (stay)	weavil	**wee·vil**
waterey	**wa·tery**	webing	**web·bing**
watermellon	**wa·ter·mel·on**	Wedgewood	**Wedg·wood**
watle	**wat·tle** (fold of skin)	weding	**wed·ding**
watress	**wait·ress**	weedling	**whee·dling**
wattege	**watt·age**	week	**weak** (not strong)
watter	**wa·ter**	weekley	**week·ly**
wattery	**wa·tery**	weel	**wheel** (disc)
wattle	**wad·dle** (toddle)	weel	**weal** (ridge)
wauk	**walk** (stroll)	weelbarrow	**wheel·bar·row**
wauk	**wok** (pan)	ween	**wean**
wave	**waive** (give up)	weener	**wie·ner**
waveing	**wav·ing**	weepey	**weepy**
waver	**waiv·er** (a relinquishing)	weesel	**wea·sel**
wavey	**wavy**	weeve	**weave**
waxey	**waxy**	weevle	**wee·vil**
way	**weigh** (measure weight of)	weeze	**wheeze**
way	**whey** (milk product)	wege	**wedge**
wayfer	**wa·fer**	wegies	**wedg·ies**
waywerd	**way·ward**	weild	**wield**
wazn't	**wasn't**	weiner	**wie·ner**
wead	**weed**	wellcome	**wel·come**
weak	**week** (seven days)	wellfare	**wel·fare**
weakend	**week·end**	welp	**whelp**
weal	**wheal** (pimple)	welth	**wealth**

WRONG	RIGHT
wen	**when** (adv.)
wench	**winch**
	(mechanical device)
wendow	**win·dow**
Wensday	**Wednes·day**
wepon	**weap·on**
were	**where** (adv.)
were	**we're** (we are)
we're	**were** (pt. of be)
werever	**wher·ev·er**
werewulf	**were·wolf**
wern't	**weren't**
werth	**worth**
wery	**wea·ry**
westerley	**west·er·ly**
westurn	**west·ern**
westwerd	**west·ward**
wet	**whet** (sharpen)
wether	**wheth·er** (if)
wether	**weath·er**
	(atmospheric conditions)
wey	**weigh** (measure weight of)
wey	**whey** (milk product)
whale	**wail** (cry)
whale	**wale** (ridge)
whaleing	**whal·ing**
wheather	**wheth·er** (if)
wheedeling	**whee·dling**
wheel	**wheal** (pimple)
wheel	**weal** (ridge)
wheelbarow	**wheel·bar·row**
wheet	**wheat**

WRONG	RIGHT
wheezey	**wheezy**
wherabouts	**where·a·bouts**
wheras	**where·as**
wherl	**whirl** (spin)
whether	**weath·er**
	(atmospheric conditions)
which	**witch** (sorceress)
while	**wile** (trick)
whimsey	**whim·sy**
whimsicle	**whim·si·cal**
whine	**wine** (drink)
whinny	**whiny** (complaining)
whiny	**whin·ny** (neigh)
whiping	**whip·ping**
whipoorwill	**whip·poor·will**
whirl	**whorl** (fingerprint design)
whispring	**whis·per·ing**
whissle	**whis·tle**
whistful	**wist·ful**
whistleing	**whis·tling**
whit	**white** (color)
whitch	**witch** (sorceress)
whither	**with·er** (wilt)
whitle	**whit·tle**
whole	**hole** (cavity)
wholesell	**whole·sale**
wholesum	**whole·some**
wholistic	**ho·lis·tic**
wholy	**whol·ly** (totally)
whoose	**whose** (poss.)
whore	**hoar** (frost)
whorf	**wharf**

WRONG	RIGHT	WRONG	RIGHT
whorl	**whirl** *(spin)*	winry	**win·ery**
who's	**whose** *(poss.)*	winse	**wince**
whose	**who's**	winsum	**win·some**
	(who is; who has)	wintrey	**win·try**
wich	**which** *(pron.)*	wintur	**win·ter** *(cold season)*
wicket	**wick·ed** *(bad)*	wipeing	**wip·ing**
wickit	**wick·et** *(arch)*	wippoorwill	**whip·poor·will**
widdow	**wid·ow**	wireing	**wir·ing**
wierd	**weird**	wirey	**wiry**
wiff	**whiff**	wirl	**whirl** *(spin)*
wiggley	**wig·gly**	wirlpool	**whirl·pool**
wigle	**wig·gle**	wisacre	**wise·acre**
wikker	**wick·er**	wisdum	**wis·dom**
wikket	**wick·et** *(arch)*	wishfull	**wish·ful**
wile	**while** *(time)*	wisk	**whisk**
wiley	**wily**	wisker	**whisk·er**
wilfull	**will·ful**	wiskey	**whis·key**
willderness	**wil·der·ness**	wisper	**whis·per**
wilow	**wil·low**	wistfull	**wist·ful**
wily–nily	**wil·ly–nil·ly**	wistle	**whis·tle**
wimen	**wom·en** *(pl.)*	witch	**which** *(pron.)*
wimsical	**whim·si·cal**	wite	**white** *(color)*
winch	**wench** *(woman)*	withdrawl	**with·draw·al**
windey	**windy**	wither	**whith·er** *(where)*
windless	**wind·lass** *(winch)*	withold	**with·hold**
wine	**whine** *(cry)*	witicism	**wit·ti·cism**
winerey	**win·ery**	witnes	**wit·ness**
winfall	**wind·fall**	witth	**width**
winlass	**wind·lass** *(winch)*	wittle	**whit·tle**
winner	**win·ter** *(cold season)*	wity	**wit·ty**
winney	**whin·ny** *(neigh)*	wizdom	**wis·dom**
winow	**win·now**	wizerd	**wiz·ard**

WRONG	RIGHT	WRONG	RIGHT
wobbley	**wob·bly**	worn	**warn** (caution)
woble	**wob·ble**	worp	**warp**
wock	**wok** (pan)	worrant	**war·rant**
wodding	**wad·ding** (stuffing)	worrysome	**wor·ri·some**
woddle	**wad·dle** (toddle)	wort	**wart** (blemish)
woffel	**waf·fle**	worthey	**wor·thy**
woft	**waft** (float)	wort hog	**wart hog**
wok	**walk** (stroll)	worthwile	**worth·while**
woll	**wall**	wosh	**wash**
woman	**wom·en** (pl.)	wosp	**wasp**
women	**wom·an** (sing.)	wossel	**was·sail**
won	**one** (a unit)	wott	**watt**
won	**wan** (pale; feeble)	wottle	**wat·tle** (fold of skin)
wonder	**wan·der** (stray)	woud	**would** (aux.v.)
wonderous	**won·drous**	wouden	**wouldn't** (would not)
wont	**won't** (will not)	wrak	**rack** (framework)
wont	**want** (lack)	wrak	**wrack** (torment)
wonton	**wan·ton** (unjustifiable)	wrangel	**wran·gle**
woodden	**wood·en**	wraping	**wrap·ping**
woolf	**wolf**	wreak	**reek** (smell)
wooly	**wool·ly**	wreath	**wreathe** (to encircle)
woom	**womb**	wreathe	**wreath** (a band)
Woostershire		wreckedge	**wreck·age**
	Worces·ter·shire	wreckless	**reck·less**
woozey	**woozy**	wreeth	**wreath** (a band)
worble	**war·ble**	wressle	**wres·tle**
worden	**war·den**	wrestleing	**wres·tling**
wordey	**wordy**	wretch	**retch** (vomit)
workible	**work·a·ble**	wrigle	**wrig·gle**
worl	**whorl** (fingerprint design)	wrinkel	**wrin·kle**
worldley	**world·ly**	write	**right** (correct)
wormth	**warmth**	writen	**writ·ten**

WRONG	RIGHT	WRONG	RIGHT
writting	**writ·ing**	yashiva	**ye·shi·va**
wrote	**rote** *(routine)*	yaun	**yawn**
wrung	**rung** *(crossbar)*		*(open the mouth wide)*
wry	**rye** *(grain)*	yeer	**year**
wunce	**once**	yeest	**yeast**
wundrous	**won·drous**	yeild	**yield**
wurd	**word**	yellowey	**yel·lowy**
wurld	**world**	yesheva	**ye·shi·va**
wurm	**worm**	yestirday	**yes·ter·day**
wurry	**wor·ry**	yew	**ewe** *(female sheep)*
wurse	**worse**	yewe	**yew** *(evergreen)*
wurship	**wor·ship**	Yidish	**Yid·dish**
wurst	**worst**	yodle	**yo·del**
wurth	**worth**	yogert	**yo·gurt**
wuz	**was**	yogey	**yo·gi** *(yoga practicer)*
		yogi	**yo·ga** *(exercises)*

X

WRONG	RIGHT
X–rey	**X–ray**
xylaphone	**xy·lo·phone**

Y

WRONG	RIGHT
yack	**yak** *(animal)*
yaht	**yacht**
yaking	**yak·king** *(talking)*
yamaka	**yar·mul·ke**
yamer	**yam·mer**
yander	**yon·der**
Yankie	**Yan·kee**
yardege	**yard·age**
yarmulka	**yar·mul·ke**

WRONG	RIGHT
yoke	**yolk** *(part of an egg)*
yokle	**yo·kel**
yolk	**yoke** *(harness)*
yoman	**yeo·man**
yon	**yawn**
	(open the mouth wide)
yool	**yule** *(Christmas)*
yore	**you're** *(you are)*
yore	**your** *(poss.)*
you	**ewe** *(female sheep)*
you	**yew** *(evergreen)*
you'l	**you'll** *(you will)*
your	**you're** *(you are)*
you're	**your** *(poss.)*
your's	**yours**
yowel	**yowl**

WRONG	RIGHT	WRONG	RIGHT
Yugaslavia	**Yugo·sla·via**	zigote	**zy·gote**
yukka	**yuc·ca**	zigurat	**zig·gu·rat**
yull	**yule** *(Christmas)*	zigzaged	**zig·zagged**
yull	**you'll** *(you will)*	zilion	**zil·lion**
yungster	**young·ster**	ziltch	**zilch**
yurn	**yearn**	zinfundel	**zin·fan·del**
yuth	**youth**	zink	**zinc**
		zinnea	**zin·nia**
Z		ziper	**zip·per**
		zirkon	**zir·con**
zaney	**za·ny**	ziro	**ze·ro**
Zavier	**Xa·vi·er**	zithur	**zith·er**
zealet	**zeal·ot**	zoalogy	**zo·ol·o·gy**
zealus	**zeal·ous**	zodiak	**zo·di·ac**
zeanith	**ze·nith**	zomby	**zom·bie**
zeel	**zeal**	zoneing	**zon·ing**
zefyr	**zeph·yr**	zonel	**zon·al**
zelot	**zeal·ot**	zoologecal	**zo·o·log·i·cal**
zenia	**zin·nia**	zuccini	**zuc·chi·ni**
zepelin	**zep·pe·lin**	Zues	**Zeus**
zepher	**zeph·yr**	Zurick	**Zur·ich**
zeppalin	**zep·pe·lin**	zweeback	**zwie·back**
zercon	**zir·con**	zylophone	**xy·lo·phone**

878 9454